What Others Are Saying

"Thanks for sharing another good chapter. I have to say though that I'm hoping the book is available soon because I get withdrawal symptoms when I finish each chapter and want to keep reading!
I've read both chapters and will buy your book just to see how you turned your life around. Most people would have given up".

Linda Skehan

"Amazing read mark, I didn't know you'd been through all that, you were always very different from the rest your family as I remember, obviously had a lot going on inside, and had this feeling about you from the start your life would go in different directions, a depth and a hunger in you to strive for more, that's what I remember about you, you were just passing through"

Debra Davies

"Have just read your first two chapters and about to hit the pillow to read the third. Incredibly well written with such profound raw and real emotion. Thank you."

Donna-Leigh Perfect

"Wow Mark... I've just finished chapter 3! Thank you for sharing your story. When can I buy the book? So very sorry you had to go through all of this pain and suffering as a child. You are a beautiful and inspiring man. Obviously making great choices in life to get where you are today. You should be so proud!! Much love to you"

Belinda Marks

"Wow...just wow!!! I REALLY REALLY want to buy your book, young man. Have only read this one chapter, but I want more. And my hat's off to you, matey... for your endurance, resilience, and never-to-be-broken spirit. BIG hug to you, Mark"

Inge Lass Verhoef

"Thank you Mark for sharing your story. Such a powerful confronting journey on so many levels."

RoseLyn Haigh

"A very inspiring read, your life has had many a road to it, and so wonderful for you to share that with us, look forward to the next chapter."

Sharon Neville

"Was emailed to me last night! I can't wait to read the rest! Very interesting read. Can't wait to read the book! Both chapters are a brilliant read."

Rachel Ann

"It generally takes me to chapter 3 to get into a book but this first chapter was straight to the point. Would have been interested to see if you only got a couple days inside then went to Pakistan. Life would have been very different and possibly not for the best. The only issue is, once I start reading a good book I can't put it down and generally read it over a few days, so to read one chapter and then nothing similar to the plane landing and your half way through a good movie. Very annoying, Thanks for sharing."

Robynn Sinclair Shave

"Amazing first chapter mark, I can´t wait to read the rest of the book."

Brooke Colella

"I normally don't read books that much, but wow I couldn't stop, the 1st Chapter was just fantastic. Can't wait for the book to be released."

Matthew Chenhall

"How soon can I read the whole book, it made me sad reading your first chapter Mark Anthony......but you are an amazing man and I had the pleasure of meeting you on the radiance of the seas in 2014. I can't wait to find quiet time to read the next chapter."

Lexie Clements

"Wow Mark. What an amazing read so far. I don't usually like reading books, however I am now hanging for the book to come out. I know it will be hard to put down. Well done."

Craig Needs

"Oh, my goodness Mark! I just read your two chapters. I was captivated, they are amazingly well written ... but, I'm so torn because I know what a successful person you have become but my heart breaks reading those things happened to you. It's so raw and descriptive, reading it you are just submerged into each scenario. Very brave of you to share."

Emma-Louise Waters

"O wow loved this just want to read more."

Michelle Smith

"My husband was reading all 3 chapters last night. Totally absorbed. I asked him something and he did not respond, that's how I know he's really into something!"

Sharon Chapman

The Rogue Hypnotist

Mark Anthony
As told to
Sara Garrido Díaz

First published in Australia in 2017 by Mark Anthony

First Floor, 31 Crombie Avenue, Bundall Queensland 4211

www.TheRogueHypnotist.com

Copyright ©2017 by Mark Anthony. All rights reserved.

This book is copyright.

Apart from any fair dealing for the purposes of private study, research, criticism or review, as permitted under the Copyright Act, no part may be reproduced by any process without written permission.

Inquiries should be addressed to the publisher.

Disclaimers:

This book is to serve as a reference only, and the material in this book is for the purposes of general information only, and does not intend to be legal or therapeutic advice in any way, shape or form.

The memoirs of this book are true to the best of my recollection, and although in many cases names, places, and or dates have been changed to protect certain identities, the memoirs are as true to the written words as can be.

I do not condone any of the rebellious and damaging things that I did in my past, neither do I advise anybody else to attempt to follow or imitate what I have done in the past. However, I have used all of my wrong doings, my adversities and right doings as learnings, and simply advise you to do the same.

Contents

Acknowledgments 13
What this Book Will Do for You 17
Preface 23
Short, sharp, shock 29
Inferno 37
No Sweet, No Home 59
Svengali 81
The Queen Bee 93
I See Red 109
The Ferrier 137
Glue in a Concrete Jungle 145
Food Stamps, Ham Sandwiches, and Small Jobs 149
The Gang 155
I Pushed Her 161
Sacred Island 165
Glue 177
No Lives Left 185
Not Everything Lost 207
Cleaning Products in the Middle East 211
Canada 215

Left High and Dry	221
Back to Canada	229
Loyalty	235
Across the Sea	247
Down Under	251
Cigarettes and Mop Sticks	255
A Lit Darkness	259
The Success Group	263
Seeking the Right Herd	273
Beta Videotapes, Broken TVs and Another Gypsy	277
Love Letters	293
Learning to Love	299
Migrant	305
A Cold and Metallic Humming	311
The Show Must Go On	317
Karma	329
The Final Beginning	339
Miracle is Mind	353
Reach Out	363
Inspirational Books to Read	365

Acknowledgments

I dedicate this book to the following people:

To my beautiful wife Marina, who has decided to share the rest of her life with a man who probably wasn´t the sort of person she would have married or even talked to many years ago, but has decided that he´s not a bad guy after all. I love you very much, thanks for believing in me!

To the apples of my eye, my children Oliver, Evan, Vegas and Voe.

Oliver who has taught his Dad the art of being a man, that it´s good to stand on your own two feet and not rely on others early on in life. A young man that I´m more proud of than he´ll ever know, determined and a fighter. Thank you for being you. I love you, handsome boy.

Evan who although I haven't seen him for many years, I hear is a great young man, full of energy and who loves his brother dearly. And come the day he meets his younger sisters, it´ll be a wonderful day indeed. You´re loved and missed by all of us.

Vegas, who is the most caring young lady I know. So determined to please and look after everybody, especially the under dogs. And yet a real resilient young lady, every time she falls down, she gets up and does it again and again until she achieves her goal. With a drive and perseverance that I haven´t seen in many people. She never gives up, and persistence should have been her middle name. Thank you, beautiful girl, I love you very much.

Voe, a young lady who asks me more questions than the host of a millionaire hot seat show, won´t stop asking until she gets the answer she´s looking for. A natural at many things in life, and always remains the lady. Thank you, my little darling girl, I love you lots and lots.

I learn so much from my beautiful children in so many ways, and loving them comes so easily as it does with many parents. I love you all so much! I love you to the moon and back!

To my sister Rose, a young mother to her siblings before she could even bear children, a caring protector of many, a wonderful mum and wife. The world is a better place for having you in it! Thank you, I love you and miss you.

My brother in law Djah, who has looked after my sister and their children with everything he has to offer in his heart and soul. A hard working and loving family man, who not only is a brother in law, but probably without knowing, one of the best friends I´ve ever had. Love and miss you mate.

My older brother Amedeo, a man who decided to stay in Italy, joined the Carabinieri –the Italian Police, bizarrely enough-, is still the man I´ve always known him as. You can´t teach some old dogs new tricks, but I love you and miss you brother.

My sister Sylvan, the life and soul of most parties. Although with problems of her own, she is always there to help with other people´s problems. A good mum and a great sister. Always love and miss you.

Ali, the youngest sister of the family, once an aspiring singer, a dreamer and determined young lady, who lost her way in life for a while, however is now bouncing back and achieving more than she could ever imagine. Love and miss you Al.

My nieces and nephews, you make your uncle very proud by what you've done in life so far, by what you give to not receive, and Jamesy, not only my nephew, my mate, and now an amazingly good family man himself! My nieces and nephews, you're very special. Love and miss you all every day.

I have some very good friends who stuck by me through bad and good times, and if they aren't mentioned throughout my book, it doesn't mean that I don't appreciate your amazing friendship, and I thank you for being there for me through thick and thin.

To my friends who were my group of friends that I grew up with, and although I have now lost many of them to drugs, none were dreamers or doers, their choices were just different to mine. I miss you my friends, may you all R.I.P… Rest in Paradise.

And lastly, but certainly not least, to one of the strongest, most loving and caring people in the world, who did the best she could with what she had: my wonderful Mum. You remained strong and courageous for your children when times were very tough. I know I wasn't an easy son to put up with, but that doesn't mean that I didn't adore you. I thank you and I love you very much.

Mark Anthony

What this Book Will Do for You

In pretty much every chapter of this book you will find issues and adversities that I have gone through. Some of you will relate to them, and some of you won´t. I hope this book will inspire, motivate and encourage you to believe in yourself. Believe that there is always a way out, no matter what you are going through, or what you have gone through in life.

Other websites from the author:

www.TheRogueHypnotist.com
The Rogue Hypnotist Book - 'From Mindless Delinquent To Mindful Hypnotist'

www.HypnotistMarkAnthony.com
If you are looking for hypnosis therapy, or wanting advice on hypnosis, this site will help you.

www.Hypnotist.com.au
This website is for the person looking to see what and where Mark is performing shows, seminars or courses.

www.MarkAnthonyAcademy.com
This is a website where you can find out about becoming a Certified Hypnotherapist, training courses run by Mark

himself.

www.SimplyEasy.com.au
Mark took many months to develop his very successful method for helping others to become 'Happy Non Smokers', due to having smoked for many years himself.

www.WeighTooEasy.com.au
Mark being very much overweight in his past, prompted him to write a weight loss system to help others, and it can help you too!

www.EthicalHypnotists.com
A website featuring 'Certified Hypnotherapists' throughout Australia, for the person/s looking for an 'ethical' hypnotist, to help with issues and problems through the use of hypnotherapy.

My book of memoirs has taken three long years to write. I have been let down by two other writers many months after we had started, so it´s taken much longer than expected, but is finally here!

So, I want to say a huge thanks to my very talented and patient writer Sara, who has done exactly as I had asked from the start, and stuck with it, unlike the other two writers.

I asked Sara to write the book exactly as I speak, I wanted a story, not just memoirs, no fluff, leave all swear words in, leave the confronting chapters as they are, and for those people that might be a little prudish, I´m sure they will see past the swearing and look at the story and it´s content.

Sara has a writing ability and skill that just draws the reader into the story, and will no doubt become a very successful, recognised writer, author, and no doubts will win many awards, for which she deserves.

I want to thank my book cover designer for an amazing job, Simon Critchell. Also, a big thanks to a man who helped me in many ways with believing that I could, Sydney Matthews.

I would like to acknowledge too the great job of Jenni Brennan-Westlake, who did a fantastic job editing this book.

Mark Anthony

"Every failure has an excuse behind it. Don't be that excuse. Do your best however hard it seems"

Mark Anthony

Preface

My life has changed dramatically, but it was me who had to change the direction in which I was heading, no matter what adversities I went through I kept moving forward.

Believe me when I tell you, I wanted to quit many times, it has never been easy, but just like the quote from Sir Winston Churchill says "if you are going through hell, just keep going!", and I did!

I now perform my shows in front of hundreds of thousands of people, on some of the most luxurious cruise ships in the world. I perform in theatres, RSL´s, clubs, I have appeared on TV, radio and performed for some of the most recognised corporate companies in the world.

I´ve travelled the length and breadth of Australia more times than most Australians performing my shows, running seminars and treating therapy clients.

My hypnosis clinic is becoming busier than ever with an expansion as I write these paragraphs, with a client list consisting of not just everyday people, but many TV and radio personalities, millionaires and even billionaires.

I now have a training academy where I train everyday people to become professional clinical hypnotists and stage hypnotists.

My eldest son and I have a wonderful relationship once again, and I am married to my beautiful wife who I met on the ship.

I´m not trying to impress you when I tell you these things, I´m trying to impress upon you that "if I can do it, so can you!"

No matter where you are in your life, no matter what age, young or old, there is a way out and a way up!

The adversities that we go through in life are just hurdles, and they're put in front of us to see how many times we will keep jumping them.

Many people give up too easy when things get tough, but keep pushing yourself, keep jumping the hurdles put in front of you, and eventually the hurdles will start becoming less and less, that's when you know that things are getting better and better... Perseverance!

Mark Anthony

From Mindless Delinquent to Mindful Hypnotist

"If you think that working to become financially free is hard, poverty is even harder"

Mark Anthony

Chapter 1
Short, sharp, shock

Rose was at the back, quietly looking through the window. My mother was in the passenger seat. Neither said a word, yet both were equally worried. Nothing preoccupied me, although I was annoyed and didn't feel in the least like going. The car was on its way to Bexleyheath Magistrates Court. I was expected in the courtrooms, again.

I had already turned eighteen, but was used to being treated as a minor. This appearance would be no different. Smart, cunning and awfully cocky, I knew from the occasions they had managed to catch me, the punishment was never too bad. Just a couple of days off the streets.

In a sense, it felt like a rest from all the other shit out there in the cruel world I had to face every day. Don't get me wrong, it wasn't a peaceful retreat. There was as much shit inside as there was outside, just without the freedom.

But how else could I take it? After all, I had been secluded for most of my life since I was eight-years-old.

The weekend would be slow and tedious, sometimes awfully and physically painful. The body never really gets used to the abuse, but the head learns to numb it just enough to keep going. And this time was only going to be two or three days, like many occasions before. Then I would see the daylight again.

I was optimistic, exceptionally positive and had a certain peace of mind, because this day was different. It was the last day I would be called into the courtroom. I had always wanted to go overseas. There was not much travelling in trafficking small goods, and I was stuck among the wrong sort of people to aim for any success. But I desperately wanted to travel overseas. It was more than a craving; it was a vital need. I always knew in my mind that I would do it, but I knew it wouldn't happen from where I was then.

I saw an ad in a newspaper for a job working as a salesperson in Pakistan and other countries. It brightened my eyes. I didn't need to think twice about applying for the position, despite believing it was far beyond my reach as an eighteen-year-old, uncontrollable rogue. I was called for an interview, and I found myself in a big room with what looked like about three hundred or more other candidates, all well dressed and much older than me.

All of them walked around with a firm step and an air of knowledge and expertise. I thought I didn't stand a chance. But I was there, and despite feeling intimidated and somewhat scared, I also realised that there is no risk when there is nothing to lose. So, I decided to stay.

A couple of guys gave us a speech for an hour or more, explaining what the job was about. Then one of them said to the crowd: "Take the pen and paper and write your name on it, with the reason why we should choose you".

I had not the slightest idea of why they would choose me. I

looked around and saw all of these older, much more experienced men and women writing on their papers. Some of them had a look of confidence; others would meditate over an answer.

A couple of them, two rows to my right, looked worried. I took the pen and wrote: "Just give me a chance and I'll show you I can do it."

They picked up four pieces of paper with the chosen candidates and said the names aloud, everybody in the room waited with bated breath for their name to be called. Mine was among the chosen four. In two weeks I would be travelling to Pakistan. I confirmed to myself once again that I could do anything as long as I put my mind to it. I felt invincible.

I felt invincible every time I stepped into a courtroom, which was a regular occurrence with me. In fact, trips to court had become a big part of my life's routine. I would be called before the magistrate, and they would scold me, tap me on my hand for my bad behaviour, and give me yet another weekend in the juvenile detention centre.

I left the car in the rear car park, by the shopping centre. We walked around the building to the main entrance. It was a grey block of concrete with three storeys adjusting to the terrain levels. Sometimes I thought that it must have been the same architects that had built the Ferrier Housing Estate. The main door was on the third level from the parking lot but in the second one from the front street. A long set of steps raised from one of the corners of the block, narrowing as it reached the top and escorted at each side by a steel handrail that stood out with its bright red paint. The three of us walked up the stairs. My mum was worried and muttering some advice and warnings about my behaviour in court. My sister was silent as

I bounced eagerly up every second step. Let's just get this over and done with, I thought. Hands inside my pockets, I wore a bored look whilst staring down at the floor, muttering and cursing the police, the court staff and whoever the fuck else had put charges against me and was wasting my time like this.

I presented myself to the court guards, and they took me to the waiting room. My mum and sister would be seated inside courtroom number three, to wait for my hearing. My turn soon came, and I was summoned; a policeman asked me to accompany him with a dull gesture, and another one grabbed my arm tight enough to make me twist in protest. He shook my arm violently and looked at me sternly. I was smart enough to know retaliating would not help me out of that place any faster.

The policeman pushed me all the way down the aisle to the courtroom. My mum and my sister were anxiously waiting on the wooden viewing platform. My mind was somewhere else; I was impatient and bothered. I would get a weekend sentence, and then be flying to Pakistan, to my new life. I needed that stupid judge to do his job fast. I was eighteen years old, untouchable and in a hurry.

The judge looked at me. My arrogance and haughtiness shone through my well-rehearsed feline smile. "Come on, get on with it, you fucking faggot; I need to go home and pack my suitcase," I muttered. The room was so familiar by then it caused no fear in me at all. It was plain and dull, a mere part of my life's routine. There was no real worry, I had faced worse, but the obnoxiousness of the process really bothered me. I needed to get out of there and start again, overseas. I made it, in front of a few hundred fucking twats in bloody suits. I had outsmarted them all and got the job. In the afternoon I would be holding my passport and off.

A judge's frown never impressed me. A Cheshire cat smile would draw almost unconsciously on my face. "You can't get me. Fucking get on with it, give me your pathetic punishment so I can get out of here."

Finally, the judge spoke. "Enough is enough. I'm going to give you three months in the juvenile detention centre. It's called a 'short, sharp shock.' You'll either straighten up and turn your life around, or you'll spend the rest of your life in and out of jail."

There was no time in between the words and the gavel hitting the block. The words echoed around inside my head. I lost my peripheral vision. I saw the gavel and heard the thump of it on the wooden block, and everything in my surroundings disappeared. I could hear my mother shouting, screaming emotionally and crying. I could hear she was there, but I couldn't see her. I was blank. I had awoken into a nightmare.

My pupils were frozen on a distant point. All of a sudden I had tunnel vision, seeing nothing but a space in which I didn't belong anymore. I felt someone grabbing me violently by the arm, the fingers digging into my flesh felt like a memory of pain that my body couldn't summon. All was silent and empty within, but in the far distance I heard the sobbing and cries of females voices.

I knew they belonged to my mother and my sister, but I couldn't connect them in my mind firmly enough to produce an emotion. My mind was motionless. I was somewhere else, in a limbo of things that cannot be because they defy the possibility of their own existence. And yet I was there, and I was me, defeated by a judge in a bad dream that I still could not conceive as a reality.

It was then the fear shook my body, and I was brought back for a second to my senses. I was pushed into a cell and asked to take my shoes off and put the shoelaces on a metal table.

I sat down in the cell staring at the floor, seeing nothing but grey, dirty, dull and colourless surroundings. On the wall, names were engraved on the cement, etched out with anxious hands trembling with fear or rage. Beside the names were profanities carved out with whatever object could be found in the cell, created by souls shrunk by depravation. I was paralysed in terror. Everything was gone. I had been invincible. I had cheated death as many times as I had cheated the law. No one could get me. I could laugh in Death's face and say, "fuck you , you won't get me." But that gavel did it. The thump resonated in my head. Three months. Bang. Three months. Bang. Three months.

It was not the weekend away that I had become used to and was expecting. Three months was a lifetime. Yet, I couldn't cry. You cannot cry in dreams. The meaning of reality was inverted, my senses could not accept the solidity of the prison cell, the bars, the cold floor, the putrid smell, not even my own body, which I could hardly feel. My mind was blocked and blank. I couldn't work out if it was despair or fear that was covering my brain like sticky tar. In my head, I could only summon with my stupefied eyes the grey concrete floor of the prison cell and a sense of doom in my heart.

Time elapsed, and it felt like an eternity of inaction. Every now and then I would regather my sanity to realise they were finishing the paperwork before taking me to the juvenile detention centre, Feltham Young Offenders Institution. I would then gasp in panic and incredulity knowing that I had lost my freedom, and my chance to travel to Pakistan.

Then my mind would go blank again, and I could only hear the gavel, like a dull thud, over and over in my head, on the grey concrete, on the cell bars. Three months and all lost.

A policeman came to the cell. I heard his steps and his voice but couldn't make sense of it. He snapped at me sternly: "Come on, move! Let's go!" and I was back to the physical cell, the tangible space my body was shaking in, the raw reality my mind was avoiding. The nightmare took a harder consistency, one that you can touch. While in shock, it was there like a sledgehammer banging the chest so hard it had numbed my whole body and became ethereal to my mind, but now it took over everything, and I could see, and the dread and fear sank deep in my heart.

I was led to the van. There were several cages. I was forced into one, my body could hardly move inside. An armoured wall with just a small hole breaching its integrity was my only passage to the world I was leaving behind.

I kneeled on the hard plastic that pretended to be a seat inside my cage and looked through the window. It might have been the darkness of my birdcage or the realisation of where I had ended up, but the grey of South London's sky seemed to shine. People walking and breathing at will on the street. My eyes, which minutes earlier were numb and dead and focused on nothing, suddenly sighted happiness in people's bodies as they moved with no greater purpose than getting to their destination.

The beauty of a couple holding hands suddenly stirred my heart as never before, in jealousy and sorrow. The fear became sadness, then fear, then sadness again. There was silence as the van set off for Feltham Young Offenders' Institution.

Chapter 2

Inferno

Three hours later the nightmare gained its full body, and its consistency made me shiver in terror. A cat only has so many lives.

I cannot recall any thoughts. My stomach was full with emptiness; however that is possible. In every second breath the air inside my body, polluted with despair, would push up into my throat. How the void can have such force to make one retch and urge the body to spew nothing is something I cannot comprehend. But the sickness I felt during the journey to the detention centre did not vanish when the van stopped.

The sudden stillness brought my mind back: we had arrived. I heard voices outside. The guards were greeting each other in a friendly tone. I heard one of them joking about the fucking shit-bags in the van. Another one burst into a vicious laugh at the word "fun". My heart sunk in fear.

The irony of the detention centre was that the punishment for the crimes were crimes themselves. The violent and lawless acts committed inside were met with such impunity that the only way to survive was to consistently breach any behaviour that might let you out of the vicious circle. As a result, criminality became a way of life until the mind, and then the body, broke apart.

The rear doors of the van opened. I covered my eyes with my arm, blinded by the outside light. The gate of my birdcage slammed open, and a rough hand grabbed me by the arm exposing my face to the filtered sun, and dragging me outside.

I was thrown against another guard that pushed me away from him shouting, "you fucking little cunt, move!" The shock was over; my eyes were now wide open, and I could look around and see where my dream would come to an end.

I was in the wrong place. I hadn't moved ahead as I had planned but backwards. I was back there again, back where I could not escape from violence because it flourished within the four walls I dwelled. Wherever I went, hell was waiting to break apart my mind and my body.

**

The black jaguar was the most majestic of all the creatures in my collection. I would also look at the tiger and admire its striped coat, elegant paws and almost evil yellow eyes looking at me, over and over. Then, I would align the cards in front of me on my sheepskin rug, in two or three rows. They were mauled and torn, my little greasy handprints all over them. I would sit on the floor cross-legged staring at them, slowly rocking my body, contented to have a treasure only for me. Just mine. I was not to share with anyone. A treasure that would take me to far away lands, away from the raw reality.

My skinny legs were not prone to much stillness. As soon as I got tired of being on the floor, I would jump up all of a sudden with the energy of a five-year-old child. I would pack all the cards in a tin box and walk off into the streets.

Sometimes Sweep would be sitting beside me. His humid nose breathing irregularly on the sheepskin rug. The rest of his body on the floor didn't belong to my woollen sanctuary, still and ethereally heavy, tired of life. He was as bony as could be, as bony as me.

My clothes were old and ripped, torn by use and covered with stains. His black fur was thin and matted, he had a bald patch on one paw and his nails were either too long or broken. And yet I could see a mighty black jaguar in my labrador as I looked at him with love and warmth.

I would call him to my bed in winter, when the bills were not paid and the chill invaded the house. The blankets stretched so skimpily over my body that I could not stop shivering. Sweep would crawl under the sheets and curl his body, covering my cold feet with his belly. I would feel his breath, damp and warm against my legs and my hand would reach to his head.

By my side on the sheepskin rug, he would follow my movements with his yellow eyes and tremble for a second as I stood up energetically, "Let´s go Sweep!"

He would never follow me straight away, as if he were pondering whether to leave the house again. Sweep knew as well as I did it was hard to decide whether home was safer than the streets. Then slowly his paws would follow me to the front door and once we were outside he would become a happy puppy dog, wagging his tail behind me.

The tin box was my token, my "mine". A thing that doesn't belong to one's body but feels so integrated that a child could not tell the difference between object and flesh. Separation feels like a laceration of the body tissue. So mine, so part of me. Just a tin box with all those creatures I would only see alive when I grew up.

I knew even then I would see the world. Off I would go, far from Ellison Road in the scummy South London that people of fine upbringing avoided. Far from the loneliness and the pain. Off I would go to all those fantastic places where big cats sport their elegance among bright green leaves and hot, humid weather. Where juicy fruits hang from trees crowded with tropical birds of a hundred different colours. I would see all that was shown on my cards and beyond. The cards were so mauled already that the corners had started to fade, and the layers of thin cardboard had puffed making the stack double its original thickness.

Most of the time I didn't want to go back. The street was safe for a while. Other children and adults paying me vague attention would content me well enough. I would jump from one person to the other, showing them my cards and quickly putting them back again, the box tight against my chest, everywhere I went.

Sweep would copy me with a wagging tail and a loose tongue seeking a pat, a kind gesture, a sign of being loved and attended. Back home there was no warmth waiting, no nice meal, maybe not even Mum. I would wander for as long as I could on the street or visit a neighbour in the hope of simply being seen.

Eventually dark would fall. Even when home is not really home, darkness scares children. It is a matter of survival.

As any other day, I came back home without knowing to what I was returning. Maybe I was coming back to the emptiness of an adult-less home, with my sister, hardly three years older than me, managing to magically produce dinner out of dry white bread and tomato sauce. Maybe I would hear the cries as I was getting closer and run towards the house to join my sister and her tears of panic and pain, begging him to stop. Sometimes my mother would already be senseless, bruised and bleeding on the living room floor.

Sweep would shake at the sight, moaning in terror, not knowing what to do. He would rush to her but somehow moving backwards, as if the duty of protecting me was stronger than his will to respond to Mum. The paws would move nervously on the spot, as if wanting to retreat but not able to move. His tail dropped between his legs and drops of dark yellow urine would fall on the floor. The wailing of his grief and fear would blend with our own cries.

Only a few times, on exceptional occasions, there would be a combination of presence and relative peace. Then I would not be scared, or not that much at least, and my sheepskin rug would seem a good place to lay and my cards a good way to hope for the next day to be the same.

I do not remember my father in South London with us, just Mum, Rose and my younger sisters. He took our elder brother with him back to his family in Italy where Mum was the English woman who would never achieve their standards of a good wife. We were left behind as Rose was not a male, and I was a dubious part of the family.

Eduardo Colella was a handsome Italian man who brightened my mum's life with their marriage and gave her two beautiful children, Rose and Amadeo Colella. Marco Antonio may or may not be his son. That was me, with the name of a Roman military leader and politician, but born in a caravan.

I will never really know, no one knew then, if the attributes I showed early in life for crime and master manipulation was an Italian heritage. I always saw Eduardo as my father; I wanted him to be. I had too small a heart to be deprived of my right to a father. Even if he didn't want me, even if his consistent rejection tore my heart apart. An absent father and a feeble sense of belonging was worse than the emptiness and uncertainty of being an orphan.

Mum married again with Tommy. Sometimes the dinner table conversation would centre around the mystery of who fathered me. The adults would ignore my presence and wonder whether I was conceived by the Italian or Tommy, perhaps someone else. I did not like the idea of someone else because there was no someone else that I could put a face or even a name to, and that was like being completely fatherless, a little bastard. They would go on talking quite openly, with no regard to my presence or the heart of a young child craving the love of a father figure, or any figure at all.

I decided myself that I was of Italian descendant and soon after everybody agreed. No one consulted me but my features seemed to show enough resemblance to please the requirements of my Italian family.

I came back home with my tin fused to the body, my only possession. My flesh. My belonging to something; my something belonging to me.

That day the house was empty and silent. I feared mum would not be there for the night. I sighed, as only a child rushed into maturity would do, secretly wishing for a nice meal and a motherly embrace. Walking in I accepted that no one would tuck the blankets in for me that night and my stomach would growl like a beast till the next morning.

Rose was home and made me toast with butter and a bit of jam, It was nice. Her little body emanated maternity from an early age. She could hardly make for a mother with her little and infantile body, but she tried hard and lovingly. I would see in her the kindness of the world personified in a house that lacked the warmth of a home.

I cut a piece from my toast and tossed it to Sweep. He caught it in the air and swallowed it straight down his throat without chewing. Then looked at me eagerly for a second. But Sweep knew better and went on chasing his own tail with a dull pace before curling on the floor. There would be no more food for him that night.

Rose asked me to go to bed, and I diligently disobeyed her. It was never in my plans to listen to or follow instructions. It was beyond my nature to allow others to decide for me. I only understood my own authority and I would see any attempt to confine me with requests or rules as a good reason for defiance. I ate my toast and grabbed my tin box almost viciously while running outside again. Rose came after me yelling, "It's dark Mark! Please come back!"

I waited crunched behind a corner for her to stop calling me, protected by the evening shadows. The street was moving some ungraceful bodies up and down in clouds of cigarette smoke and annoyed voices. Sweep had decided to stay with Rose and I lacked the warmth of his squalid fur against my legs. It was cold. I peeked and checked she had given up and gone back into the house. Only then I decided it was time to go to bed. I walked back in and threw myself on my mum's bed, empty of her, hugging my tin box and snuggling against Rose's back.

Rose rolled towards me in her sleep. Mum wasn't there, but at least we could smell her scent by digging her pillows with our little nostrils. I would inhale deeply and feel she was there somehow. It was a meagre sense of protection that did nothing to keep us safe, but allowed us enough peace to sleep.

I don't know where Sweep was. Maybe he had been with us that night, or maybe he just ran and hid before *he* came into the room. Sweep had that canine instinct that foresees danger, and a cowardice I don't blame him for.

I wished it had been just a bad nightmare. Maybe I thought it was at first but when the weight of a wound hits the bones you can be certain that it is not. The boogieman's hands striking hard with wrath into the flesh of a tiny body resonates deeper than just the skin. The blow travels down to the abyss, where the soul doesn't have a shield anymore.

He slammed the bedroom door open in the middle of the night. The boogieman had mighty strength driven by the rotten fury of an empty soul. We had no time to react. As I opened my eyes I saw a blurred dark shadow leaping towards us. My stepfather pulled back the blankets with rage. I was naked and the shudders ran throughout my body like a current that burnt and chilled my bones at the same time. He grabbed me by my bare arm and yanked me viciously up in the air, "You fucking dirty cunt! You've shit the bed!"

I was disoriented, and the shock didn't allow any sound out of my throat till I got the blow. He smashed my nose furiously with his open hand and blood splashed on the sheets and night table. I cried in terror. He dropped me violently on the bed. I saw his head coming close to mine. I could feel his breath like sharp needles repugnantly pricking my skin. The polluted air from his mouth was drenched with booze and ran up my nostrils making me gag. Then his voice was thundering in my eardrums, "Where is your fucking mother, you little cunt?"

I covered my ears, everything hurt. He dropped me back on the bed and paced the room, abusing me and kicking everything around. Mum wasn't there. I didn't know where she was. I didn't even know whether I wished Mum was there.

My stepfather went to my mum's closet and slammed the doors open. He pulled out all her clothes. Then I saw the knife. The sight of the blade chilled every cell in my body. He proceeded to pull Mum's clothes out of the closet and started to stab them as if they were full of human flesh. He cut them open with the knife and then used his hands to finish them, tearing them apart violently. I was paralysed with terror, covering my head to protect it, expecting the knife to sink into my flesh and my organs to be ripped like the fabric of Mum's dresses.

I lifted my eyes for a second and saw Rose. She was in the doorway beckoning me with talking eyes to get to the doorway, tears sliding down her face. She made a sign with her hand to follow her and I ran towards the door as fast as I could. The boogieman turned around suddenly, "Where are you going? You fucking kids".

We ran to the toilet, and Rose slammed the door behind us and locked it. I was already crunched against the wall expecting him to fly through the door, but he never did. He was too busy destroying the remains of my mum's possessions, the only evidence of her he would find at home that night.

Rose and I were petrified. I sat on the toilet shivering in terror and crying. Tears slid down my cheeks mixing with the stream of blood coming from my nostrils. Rose sat on the cold floor crying, but consoling me all the while, not even paying attention to the blood still pouring from my throbbing nose.

She came to me and held my hand, stroking my hair and maybe saying some soft words in my ears. I'm not sure if that is part of a memory or I just made it up. But as I look back, it seems to me that her voice calmed me down. Even if I didn't hear it, even if she hadn't really said a word.

She was also shaking, and her feeble body was not much of a protection for mine. She did not possibly have the strength to face our aggressor. Maybe we would both die there.

But there was only a violent blow on the door and then steps fading down the corridor. We heard the front door bursting open but never close again. Ugly words of disdain and threats would dissolve into the dark night.

Rose told me to wait. She cautiously checked we were alone again. When "alone" means "safe", children mature quickly.

I couldn't move. I started to feel the pain in my face. I heard how she closed the main door gently, and I left the safety of the toilet with scared feet. That night she cuddled me on her bed, and I felt as safe as I would ever feel for many years. Never more but so often less.

Tommy, my stepfather, was once a nice guy. When my father abandoned Mum, she started to go out with him. He would play with me and sell himself as a good man by bringing home little treats. As I held my tin box with the treasure inside, any other present was well received. My gratitude would show in my eyes, open wide and bright. We had nothing, or what is just above nothing because we could still have less, I guess. Back then, Tommy was a good and generous guy who earned our infantile approval with his treats.

Mum and Tommy married and with marriage the inferno started. He gave her two more daughters, or just one, as Ali was like me, a strayed baby who came with the uncertainty of her forefather. He also gave her excruciating pain, drove her almost to her death and made her lose whatever dignity she could hold in her own home.

Tommy would hit and kick my mum senseless. He would do it in front of us more often than not. Once I saw her pulling her head away just in time as he was trying to put it through the kitchen window, and as she fell to the floor he kicked her again and again and again. I had nightmares depicting my mum's headless body for weeks.

My sister and I would stay impotent, yelling and screaming not knowing what to do, begging him to stop. Then, when her body finally lay almost lifeless on the living room floor, he would storm out with a distorted face, half way between acrimony and hatred. I would poke my mum's body and beg her to open her eyes. Rose would call for help, and my mum would be taken to hospital by a friendly neighbour, whose home became Mum's lifeline on many occasions throughout a war she didn't know how to win, or survive for that matter.

Sometimes she would come back to consciousness by herself and prepare a cup of tea with the eyes lost somewhere unknown and her beaten body shaking and convulsing, as if life had to go on ahead regardless and she just had no option but to catch up.

We could not hug her as much as we needed it, as much as she needed it. The wounds would burn her inside and out; too broken outside to bear a caress, too broken inside to hold a sense of worthiness. Sometimes she would be away in hospital for a couple of days and then come back with a smile only for us that would erase the terror of the nights without her. Until the next one, at least.

But there was only so much a broken body could do for her children. Our neglect eventually manifesting on our skin.

It was itchy, so itchy it burnt. I couldn't sleep at night. While I was trying to rest with my eyes closed, my mind half way into my dreams, I would not notice my nails lacerating my skin in an attempt to stop the itch. I would wake up crying in pain, the open wounds blazing like red-hot needles. It wasn't just me, but Rose, Mum and my baby sisters too. We didn't complain much at first, as we feared it would be adding more suffering to our already messy situation, but Mum noticed eventually and she took us to the doctor.

As children, we learn to see the doctor as a saviour, someone who is on our side, protecting us and taking care of us. And I wasn't any different. I was hoping for that old man with the white coat to solve everything; the scratches, the burn, maybe even the hurt deep inside.

I had set my expectations high when I thought after that visit I would feel better. Unfortunately, the treatment for scabies in the seventies wasn't painless. As we left the doctor's, my mum would then drive us to another clinic.

The car was a rattling tin of metal pieces. It had no brakes, bald tyres and wasn't even worthy of a scrap yard, but it was our lifeline to get around. Rose and I, were contorting as we walked, trying to get the most itchy spots and Mum would growl at us and ask us to stop that for once. What was burrowing into our skin seemed to burrow her from the inside out, because her itch came from her mouth in the form of irritated words and stress. But we were too busy suffering from the mites digging deep into us so her bad temper didn't affect us, nor did it stop us from scratching.

We arrived at a small clinic that was no more than a small reception and a room of old yellowish tiles on the wall and floor. There was a woman dressed in white pyjamas who asked my mum to come into the next room and undress the kids.

It was cold and the smell was sickening. It was a thick, alcoholic stench mixed with damp plaster and a timid touch of flowery air freshener. I didn't want to take my clothes off, but Mum was not up for any argument that day and I could tell. Rose had already stripped off her clothing diligently and she urged me to do the same, reassuring me they were going to heal us. They did, but not before we went through a real martyrdom.

The woman in pyjamas came in and closed the door behind her. She was carrying a bucket with a thick white liquid in it. She asked my mum to tell us to stand very still while she put it on our bodies. She didn't talk to us when she warned Mum it would sting a bit. Then it started. The woman took a wide brush and covered our bodies with that white paint, head to toe.

The first time she did it, I didn't feel anything but the cold of the concoction on my skin. Suddenly, the heat started to burn and in seconds I was feeling every pore of my skin twinging. I yelled and cried in pain, and my mum shushed me. I cried through the whole process but contained myself the best I could. It felt like someone slowly ripping my skin off, over and over.

When she finished, the nurse told my mum to dress us and not to bathe till the following night.

Even though the mites came to symbolise the neglect we were going through, it made Mum more present somehow. She had to be there, making sure we got the treatment and washed it off the next day.

Every Tuesday, for six weeks, we would go through the white paint torment. It never got easier, we dreaded the times we went there, but it got rid of the scabies eventually. It also got rid of an excuse to demand my mum's care.

My little body and my tin box were no match for the lack of attention. My heart was yearning to be with Mum, but she was either away or too sore to bestow love. She always did her best, and the memory of her cuddles, even if scarce, is still with me. There is only so much you can ask from people who are on the brink, fighting for survival.

Now, as an adult, I am never tempted to blame the woman who brought me to life. There is no more to do but appreciate the love that others give you, because it has always been given within the context of their best capabilities.

Violence drains away the love a person can offer. It confuses the way the emotions that remain are released into the world, mixing care with apathy. She was not the greatest of mums, but she was a mother who loved us and would fight to the death for us, literally.

I remember her hugs as precious. Although, as often as she would share them, they were never enough for me, I wanted more. As a child I needed them to know that I was there. I didn't like to feel absent when I was present. I yearned the love, the care and the attention. I guess I determined that any attention would be a greater treat than none at all. My tin box and my mauled black jaguar stopped being consolation for my yearning heart. Sweep, with his thin and sad fur was as needy as I was, and would wander off to the streets for days, as invisible as me.

I wanted them to see me, to acknowledge I was there, and even to be called a "fucking little shit" seemed better than nothing. I defied adults and discovered the Machiavellian way to get whatever I wanted. Running away from home was not simply a way to misbehave. It was in many cases a matter of survival. Sometimes, an escape to the unknown seemed to be a better place. Even though my presence was like an absence, the emptiness of not physically being home when Mum assumed I was would alarm her.

Rose would look for me. Sometimes they'd find me, sometimes they would give up and wait for me to come back. I just wandered in the streets, running into busy roads carelessly, stealing lollies from the store or visiting my gypsy friends.

I was in South London, a jungle on its own. A jungle is what a black jaguar needs to move freely, and wait for its prey. I learned the ways of manipulation very early. I always trusted my mind and believed in it, even if I didn't understand the notion of "mind". I naturally learned to use it for my benefit. I realised some people were susceptible to my wishes if I showed the right manners, words and tone of voice.

Then the Cheshire Cat smile came to me as a feature that would eventually bring me more trouble than good.

I don't know how it came to life, whether I saw it in someone else or it came naturally to me as a defence mechanism. But I do remember when I drew the cheeky smile on my face for the first time. I can clearly recall the cane cutting the air like a whip, the whizzing sound and the smack on my bare hand or my lower back.

The pain was a stinging burn that would leave its trace on my skin for days. The teacher would be wild with me for something. I wouldn't even bother thinking what it was as I was aware that anything I did was out of bounds. I just couldn't help it. I had an earnest commitment to myself to break any rule possible, to undo what was to be kept done, to twist any deed or thought that required rectitude.

The excruciating pain as he stood on a chair and then jumped off it to gain even more momentum, as he thrashed the cane against the palm of my hand, the hurt inside and the burning on the skin, was attention after all. It was a focus on my little being, which was craving the care of an adult and the recognition of its soul.

Nonetheless, a cane against the tender flesh is not a treat to anyone. I would twitch in pain at night under the blankets, where no one could see me. I fought the cane and the hand that grabbed it. I would defy any teacher, their rules and their useless authority. But there was one whose cruelty stood out amongst the rest. My mischief was the excuse to release his frustration.

He would hit me so badly I couldn't help the tears, as much as I fought with them to stay tight and dry within my eyes. The more I resisted, the worse the punishment. It was David against Goliath. And as the tale goes, David found a pebble.

Again, how could I know it would work? But the brain is amazing, and its ability to find a way to protect itself engenders creativity. I stopped fighting and I started smiling. The cane would incise the air, hissing loudly, and at the sharp noise of the blow against my body the class would shudder in silence. Some would hold their leg quietly under the table disguising the fear of their shaking body, others would shrug with a grimace in their mouths at each hit.

Then, one day, I didn't offer any resistance. I didn't oppose the cane. Instead, I turned to my enraged teacher, and smiled cockily, bright eyes, sweet cheeks and a sense of triumph. And that did it, his teeth clenched with frustration as I mocked his abuse. He told me I posed a Cheshire cat smile.

It didn't save me completely from the cane, but I learnt that I could manipulate abusers and bullies into giving up to an acceptable and very useful extent. Neither did its beneficial effects last forever. While my face kept its angelical appearance, it worked for long enough to give me the sense of invincibility, immunity and arrogance that would mark my career as a mindless delinquent in the years to come. A paradox that would play in my head for years: a powerful mind which when misused results in a mindlessly driven life.

I would wander around without any direction. There was a gypsy camp close by and every time I'd come close, I'd enjoy seeing them around an open fire. I became fascinated by fire. It was big, hot and explosive, like the one thing burning inside me. The gypsies would sit around it, the music on the radio playing and people smoking pot, swearing and bursting into coarse laughter. They would fight and snap at each other. Fire is a force that attracts human hearts, in love or in fear. Elements have this property, they give us life, or they take it from us.

I couldn't know back then about the mystery of fire. Neither was I able to explore that fascination in an analytical manner, although I could feel its attractiveness and was very drawn to play with a box of matches, as any child would be. However, my boundaries were far beyond any conventional expectations of behaviour.

I was out walking, repeatedly kicking a soft drink can on the dirty concrete, when a pile of rubbish caught my attention. It was right outside one of the open garages, a low-level floor where residents parked their cars. I had a box of matches in my pocket which I had stolen from my mum's handbag earlier. There was no premeditation, and on reflection, I cannot recall any thread of logical thought at all, just the fancy of seeing flames lifting high over the ground floor and hearing the crackling sound.

I lit the pile of rubbish and the plastic fed the flames with exuberance. Within seconds a fire was crackling loudly and expelling the sparks high in the air. The pile was too close to the cars in the garage. A lit plastic bag rolled down the pile towards one of them and set fire to one of its tyres. All of a sudden the whole garage was on fire and spreading quickly to the adjacent garages.

The fascination I was experiencing till then rushed up my neck in a shot of adrenaline. Once I realised I could not control the power of nature and envisioned the consequences of my actions, I ran as fast and far as I could. The fire spread inside the garage, and three cars got reduced to nothing but a black, crispy metal skeleton.

By the time I caused this fire – my first fire – I was regularly visiting a child psychologist to determine what was wrong with me. The truth is, there was nothing technically wrong with me. Whatever the cause of my savage behaviour, the reality is it was just a defence mechanism. The only way I could possibly behave to survive the lack of love, care and attention, and also to protect my physical integrity.

I know that even back then I was somehow aware of the power that lay within my mind because dreaming big was not inhibited by physical pain or emotional stress. The psychologist's clinic was a nice place to be. I was listened to and I enjoyed the visits. I got the attention I was yearning. A victory of my infantile manipulation, but just as ephemeral as a short breath. As soon as I was back into the outside world, the little attention I received in exchange for my measured good behaviour within the walls of the child psychologist´s was not there any more. The only way to be heard was by hurling insults and acting up to my worst.

The violence never stopped at home. Tommy had a car accident and hit his head. When we thought it couldn't get any worse, we all fell into an abyss of desperation from which there was no escape. Now my two younger sisters were crying their lungs out in terror too.

Broken bones, open wounds and bruises to the skin. Apathetic furniture suffered the rage of a mad man destroying anything in his road to nowhere. A lost man looking for his own soul. There were blood stains on the floor and wrecked old furniture that insisted on holding its ground, as if those objects were the only ones with pride enough to stand up and face their fate. They would not beg or crunch under Tommy's fist. They would stoically bear the boots ripping off the paint and splitting their wood, boarded up windows hiding their scars.

They were not flesh, and so I wished we weren't either: not Mum, nor my sisters nor me. I wished we weren't there, but I could not conceive where else we could be. And as my mind would fail to find an escape, we would hold each other tightly, as if our squalid bodies could offer any solace.

Alcohol ended up tearing apart Tommy's heart and mind, and he became ruthless. Again cutting Mum's clothes with a kitchen knife. Again beating her almost to death. Again provoking in all of us a fear I cannot even describe. Again, Mum's breath becoming just enough to keep her alive a few hours till help arrived, her hair stuck to her face with fresh blood. Rose and me crying and praying to a God we didn't know, saying, "please, please, please." Little Sylvan screaming out her terror. And Ali, still a baby, laying on her back in a cot not knowing what was going on, howling the high pitch cry of a baby sensing the danger.

Again, there was Tommy's insults and cursing and the front door slamming shut, with his rage fading away as he stepped off into the darkness of South London's streets.

I learned there is always a level beyond what has been reached, in any matter, good or bad. Whenever you believe things cannot get worse, they certainly can.

On my way to nowhere, away from the war that was ripping off my mum's clothes and flesh and that threatened to tear apart my mind and body at home, I sought refuge on the streets. Fiddling with the box of matches in my pocket, thinking of nothing. I saw a bunch of dried branches and leaves besides one of our neighbour's sheds.

Once more I thought, maybe without thinking, of the warmth of fire, and I craved for the heat and the orange light. A magic element that could emphasise my being, soaring high enough for others to see. Would others be as fascinated as I was, and in looking upon the flames would they find me and notice me?

I lit the heap of dried weeds with a match. I walked backward slowly, admiring the flames growing taller. I stared at them for a few seconds, and then I ran to hide and escape the guilt that suddenly hit me, as if I could.

I was running on the concrete pavement towards nowhere in particular, just anywhere away. Anywhere I wouldn't be caught. Then I heard four explosions. The fire had reached the shed inside, where countless tins of paint had been stored.

I was labelled uncontrollable. No one could handle me at home. I must agree with this label, but it is fair to say that nothing was handled at home. Everything and everyone were mauled, kicked, punched, cursed, abused and almost killed more often than just "handled".

I was sent to a children's home, a home labelled either as an orphanage or a place for uncontrollable delinquent little shits. I was the second one.

I fought the social workers and stood my ground with all the strength I could possibly summon. My place was with Mum, wounded to the bone, with her esteem shrunk almost to nothing by the violence thrown upon her. Even if she was absent. I had parents; I had a mum right there, in South London, and a dad somewhere abroad. Maybe not great parents, but I loved them. I would stay with Mum even if that meant I had to go through the inferno that Tommy had created for us. But at eight-years-old I was no match for the men who came to grab me.

As I walked through the front door of the children's home, carrying a small bag with all the clothes I had, I saw in front of me an aquarium with colourful fish swimming slowly in the water. The glass tank uplifted my heart timidly. This would be one of the very few good memories I would gather in that place. Thinking back now, I often wonder if the bright colourful fish tank had been placed in that spot for a reason.

Chapter 3

No Sweet, No Home

The guards forced us in pairs into a double line. The guy beside me was a very skinny boy. He looked younger than me and quite feeble. However, as we were walked towards the reception area of the Young Offenders Institution (the YOI), I saw how his shoulders drew back firmly and his chin raised as much as the situation would permit it. A show of arrogance that would certainly be punished if detected but just enough to make clear to the rest he wasn't one to mess with.

I walked in with a similar attitude. I had lost the confidence that I was holding onto in the courtroom. I was not invincible anymore, but neither was I defeated. The judge had swept out my arrogance only momentarily, and as I was coming back to reality, images were less diffused. Even though fear was still shaking me inside, it was fear and arrogance that had been keeping me alive all those years.

We were told to strip off and walked naked into the nurse's room. A doctor was expecting us for a medical examination.

It was January, and we all stood as straight as the freezing cold would allow us to hold our spines. The doctor was a broad man, bald and with mighty rough hands. He had a frown like every other guard in the institution and a filthy grin that made you expect the worse. I was second in line.

The doctor questioned the skinny guy first, "Do you have any medical condition?"

"Ulcer," he answered.

"Ok, move." And off he went.

The doctor stopped in front of me and smiled with a vicious look.

"Do you have any medical condition?"

"Ulcer," I said. Then he punched me in the stomach with all his strength.

I dropped to the floor in a heap trying to catch my breath, my guts in excruciating pain, the wind knocked out of me. I couldn't stretch my spine, and I made myself into a ball on the cold tiles.

"Fucking move!" the doctor shouted.

Another guard scooped me off the floor by the armpit. I could hardly stand, my legs were shaking, and I wanted to spew.

The doctor had curled his fist against my stomach, pushing my guts up into my ribcage. I found it very hard to breath in, but the fear of receiving another fist on my face gave me enough strength to follow the guard's instructions and put on the wool uniform I had been given.

I was thrown into my cell. The short skinny guy turned out to be my cellmate. He was called Barry. We shook hands and nothing else was said. We both lay on our beds, a thin mattress on a metal structure. The cell had a small table and a chair, and that was all aside from a window with iron bars.

My stomach was still hurting, and I tried not to breathe too deeply as it would make me gag. I just turned to the wall, curled up with my hands on my stomach and looked at the grey masonry in front of me. My blank mind was now recovering images of all that was dear outside. All that was already lost.

***

I know a person, a good man whom I have worked with while performing on cruise lines. We met again recently and afterwards I thought about him. He has a trait that I dislike very much. I do not appreciate it in the least. I have even offered him my help as a hypnotist to overcome it.

This person was unfortunate enough to suffer sexual abuse as a child, as many of us did. Child abuse is a scourge this world never seems to eradicate.

He walks around telling his story to any female who wants to listen to it and the usual response from women, in their kindness and well-intentioned manners, is to come closer to him and offer him their pity. An instant hand on his knee, or even a stroke on the head if they feel motherly.

This attention is plain sorrow; it is sympathy, not empathy. Sympathy stands for a sense of superiority, and they touch his shoulder and offer him a few nice words of comfort. Yet, this is a treat for him, a valued reward or compensation for how he felt back in those days when his soul was ripped out by the shame or sense of betrayal or the fear. Whatever it was he had individually experienced upon the abuse. He doesn't want empathy because empathy involves respect but also bluntness: "I know how you feel, but you need to get over it and move ahead". I offer him empathy, but never sympathy.

Now he is in his mid-to-late forties. Year after year, since he became an adult and no longer abused, he recalls his trauma in order to receive a bit of fake love, even if it is just vague attention.

Because I have been through all sorts of abuse myself, I cannot help but feel frustrated by his attitude. I have offered him my services as a hypnotherapist for free to stop him soliciting crumbs of appreciation and gestures of pity and to start living and receiving real love. The power of the mind can release the pain and bring a better present and future.

However, my help was refused as the secondary gain for him was a stronger stimulus than the unknown primary gain. The release of a load that has been carried for years cannot possibly be a burden like the one he is suffering in the present: living over and over the emotions and the pain the abuse caused him. But for the release to happen, one has to make a decision to move forward towards the unknown and risk leaving behind the secondary gain.

***

I was curled up under the blankets, my head sunk beneath them. I did not want to be awake. I wished I had been in a profound sleep, in a dream or a nightmare. Anywhere within the realm of fabricated images, just not hearing the pain spitting out of the supplicant's mouth with every lunge.

I could imagine the grimace on his face and the tears mixing with foamy saliva. I could hear the sobs, the cruel laughter and the moans. We all could, no one could sleep through that. But if we weren't seen, they wouldn't touch us. There under the blankets, it was a frail shield, but it was as much as we had. The rest was just a matter of luck.

Eventually they would stop. We would hear a last moan of ruthless pleasure from one of the older boys. Then silence, timidly broken by the sobs of their victim. They would never come alone, always two at least. I didn't even wonder if that could happen to me. If it did, how could I possibly escape?

I think now I would have fought, yes, I would have. But there is only so much a bunch of skinny muscles can do against two teenagers that were double my weight. I wasn't raped, as in I wasn't penetrated but my intimacy was violated in other ways. In ways a boy doesn't learn till he is exposed to the vice of hungry predators. These were not grown up men, not even only males, but other children with no notion of right or wrong.

Someone asked me how I felt when I was sexually abused, how I felt when I was witnessing the abuse of others. In the latter, I didn't feel, I just feared and then thankful it wasn't me. When adults don't play their roles as carers in a children's home, children don't learn to understand or differentiate between wrong and right.

There was no place for bravery when one is certain to suffer the same fate should they stand up and expose themselves. We were just children. It is not the child's role to protect but to be protected. It is not up to children to decide what is right or wrong. A lack of guidance in this matter leads you to a state of numbness, an acceptance that the wrong is inevitable , not recognising the good beyond a short-term satisfaction.

I don't know what I felt when I was abused. I did not like it in the least, I can say that. But, without the parameters of healthy relationships or anyone to guide me and help me discern right from wrong, sexuality was for me something where feelings were not identified as one or the other.

I only knew I would not abuse. I could certainly sense the emotional and mental pain rape would have brought on me. Even hiding under the blankets, I could understand the suffering. Even though I did nothing. I was just a kid, like all the others under the blankets.

Maybe the development of sexuality was just a manifestation of the lack of love we suffered as kids. I am not sure if this in itself could be considered as sexual abuse or whether there is more beyond it, not to excuse it, but to pay it a different attention. A children's home – like the one I was sent to – is no place for a child to grow into a balanced, well-adjusted young adult.

The sexual abuse is a chain that goes from the top down to the defenceless, from the first adult that started it. Then it spreads like the plague. I am glad to say that I made it to adulthood without bringing that virus into my life. I grew out of it with the power of my mind, and a desire and yearn for a better life. I am glad I didn't choose the secondary gain in this matter and did not conform to a label of pity, which never allows us to move on.

My time in the children's home was marked by a constant expectation of pain and suffering, but also moments of camaraderie and friendship. For years I couldn't be certain whether our carers were aware of the nightmare the children were going through at night. I do know now that they were and chose to look the other way. I also guess they didn't really care.

I knew the carers ignored what happened because not very long ago I met one of them, who also migrated to Australia as I did. Bettie was one of the "good ones", as we would describe them.

I told her, "Bettie, I am writing a book, and you'll be in it."

Her eyes widened, and she nervously nodded first and then exclaimed, "No, no, no!" She almost fainted in desperation as she pronounced the last one. "No, Mark, no! You cannot tell what happened there. You cannot!"

Maybe she wasn't referring to the sexual abuse. Maybe she was referring to all the emotional and physical abuse we would suffer over and over. But I cannot just accept they had no idea what was going on in the dormitories.

On Sundays, a man called Daniel would visit us. He was an older gentleman, respected, well dressed and friendly. In the children's home we all liked him and looked up to him. He had a soft and comforting voice. We loved his attentive tone and caring manners.

Daniel would spend a few minutes with the young kids, entertaining us with his conversation, fun and wit. Then he would take two of the older boys to the markets. The boys would come back for dinner with some pocket money that Daniel had given them.

I remembered that I wished he took me out on a Sunday with him. I thought it would be nice to spend the afternoon somewhere in the markets, as that was what the boys would claim they would do. But he would only take the older boys, never us.

I met Daniel years later on the street. I was fifteen by then and I recognised him. I went towards him to greet him, I was glad to see him and we chatted for a few minutes. Daniel asked me if I wanted to have a cup of tea with him at his place. I accepted. He was nice and fun and I did not see anything wrong with it.

Even as cunning as I was I could not conceive of certain behaviours that I was too naive to perceive. We walked to his house, only two blocks away, and he let me in. He invited me to sit down while he prepared a cup of tea for me. Then he said he had to go upstairs for a moment.

He was taking too long up there. I was pondering whether to leave when he called me from a room upstairs and asked me to go up, claiming he wanted to show me something. I went up and found him in his room lying on the bed completely naked and his genitals covered in baby powder.

"Mark, would you like to rub me here?" he said pointing to his penis.

I had no time to be shocked. I told him to fuck off and ran as fast as I could out of his home and out of the sight of it. I understood then. I felt betrayed and embarrassed when I thought I wanted to spend Sundays with him as a child. I suppose I must be grateful that I wasn't at the age he fancied back then.

Bettie was one of the good ones, as were Julia and Victoria. I remember they were good people within the limits of goodness and kindness that a ruthless environment would allow. They weren't abusive like Pia and the other two, whose names I have erased from memory more successfully than I have erased the memory of their abuse.

In a way, I like to look back and be able to tell this story. Pia was the principle of the children's home. She was divorced and her daughter and son lived with her at the children´s home. They would mingle with the orphans and those three or four of us who were there with the label "uncontrollable". Pia's cruelness knew no bounds. She wouldn't think twice about hitting us viciously, and no excuse was too banal to slap us in the face, with or without a weapon of some type. Some people find the way out of their frustration by releasing physical energy upon others in the cruelest way. Pia had landed in a paradise of impunity where she could pour her rage on a bunch of children no one cared for.

She earnestly seemed to dislike certain children, particularly me and Scott. I made good friends with Scott in the children's home. He was one of the uncontrollable kids, and we used to get into trouble quite often. To be fair, our delinquent behaviour never matched what we would do on the outside and the reasons why we were in the children's home in the first place. But every single act outside the rules, even if small or not really serious, would bring disproportionate consequences. They called it consequences, but in reality it was plain abuse, an excuse to damage, sometimes permanently and without regard to a child's emotional and mental health. Physical and emotional abuse would take place in parallel with sexual abuse. While sexual abuse among the children and perpetuated by children was overlooked by adults at night, the carers had their shot at every opportunity during the day.

Scott was with me that night. I had just come back from the main bathroom. My mouth had been washed viciously with soap as a consequence of swearing in the children's home. The sour taste still on my tongue urged me to scrub it with my pyjama sleeve, pulled and stretched against my palm. Scott was laughing at me, and for a second I admitted with a smile I was making a joke. Too soon, that timid smile attempting a warm moment was broken.

She came thundering into the dormitory, and stomped all the way to our beds. Then she grabbed me by the arm and pulled me behind her all the way back to the door. I didn't resist her power not because of my complacency and respect for authority, which barely existed, but rather because I was too shocked. I had already been punished, I couldn't understand what was going on.

Then we reached the bathroom. She pushed me inside and stayed guarding the door while pointing at me with her finger, "This will teach you. You can sleep in the bathtub tonight!"

The chosen bathroom for my redemption was upstairs. I suspected the choice was made to make the punishment more unbearable. The heating was virtually nonexistent, there were no hot water pipes to be seen and the heat from the rooms didn't reach the bleak tiles. I had to try and get some warmth from the cold bath. I curled myself inside the bathtub in the unavailing hope of conserving some of my body temperature. I had no blankets or anything to cover myself with. Shivering with clacking teeth, waiting for the night to end, I had never wished so strongly for my bed in the dormitory.

I can clearly remember the feeling of losing control of my body, how my hands were shaking so much. I wanted them to stop, but I couldn't stop them. I was eight years old and had been separated from my parents. That was chilly enough for the heart, but someone still abused their power to condemn me to an icier place.

It is fair to say that when the body is suffering and survival mode activates in the brain, the mind selects what is important to keep us alive. I could not feel any emotion troubling me, just the external cold, the fingers trembling, the teeth uncontrollably clacking against each other. Maybe it wasn't that bad, maybe it was best to be there risking pneumonia than under the blankets. Yes, maybe it was.

Although then I wouldn't have been thinking about it. I would have preferred to be back in bed and take the risk of the dormitories. Children's home is a funny name. While it involves children and a home there is no sweet, no home here. Children become adults with the tainted traits of a child who does not know integrity. Home is a word that just made sense for me within those walls because of Tommy's presence in my own house.

Some times were enjoyable, because regardless of all the cruelness – and a fish tank that only could bring limited happiness when looking at it – we were still a bunch of kids. Somehow, we would find the way to a kind of wellbeing and joy, as any other child would.

Hunger was something that blighted our lives in the children's home. Whenever abuse is talked about in institutions there seems to be a lot of focus on a lack of nutrients. But as kids, we couldn't care less about nutrients. Nutrients was an alien word, fuck the nutrients. Whatever we could get into our belly to fill it up was good enough. Growling stomachs are terrible and the pangs of hunger that would make us gag nothing was just another mistreatment we would suffer every single day.

One night, ready to go to sleep in the dormitories, Scott and I had an idea. It was a calm night with no hidden places or painful moans, one of those nights where children remember they are children and chat in whispers.

We were forbidden to enter the kitchen. That was a golden rule not to disobey. While lying in bed, Scott and I started to talk and fantasise about an apple. The saliva started to roll down the corners of our mouths. Dribbling was the only motivation we needed.

I was already good at manipulation, not only with adults. My self-confidence, wherever I got it from, could entice any other kid to do whatever I wanted them to. This is what hypnosis is about, even when I did not know I was already practicing it.

I talked Scott into coming down to the kitchen cupboard with me in the middle of the night to steal a couple of apples. Looking back, I realised how naturally hypnosis came to me. At ten I was able to talk almost anyone into doing something terribly wrong that would lead to a harsh punishment that would make any of the orphans or school kids shake in fear. They would follow me for no reward whatsoever.

Scott and I managed to sneak past the older kids and carers on duty. They were in the lounge room watching TV and we slithered past the door with feline skills. We were thrilled; two ninjas fooling the enemy was a fine game for us.

We snuck into the kitchen and brought two apples back to the room. Scott and I ate them delightfully and carelessly, throwing the cores out of our bedroom window into the garden below. The garden was an incongruent mix of grass, weeds, broken pavement, stones and gravel, disposed in an attempt to mark a path, and the apple cores fell on an amalgam of dry leaves, pebbles, twigs, grit and dirt. We had a good sleep on full tummies and accomplishment, oblivious to our lack of strategy skills when committing a crime.

The next day, after we had returned from school, we were called as usual to the dining room. We waited for our food plate as we would every day. Strangely Scott and I were the last ones to be served, with carers serving plates around us and skipping us all the time, offering the food to any other. At last, we were the only ones on the dining table with no food on our plates.

One of the carers came with a tray toward us. Scott and I looked at each other puzzled, trying to work out what was going on. We knew soon enough as the two plates were placed on the table in front of us. There was nothing on them but two apple cores covered in dirt with stones and grit deeply embedded into them. The carer stared at us and said, "Your dinner. Eat it!"

There was no argument; we knew we would have to eat it. Eventually, with bleeding gums and sore teeth from biting and chewing into the stones and grit, we both finished the meal, controlling the impulse to spew and swallowing every bit. We got sick, which was the end result of most of the cruel punishments we would receive in the children's home.

There was an attempt from the social services system to pretend we were normal kids living in normal families. On weekends we would receive some pocket money. For the young ones, it was just enough to buy lollies. However, the older kids would get a greater amount, and that would also allow them to buy a bottle of Coke.

In recalling this memory, I try to understand what the wrongdoing was that led to us being so badly scolded. It is so senseless that one can only assume it is out of pure evil and perversion. Our sin was harassing the older kids to share their Cokes with us, the younger ones. While sharing is caring, that concept was not deemed a good value in the children's home. If I thought I was Machiavellian as a child, it was because I learnt it from adults.

I accept responsibility for all my wrongs, and I am grateful my past has been able to show me a brighter future. But twisted minds like this should not be in charge of children who lack adult figures to learn from. It was decided by the carers that sharing is not caring, and thus we were banned from even asking the older kids to share their treats.

The lesson came in the form of digestive torture. They filled the older kids Coke bottles with a mix of Coke, brown vinegar, salt, pepper and cold tea. I really don't want to recall whether there was anything else in the concoction. As with the apple core, we were forced to drink it till the last drop. It was clear to me that punishment in the children's home – aside from the hitting – was not only a prompt scolding, but a system for inducing sickness in the children. I assume that the most subversive way to keep children submissive is to jeopardise their physical strength and energy.

Yet, among all this abuse, our infantile souls would be bright enough to make good memories. Fortunately, the fish tank wasn't the only good image I recall from my time in the children's home. There was the chocolate factory.

A chocolate factory is the utopia of any child. A place of innocence, joy and clean indulgence, full of laughter, sweet dreams and the legitimate happiness every kid should know. Our chocolate factory was indeed a source of joy and happiness, but at a cost to other's hard work and money.

Rather than showing any sort of innocence we were street rogues with little or no sense of integrity. I calculate now that we would have robbed more than a thousand pounds in chocolate bars and other treats.

The factory was isolated in an area not far from the children's home, surrounded by empty fields of weeds, rocks and grit. We would form a party of ten or more. The older kids would lead us like fugitives in the early evening, sneaking away from the carers into the streets. Hiding behind a bush or a rock, at the back of a brick building with fuming chimneys exhaling a scent of burnt sugar and hot chocolate, we would wait for the workers to finish their shift.

We already knew the easiest spot to get in. Breaking in wasn't an issue for us, even at our young age we were dexterous and cunning with mischief. We would pick up as much chocolate as we could carry within our hands and pockets, and would hide them in the bushes or under a rock in the surrounding fields. The loot would last a few days; some of it would be stolen by other kids, or spoilt by stray dogs, or soaked with rainwater. Then we would come back to steal more. It was there, we were hungry, and there was no reason whatsoever not to steal it.

I also remember Svengali, an Austrian hypnotist. That was another good memory. And Tommy. Unexpectedly Tommy.

The boogieman had a kind side, although so small and barely existent, it had been consumed by the violence that shrank his soul. I do not feel pity for him, even when I acknowledge the torments he would be facing inside. A hell that he couldn't contain and would pour it all over my mum, my sisters and me.

I know whatever a person goes through, is not an excuse to damage others. It is not an excuse to find happiness by whatever means, it is not even an excuse to avoid searching for peace. I should know, I had never had a unique trait but my own mind and I got out and found a way. It is a matter of choices and acceptance. And Tommy would not choose to be different, he would not accept he was a monster, and without that realisation and acceptance, change is not possible.

But that tiny, slight, almost faint, kind side of him would show up with me, because he always wanted a boy, and he had only conceived two girls. Maybe there was a place for the doubts about whose offspring I was, maybe he wanted to believe that I was his legitimate son.

He would visit me in the children's home and spend time with me. The visits were pleasant. I am not the kind of person who forgets when pain has been inflicted, but in the mind of a child who seeks attention, even if the devil came to give them poisoned lollies, that would be better than indifference. Indifference makes you disappear among the crowd, as if you had never existed.

Tommy came one day to bring me a good memory among the collection of bad experiences I would suffer at the children's home. He brought an old reel-to-reel tape recorder. I was very excited. It was indeed a magnificent surprise.

One of the carers welcomed Tommy and led us into the visitor's room. We sat down in front of the tape recorder and I saw the enthusiasm in his eyes. He might have been recalling a time when he was a child, when he would find moments of peace even in a tumultuous life – as I was doing myself at that moment. Enjoying what was offered in those given moments, just then, with no past or future pestering to spoil it with its nagging. Not thinking about consequences, not remembering what was left behind.

My step-father was a huge fan of Everton football team, and we practised the Everton song first before he pressed the "rec" button. Then we sang and I would make a mistake, and we would both laugh out loud and have another go:

"Blue is the colour,
Football is the game,
We're altogether and winning is our aim,
So cheer us all through the sun and rain
Cos Everton, Everton is our name"

We rehearsed around ten times before we recorded it. Of course it wasn't good enough. So we did it over and over until the time was up or until the song was neat, I don't remember.

I would imagine I was dressed in blue and white to add more passion to the song. I would stand up solemnly pretending I was a football player in the field, aligned with my other twenty mates, my fist on the puffed chest and a deep voice looking to the audience, in a stadium packed with thousands of people waving blue and white flags and cheering and crying, wowing and roaring. Then he had to leave, and for once I did not think he would go home, have a drink and beat my mum and my sisters. I just skipped up the stairs singing "Blue is the colour", because children deserve to anchor to the happiness of a moment in order to move ahead, at least enough to allow us one or two steps.

I spent almost four years in the children's home. Never sweet and never home, and yet it was so familiar that the way I left seemed sharp and brutal for a fraction of a second. Mum had left Tommy about two years earlier. There had been a restraining order that did nothing to protect my family. Not being able to get to their flesh, Tommy still managed to destroy Mum's car with an iron bar and terrify my sisters, confining them at home, unable to feel safe going out. But along came Stace the Ace, and then Tommy left for good.

Stace the Ace was an amazing man. He was good and gentle. Mum and Stace the Ace would visit me at the children's home and we would have a joyful time. I started to be allowed to go home on weekends. I never got used to the separation. It would tear my heart apart every single time. It felt like the sky was darkening as I walked away from my mother and into the institution, not even the fish tank in the hall would change my sadness for an instant.

Mum and Stace the Ace would always drive me back there at the same time each Sunday. On our arrival, the ice-cream van would be parked in the street, right in front of the children's home entrance. I knew they always planned for it to be like that. They would buy me an ice cream, as if its smooth texture could soothe my pain. It never did. I would sob and cry my heart out, all the joy would evaporate with my tears and I would feel an excruciating void in my chest. I would suffer the agony every time, over and over, until "over and over" was no more.

Stace the Ace didn't have much money, but he would try his best to please us with gifts. On most weekends that would be an Indian curry that we would devour with a mix of hunger, anxiety and genuine pleasure. It was a meal that mum could never afford to buy for us. I would never forget the time they brought me home from the children's home for the weekend, and as I walked into the kitchen, there it was: leant up against the kitchen cupboard was a bright and shiny bicycle.

Stace the Ace was a great handy man, especially with anything that had an engine or wheels. He had managed to get a Chicco bike frame and a couple of tyres, one white and one black. He had assembled the parts, fixed the brakes, and cleaned it. The tin box with animal cards had been part of me, like an extra limb that gave me security, an external object that demonstrated my existence and my right to possess material things for my own good. The bicycle became more than that. It was also a physical resource that would break barriers and shorten the distance between me and my family. And it marked the end of my time in the children's home. Although before I left there was a finale I would not escape from.

Unfortunately, I didn't miss the yearly holiday at the children's home. They would organise some time out in the country, a camp or a farm, anywhere near South East London. It was a pleasant time for us, as long as we weren't caught breaking the rules.

Scott, another boy called Gary and I were caught smoking cigarettes. I had been smoking since the age of five, whenever possible. I used to steal cigarettes from my mum's handbag and smoke them in any hidden corner or behind a bush in the playground. I don't even remember how we got the cigarette this time, but the carers didn't like it in the least.

Waiting for a punishment wasn't scary any more. We knew it would be painful, we knew we wouldn't forget it, and we knew we would go through as much abuse as necessary and we still wouldn't learn any better from the consequences imposed. This is the apathy of the rebellious soul in an abusive environment. Either way there is always something you'll lose and no one escapes it. The physical punishment makes you immune and strong enough to cope with even worse, rather than promote any change to a better or expected behaviour.

The carers got quite creative with their punishment. They locked us one at a time in a cupboard and forced us to smoke a big long fat cigar inside it, down to the last bit, not letting us free until we had finished. We got sick to the point of nausea, and vomited halfway through, but had to keep going. However, I don't remember that torture so clearly because of the pain and the claustrophobic environment, but because it would be the last one I would suffer in the children's home.

When we came back from holidays we had time to visit our families. Since I had the Chicco bike, I would ride twenty kilometres every Saturday to meet my mum, my sisters and Stace the Ace. It was a hard ride with tough hills to climb. But no thunder or heavy rain pouring fiercely would stop me. I would get by just thinking about spending time with my family at home. A home that for once was so much better than the place I was forced to live in. That strength would push the bike without the slightest feeling of tiredness. It was always a happy ride, full of hope and expectations.

That day after the holiday I arrived home and spent the weekend playing in the familiar streets and watching TV with Mum and my sisters. Then, the sad time came when I had to leave. No one was saying goodbye this time. Mum didn't ask me to prepare for the return. There was not that feeling of sorrow and nostalgia that used to float in the air every time I was to go back.

It was a Sunday afternoon without that feeling of end or wasted hours. Instead, everybody seemed to keep going with their lives without disruption, and this continuity confused me.

Then mum and Stace the Ace called me into the kitchen and Mum said casually while setting the table for dinner, "Phone the children's home and tell them you are not going back there."

And that was it. I never went back.

Chapter 4

Svengali

The dining room was as cold as any other place in the institution. We queued up when it was time for dinner and then walked slowly to the serving line. Each of us picked up a metal tray with several compartments and waited for the staff to serve us. It was more like throwing the food onto the plate than serving it. My stomach was still sore but I could walk straight and managed to hide the pain.

There was a bit of a bustle; we were the new lot. Some prisoners looked at us with disdain, muttering some unpleasant comments. Others made sure we knew they were in charge with just a look.

I queued up in that line every day for three months, twice a day. The first time we walked in it we were the new cattle, an exhibit for the others to determine our worth in terms of strength. One of us was tacitly labelled as a moron, a nonce, and he would suffer special abuse, just because a particular trait would condition the selection. It was up to oneself to keep this tag or show otherwise with the right attitude, and yet that was no guarantee.

Safety was something no one ever took for granted inside the institution. It was the physical pain inflicted as soon as I arrived that had brought me back to reality, and it would be what would keep me alert for the time to come.

Already recovered from the shock, I observed how other prisoners moved, who would be talking and who would just be listening. Eyes lost looking nowhere would tell me who had suffered the most in the last few days. Puffed black eyes and broken lips are common features in places where impunity reigns.

As the queue moved forward to the hot plate, my stomach shrunk even more: mashed potatoes. I hated mashed potatoes. The consistency and smell were repulsive, and the lumps made it even worse. I felt the nausea as the cook dropped the paste with all its splodges on the steel tray.

I sat down with my cellmate. We did not talk at all that day. I looked at my tray: mashed potatoes, ten peas and a piece of meat, so hard and small that it could be eaten in a single bite and yet had to be chewed for ten minutes until soft enough to swallow.

With my stomach still sore and growling with hunger I saw no other option but to eat it. I played with the peas and swallowed them slowly not wanting to face the rejection I knew my body would feel from the smell of the whitish mass on the plate. It seemed infantile to debate with oneself about food on a plate when the guts are crying to get something, anything, inside. But as strong as my mind was, I certainly had a powerful disdain for mashed potatoes and when I introduced the first spoonful in my mouth, I could not help gagging.

I forced myself to swallow and I felt the bile coming up in my throat. With all my senses now back in that place, and accepting the familiarity of a ruthless environment, I knew spewing in the dining room on my first night would give me an unfortunate label. I was not willing to let anyone think I was weak enough to be a target for their cruel entertainment.

I focused on my throat and brought the bile back to my stomach. It burnt. I took another mouthful, small enough to swallow with a single move of my tongue. This time I could feel the vomit coming out, but I swallowed it. The portion on my plate was so small that I just needed one more half a spoonful to finish it. I put it in my mouth and immediately pushed it down with a piece of white bread. I felt sick but pretended I was fine. I felt sad as well but hid it successfully. I was scared and frustrated, and I looked at the metal plate with just a trace of what had been there and gagged again, closing my mouth very quick and tight so no one would notice.

After dinner, we were served the darkest of black teas with bromide, as a remedy to eliminate the only possible physical pleasure we could have left. Its flavour was terrible and yet it was a relief as it killed the taste left in my throat by the mashed potatoes . I even enjoyed it. The acrid flavour seemed a delight to my palate.

There is this constant feeling of emptiness and mild sickness that the dull food only relieves for a few minutes. It is a characteristic of any institution where children and young offenders are secluded, no matter how full of starch the stomach is.

Everyday I would line up, dreading the moment I had to eat the mashed potato, but I soon learnt I could get more food than the other prisoners. It was just a matter of wording. I sensed how the cook disliked me when I asked for a bigger portion of veggies. However, he could not refuse.

"Can you put some more on, please?" I asked.

Mum used to tell me manners never cost anything, and I understood that on a deep level. I would use my nicest voice and look directly into his eyes, not staring, but only giving him the proper attention while I pronounced those words.

"No, I can't," he would reply sternly.

I would offer him a mild smile so as not to seem too enthusiastic in a place where any act of kindness could be mocked and seen as a weakness for irrelevant and unreasonable punishment.

"If you could put some more on my tray, how much more would it be?"

There would be no answer but an extra scoop on my plate. It wasn't difficult.

***

The building in Erith was of red bricks, dark roof tiles and white timber frames. On the ground floor, to the right of the fish tank, there was a door to a medium sized room where we would receive visits and play. Sometimes we would watch a movie: another of the few good memories I gathered from the children's home. The wooden chairs would usually be resting against the walls and we would set them in front of the small screen, although most of the young kids would lie on the carpet.

I was lying on my belly, holding my head with both hands under my chin and kicking the air slowly forwards and backwards with my feet, pacing them with the suspense in the movie, to the rhythm of the music and the scenes. I was fascinated. The room was semi-dark and unusually silent for a bunch of irreverent ratbags. I was drawn into the film: *Svengali*. An Eastern European music teacher who used the power of his mind to control his female students and get whatever he wanted from them. His eyes would go blank and then he would have the heroine under his control, an innocent looking Trilby, who could only sing when Svengali was present. I was fascinated by his power.

Little did I know I had already used hypnotic powers to get others to do as I pleased. My tantrums as an uncontrollable five-year-old were only an unpolished version of my manipulation skills. I had a natural ability to pick the most impressionable children in the children's home and easily convince them to break the rules for my own benefit. However, after *Svengali*, and for the period of time that infantile enthusiasm and commitment allows, I was determined to become a hypnotist.

I was ten years old at the time and Scott was happily willing to contribute to my training as a hypnotist. I found a plastic watch in the playroom, which I tore apart from the wristband and tied to a shoelace to make a pendulum. I waved it in front of him, and I asked him to focus on the watch and only on the watch, close his eyes and go to sleep.

"Watch the watch. Watch the watch. Watch the watch…"

And so he did. And fell asleep.

I assumed he was playing as I was, just pretending that I was an amazing hypnotist. I poked him and talked to him, but he didn't seem to move. I called his name louder, "Scott!" but he did not react. Then I just resolved to give the order, "Awake now!" And back he came to the room.

I still thought he was a good playmate and I didn't conceive for a second that he wasn't pretending. But then Scott looked at me startled and asked me what had happened with a big smile, as if expecting me to explain whether it had worked or not.

I cannot tell if it was just my skills or our propitious mental states that made it work, but the romantic side of me wants to believe it was the first time I consciously used my mind as a hypnotist. Yet, even with my newly discovered powers, my situation stayed the same and I was back to life in the children's home.

Survival instinct forces you to develop your natural weapons and perfect them, in order to defend your life from threats. This must not be in spite of your integrity as an individual in all aspects: mental, emotional and physical. Life is not an easy ride for anyone, but some suffer more than others.

I grew up among violence and in a constant state of alert, I could not know what would be coming next and whether it would kill me or not. I didn't see this way, or have these thoughts as a child or even a young adult, otherwise I would never have risked my life so often and in so many different manners.

I didn't have a safe home or a reliable adult to lean on. As much as my mum loved us, she was fighting to keep herself alive, over and over. Maybe not only in a physical sense, but also in a mental battle to keep alive a fire that made her feel breathing was worth it. My special survival trait, my natural weapon, was my mind. I had a very active imagination and would visualise situations so intensely that they would become real at the right time. It was my defence from the world that insisted in putting me down.

I do especially remember me wiping the dirt off my hands onto some overalls mum had bought for me from an op-shop. The sixteen-year-old me smiled at recalling this memory, and a feeling of achievement run up through his spine. It was like the job wasn't offered to him, but he had created it. Years earlier, I dreamt of being a tyre fitter, playing in a mountain of rubbish and wasted car tyres. I would pretend I had clients and then pretend a stick was a tool. Then I would roll them to an imaginary car and acquiring a professional look, I would explain to my client what he had to do to avoid future damage while I fitted the tyre. Then nine years later I got the job – with real tyres and real clients.

More than thirty years into the future, I can be certain of all the things I built with the images in my mind. How my ability to visualise whatever I wanted was the seed for its future acquirement. This is also an example of how the logic of time allows for things to happen at the right moment. I could not possibly have been working at a tyre shop before I was sixteen, could I?

But a powerful mind doesn't mean an honest mind. Whilst I had great values regarding family and friends, I also had a hierarchy in place that would make me steal or damage others. In this instance, I stole a set of high quality tyres from the workshop after breaking in at night, and sold them to my then girlfriend's father. The next day, I came back to work with no shadow of regret or guilt.

Svengali also had a powerful mind. Still, he was an evil music teacher who would use his powers to control other people. A hypnotist must be honest and have a high standard of moral values; integrity is essential.

I was already twenty-five years old when my interest for hypnosis and the mind got serious, fifteen years after I purposely hypnotised Scott in the children's home playroom. Although the mind was an ever-present subject among my first active interests during my early twenties, I did not pay detailed attention to it, not consciously at least, until 1991 when I first saw the hypnotist Paul McKenna in action.

Paul McKenna had a show in the Orchard Theatre in Kent, and I went along with my first wife-to-be. I loved the show. It sparked in my mind, all bright and warm, the idea of becoming a hypnotist. I bought some books and learnt from them. I would practice with friends and family and we would have fun with it. I kept faithful to this interest for years, even though at times it would only be a latent call I would not pay too much attention. It was only in Australia that I would dare to leap into it and take the risk to become a full-time hypnotist. By then, I had a clear, honest attitude and a great desire to help others, I had left behind the mindless delinquent and walked towards a mindful life. But, in the meantime, I was more of a Svengali.

My manipulative nature, the Svengali within me, has always been holding hands with my entrepreneur spirit. There was not one without the other, it was my gift and I would use it to get what I needed. My entrepreneurial side showed up very early in life. My first sales were made at primary school, and my manipulation skills were also put to use.

Although I was an arrogant ratbag even as a child, there was something that would embarrass me deeply and shrink my pride to the size of a dried and wrinkled pea – like those I would eat with certain displeasure later on in the Young Offenders Institution: poverty.

Still today, poverty brings me a feeling of shame and stigma. Poverty meant no one was working at home, no one was caring for us well enough to provide. Poverty was then synonymous with laziness and thus there was no excuse. However, I lived in it, my clothes were always bought in the charity store and I would fix the soles of my shoes with cardboard. There would be holes in my trousers. There was no way around it, I was a child and had no power over it and staying secluded inside a house for such a thing was not only nonsense but impracticable.

Somehow, I learned to walk with my head held high, ignoring the signs that would tell whoever wanted to look about my hardship. But food stamps were a totally different thing. Not being able to pay for my lunch at school with money was the lowest level of humiliation, or at least that is how I felt. So I started to sell my food stamps for less than their value to be able to pay for my lunch with real money .

Cash would brighten my eyes. I loved the feeling that the exchange of goods for money would give me. It was pure satisfaction. But to be able to sell something, you first need to own it, which initially was my biggest handicap.

For a while, I sold some stationary items that my friend would give me. He was a Jamaican entrepreneur, ten years older than me. I am not sure how we got to be friends, but making friends has always been a skill of mine. My Jamaican friend would have entered into my life after a conversation on the street. And there he stayed, even holding the rings at my first wedding. He was in his early twenties then and had several businesses. Every now and then he would give me some items to sell at school, encouraging and supporting me as an entrepreneur with his provision of resources.

He was a real push into an honest and decent entrepreneurship for me. But I was growing older, cunning, and of course, ambitious. I started to steal goods not for my own use, as I had done before, but in order to get cash. However, the Svengali in me was clever enough to never get his hands dirty.

I was in my teens. It wasn't intentional; there was no start-up for the gang. We just came together. First I met Kevin and then Mick and Vince. I met Richie because my mum and his grew up together as neighbours and had been friends ever since. The last one was Brett; he was a rich boy. He had no reason whatsoever to dread his life from our point of view. His parents were millionaires and he was lacking nothing material. There was no need for him to go stealing. But he liked it; he wanted the trouble and the thrill of being chased by authority. I guess it was just the troublemaker in him, rebelling against anything and everything. Sometimes it was extra fun to hang out with a generous, rich boy, but I could see in him a violence I was not capable of, as I saw in the rest. Although, I could tolerate it as long as it was justified in my own terms.

I cannot affirm I was the brains of the gang, because our crimes would usually lack any delicacy or elegance to indicate that we used the brain intelligently, or at all. Neither were we talented or white glove burglars. We were a gang of plain, mindless, juvenile criminals. Yet, I never got my hands really dirty when perpetuating a crime that required trespassing or any sort of physical threat to another person.

It was never a challenge for me to get someone else to do what I wanted. In the same way I would get other kids in the children's home and at school to misbehave for my own benefit, I would look to these rough teenagers with no regards whatsoever for anyone's wellbeing, and say "Look at me, look at me. You are going to do that right?"

It was incredibly easy. Back then, I didn't even consider it as any sort of talent or mind power, it was just my way of manoeuvering through life, in an environment that could realistically kill me every second hour.

As Svengali did, my only purpose was to exert power over others. My manipulative ways were sometimes ruthless and I would do it with no regard to their will or need. At the end of the day, I convinced myself that they would have done it anyway. I would take my part in the crime, only so I could set some boundaries for myself to soothe my conscience in some way. And to get the easiest job and still get part of the loot.

I only realised I was using a hypnotic technique ten years later, when I became immersed in books about hypnotism. I learnt that, by getting my mates to focus on my eyes, I was distracting their conscious mind. Any word I'd say from there would tap straight into the subconscious mind. Then they would be helpless, they would not question whether I had the authority to give them commands, and would follow through.

Svengali was a first step into my career as a hypnotist, and although a lack of integrity would taint my following performances – making them rough manipulating abilities – I cannot erase them and pretend that was not part of my mind skills. The turn around was slow and painful. Good values developed over time, but if I could find the kindness within me it was thanks to the confidence I always had in my mind power. A very bumpy road, with many side paths to get lost in, and terrible weather to face, but it can be done and I am proof of it.

Chapter 5

The Queen Bee

We had two sets of clothes. The second one was to be used while the first was in the laundry. Not that often though. The pants and the shirt were of tough cotton, grey for the pants and striped blue for the shirt.

We also had a dark blue jumper in wool. I was seated on my bed, knees bent and feet on the mattress, with my back against the cold wall, embracing my legs and fidgeting with a fugitive thread from my jumper. My head was tilted to the side, and I was listening with a half smile to a funny story my cellmate was telling me. Barry was short and skinny but sporting one of those bodies full of muscle fibres that even without touching them, one can guess how firm and strong they are.

The doors were open that day. Sometimes we would spend the whole day locked in the cell, only going out for dinner time, and if the guard's were kind that day, maybe the toilet outside hours. We didn't hear them coming. They just appeared in the doorway: one of the daddies and two of his thugs. He was a big, black bloke with an unpleasant face, always wearing a grimace as a warning of the pain he could inflict. He pointed to my cellmate and told him to stand up at once.

Barry did not stand up. I recognised his arrogance, as I would sport it myself. Even in those situations, no promise of pain can erase the ego and haughtiness gained on the streets.

The daddy grabbed one of his thugs and pushed him into the cell in front of Barry, who had straightened his spine and was now tense and alert.

The daddy looked at me and said, "You fucking stay where you are, and don't even think of pressing the panic alarm." Then he turned to his thug and Barry and said, "You two solve it, now!"

The thug jumped onto Barry with a closed fist. I stayed seated as I was on my bed, observing how my skinny friend was beating the shit out of the thug and secretly enjoying the display of arrogance and consequent humiliation of the daddy's mate. All the while, calmly playing with the loose thread in my woollen sleeve.

Within a few minutes the daddy's man was laying on the floor holding his stomach, blood pouring onto the floor from his nose and above his eyebrow. My cellmate stood up and made a gesture of haughtiness, lifting his chin to the daddy who just helped his thug to stand up and walked away. My mate was bleeding too; he had a busted lip.

The fight had been solved. We wouldn't be bothered in our cell again for the same matter. It worked like the gypsy's bare-knuckle fights: when there is a winner, the loser walks away and there is no retaliation.

The gypsies I knew would not bother with bare-knuckle fights, though. They wouldn't think twice to gut you with a knife or break your legs with a bat. A fight where any sort of honour is involved was too much of a hassle and a waste of time for them. There was no sense of integrity. Respect was a two-way street, and gaining their loyalty would avoid a million problems if you lived in their territory.

The gypsies I knew were always at the heart of crime and violence. Their toughness was measured by their actions, and thus there was no compassion or empathy in their treatment. They had bodies mauled by fists and steel boots, and scars from knives carving their flesh. Tattoos all over their skin would give them the toughest look. I remember how one of the gypsy boys got his first piercing at five; his ear pressed against a wooden block, the nail waiting to go through, and his uncle banging a hammer fast and strong to make sure the nail went through the flesh with one single blow.

Hanging out with gypsies was dangerous. They would fight constantly, beating the shit out of each other with no regard for any family bond whatsoever. They were wild and savage, destroying the house in a rage for a small disappointment, stealing whatever they needed and in whatever manner. They would make a sport of torturing animals, usually the unfortunate cat crossing the street.

The gypsies I knew were not the ones who would get into a bare-knuckle fight, neither were they living in a camp. These people who would cut your throat should you disrespect them – or be thought to disrespect them – by crossing their path at an undetermined wrong moment, who would go to bed with no regrets, sporting the most irreverent lack of human values, lived in a house only four doors away from the police station. They also did something to me I will never forget. They gave me a sense of belonging that I had never had before. If you think that where the devil lies there is no chance to find, give and receive love, you are wrong.

***

I was living in the children's home when I met the gypsies. I was attending a local school with the orphans and there was a gypsy boy that was even more trouble than I was, however that was possible. His name was Pali.

We got along very well, almost instantly, joining forces and becoming the two worst little terrors around. I would run away from school and sneak out of the children's home, following him to his house whenever I had the chance. I would go there and meet his brothers and sisters, to play or just chill out with his family.

Their house was an authentic shithole. There is no better description for it. Rubbish would pile up in the driveway and front yard, the furniture inside was torn, purposely ripped off, or just completely destroyed but still taking a stance to be part of the dwelling. The walls in the kitchen were covered with old oil drops that had dried before getting to the floor and were stuck to the grey paint. The pavement would have been cleaner than the floor in their house.

They used to light a fire in the back yard and we would sit around and relax, all together, chatting or in silence. Sometimes laughing and sometimes arguing, but always together. Their togetherness and warmth were so precious to me. I didn't care about anything around me when I was there. I was content and very comfortable, not caring about the filth and enjoying the people around me. It was a fondness and acceptance that made my heart pump with the confidence that I was loved.

There was a matriarchal system in that family and the Queen Bee was the boss. She loved me and took me in like one of her own. I now laugh at the irony. Secluded in a government institution, which was supposed to care for my wellbeing and development, I was just a prisoner exposed to consistent abuse from those who were meant to care for me and protect me. However, in the nest of crime and filth, the worst scenario for a kid to grow up in, I was loved and protected, as I had never been before.

Sometimes we'd just sit down around the fire listening to the adult conversation, free of prudishness or modesty, and with no regard for our little ears.

Pam was the mother, the Queen Bee. She was a short and obese woman who could hardly move from her chair. She would always wear a short sleeve dress and her huge arms covered in homemade tattoos would spread their lushness under the pressure of the fabric opening. Her breasts rested on a round and soft belly, and her legs were almost purple with varicose veins running down to her swollen ankles. She had no front teeth and every time she laughed you could see a couple of black moribund molars and a collection of abscesses in her gums. No gold teeth to be seen in this gypsy woman, just the remains of a tough life.

Cheryl was her oldest daughter. She was a miniature version of her. Maybe just in age, as in size she was getting closer to her mum's exuberance quickly. She used to wear short sleeve dresses too, and both would sit down to listen to the radio.

Debra was Pam's best friend. She would join the party of big women with her indecent and strident laugh, her swollen feet popping out of her shoes in a mass of purple flesh and dried skin. Debra was also part of this landscape of love I still hold dear in my heart.

The three of them would sit down in an irregular triangle listening to the radio. The Queen Bee, Cheryl and Debra completing a triad of gypsy witches summoning freedom out of the broadcasting device.

There was this song, *Barbados*; they loved it. Every time it played they would start dreaming aloud of travels and going overseas, to a tropical island, to a far away land of sun and sand, to a forest in a lost mountain. To anywhere but where they were.

I loved when the three women expressed their imagination out loud. These three rogue witches, who would not hesitate to kill you if they thought you deserved it, with their too loose criteria and distorted integrity, talking with bright eyes and laughing at the thought of a better life far away. It was the gypsy blood in their veins talking. The imperative of those who were born to be nomads but are stuck to the ground with obnoxious roots. It was the yearning for a gypsy's life, the life that brought their ancestors to England.

I found them so heartwarming, the two big matrons, with those bodies that struggled to hold them in a standing position, smoking marijuana and laughing so loud and without inhibitions. Overall, I loved their hunger to fly away. The doubts about my origins don't allow me to say with certainty that my desire to travel isn't an imperative of my blood. After all, I was born in a caravan. However, it didn't matter to me back then where my urge to fly away, over land and sea, came from. I just enjoyed their singing and shared their yearn.

The mystery of whom I owe my paternity to remains unsolved. But as I have accepted Eduardo Colella to be my father, I might have inherited his craving for travel. He was a trumpeter in a circus, a nomad artist. Maybe it wasn't the troublesome Pali who lured me into this world of gypsies. Maybe it was a connection between traveller hearts.

Having the same nomad soul, it made sense that the Queen Bee loved me so much. She would treat me as one of her own, one of her children. Nothing that surrounded them in that physical space of dirt and grime, of felony and transgression, brought me dread or fear. On the contrary, the love I felt among her family would become of great importance to the man I grew into. It was slow and steady, but with the certainty that even in a shithole, love can be found. And love and passion are what drives every achievement that leads to happiness and peace.

There are many expressions of love and the Queen Bee's was a tough version. You can only show as much care as you have received; role models are important. You cannot behave in a way you have never experienced or been demonstrated somehow, not necessarily at a personal level, but just by observing people around you.

Pam's family would not share a word of encouragement or compliment with each other. They would fight and start riots at home with any whimsical excuse. Even though they would laugh together, alcohol and drugs could deviate the joy and transform it into a burst of violence. And yet, there I was feeling more loved than I had ever felt.

I was very young but I had lived more than my share for my age. I had an intuition about where my gypsies came from and how hard Queen Bee's life had been. I could guess by her missing teeth and a body that looked twenty years older than it was, that it hadn't been an easy ride. Hence, it would never have crossed my mind to judge their ways back then because they gained my respect by loving me, and not because I feared them, which would have been the usual way to attain any sort of regard.

Even now, when I remember my own deeds I let them be without any strict ruling. I have learnt that judgment doesn't lead anywhere further than guilt, a pretty useless emotion that has the ability to keep you stuck in an unfavorable place. However, observing the past, learning from it and accepting the lessons is what moves you in a positive direction.

One day the Queen Bee called me closer to her, as she would do, sitting on a chair and leaning forward with one hand on her knee and the other one stretched towards me, waving it inwards once, twice. Even that slight movement made her tired. Whenever she did that, I would start walking towards her and she would drop her body on the back of the seat and take a draw of her cigarette, breathing the fumes in deeply. That day I stood in front of her and she started to talk, but as she took air to say the first word a violent cough took over and her body fat started to tremble as she hacked. It sounded like she was expelling her lungs. All the people in the room burst into laughter and her other daughter, Deb, came to her and hit her back firmly with a wide open palm a couple of times. Then the Queen Bee stopped, sighed noisily and started laughing too. Deb was still behind her mother when she told me, "Mark, you need a tattoo."

Deb was then sixteen years old. I was about eleven, and she was the most beautiful girl I had ever seen. She wasn't like any other member of the family. She was tall, blonde and slim. I used to daydream about her and being her boyfriend. I smiled at the Queen Bee. Deb didn't have any tattoos, but surely I would look tough enough with one to attract her attention.

"When you think that times are getting tough, they get even tougher before getting better, just keep going."

Mark Anthony

Top: The handsome Italian man I call Dad, Eduardo Colella at about 45 years old.
Bottom: My aunty Giovanna and My beautiful sister Rose taking her Holy Communion in Italy, around 11 years old.

Top: More of the Italian side of the family, left to right, Aunty Giovanna, Rose, Aunty Giovanina, Uncle Alfonso.
Bottom: My birth certificate naming my home as a caravan in the middle of a field, maybe that's where the traveling man inside of me came from.

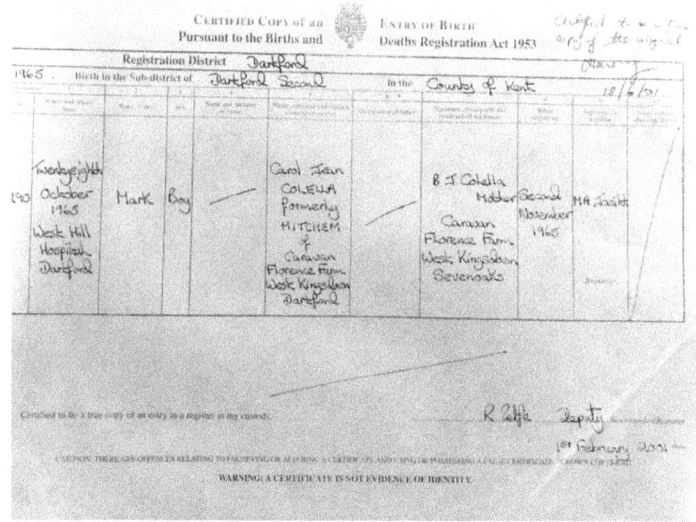

Top: My first trip to Italy to try and convince the man I call Dad that he actually was! The very angelic looking, butter wouldn't melt in my mouth: me, seated bottom second from the right. Bottom: My big brother Amedeo, Me, and my beautiful sister Rose.

Top: Some 'family' photos on top of the Italian home, from left to right, Aunty Giovanina, my protector and big sister Rose, and my Scottish Nan Sally Mitchem.

Bottom: Christmas time in the concrete jungle, Me and my niece Lou Lou.

Top: A family hug with big sister Rose and sister Sylvan
Bottom: A family photo from left to right, the loving and strong woman that's Mum, Me at my heaviest 101kg, life of the party sister Sylvan, big sister Rose, Nan and sister Ali.

"Drugs will numb it for a while, enough drugs will definitely numb it forever."

Mark Anthony

Chapter 6

I See Red

I was holding a cloth soaked in soapy water. Every now and then we would have some chores to do at the young offenders institution. They would be relatively easy tasks paradoxically turned into arduous activities due to the constant abuse and pressure we had to work under. A guard would be watching us, and whether or not we'd be humiliated would be determined by his mood, which was as volatile as any of the prisoners but with the advantage of his uniform's immunity. We would not be considered human beings with any of the dignity attached to the assumption of our humanity.

There was so much hatred accumulated between those concrete and brick walls that it was impossible not to yield to it. There would be times of laughter and something close to contentment, maybe reading the letters from your loved ones or chatting with some of the inmates. But it would be a bitter feeling, sour in the end, not even enough to remind you that good emotion can be transforming. Perhaps enough to keep awake the memory of the humanity that lay under the stiff, cotton uniform, enough to still have a bit of that dignity, and just for the sake of being alive a bit longer. It would not have worked for every one though; we knew it didn't if an occupied cell felt too still in the morning.

There were certain attitudes that would keep us from harm, to an extent. While arrogance might not have been the best, humbleness was the worst. Anyway, I had not yet learnt how to be humble. My manipulation skills and confidence in my brain had helped me to build a pride that was keeping me alive in a concrete jungle with all its crime, but would very soon cost me too much within the grey institutional walls. All that cost to the detriment of my way out of a worthless world and my genuine desires for a change. At most, my arrogance was a self defence mechanism, and so far, it had kept me alive.

My task for the day was simple and tedious. I was wiping the tables under the supervision of two guards. They were having a conversation about their families in one of the room's corners, as if they were regular men of good, caring for their wives and children as any other outsider, never exposed to the ruthless, immoral, coldness of that place.

I could hear them. They were talking in a way that would make you imagine them tucking their children in bed and kissing them good night with tenderness. Men who were unable to beat the shit out of kids just for the sake of it, pouring their hatred and frustration into every kick of the stomach. Men who would never take twisted pleasure from humiliating teenagers.

They talked to each other like that because they recognised themselves as humans. Unfortunate humans working with scum, a suffered job that would help them gain a pass to heaven.

I was wiping a table not thinking about anything but my girlfriend. She wasn't my girlfriend anymore but since I was in prison she took the generous job of writing me letters with her friendship and love, and I very much appreciated that. Still today, I remember the scent she used to impregnate her letters.

I was absorbed by the easy task, wiping the same table over and over to kill time, as nobody seemed to care how time was employed on a single table as long as the room was quiet enough. Nor was it an issue whether the task was successfully accomplished. I didn't realise they were behind me.

I heard the daddy's voice, "Give me the fucking cloth."

I kept wiping the table. "I'm wiping the fucking table," I snapped.

His voice went deeper, as if he were talking from the back of the throat and with clenched teeth, "Give me the fucking cloth! You piece of shit!"

"Fuck off, fucking cunt!" was my only answer.

The daddy jumped over me and grabbed me by the neck, lifting me in the air. As a response, I flashed him my arrogant Cheshire cat smile.

As I grew up, as I met rogue people, as I put myself into more dangerous situations, as I entered into a world of crime – even after, when I tried to wipe off my past in the same way that I wiped that table with a smelly damp cloth over and over, not really caring about whether it was clean yet but dreaming about what was beyond – there were times my arrogance and the Cheshire cat smile, the face of my haughtiness, proved to be useless. The feline smile was a defence system that worked so well when I used it as a child, with a nice voice and very good manners but with a hidden agenda. Unfortunately, I was a grown-up man now and I wasn't dealing with easily manipulated people any more. Indeed, the daddy wasn't one of them.

I saw the irritation in his eyes as I was drawing the smile on my lips and the fist raising fast and high with fury, hovering over my face. I waited for the mighty blow, staring at his eyes and my feline grin defying him. He surely would push my nose bone right into my skull. Everything happened very fast.

The casual guards' conversation, about men pretending to have some sort of integrity once they were outside the cold walls of the building, was interrupted, and their tone and words changed abruptly with a "Fucking cunts! Stop that!"

They saved me from a broken nose but still bruised my back around the kidneys and gave me a black eye in exchange. In such a place, you could never win.

I was led to my cell and informed I had lost my privileges. That meant that I would not be granted a week of pardon and an early exit for good behaviour, ever. There was no need for me to behave well anymore, where well-behaved is no more than bearing the blows of guardians and inmates and hoping for the best. I had never been built for good behaviour anyway, and even when my arrogance had cost me a precious week of freedom, I still didn't know any other way to be me, or whether I could transform that attitude and confidence into something more productive.

My cellmate started at me with a bad joke as I walked in, and I looked at him as if to say, "No shit today, mate." My back was hurting and my eye already puffed, I could feel it throbbing. I threw my belted body on the bed and covered my head with the blankets to avoid what I was starting to feel inside: the impotence, the anger, the fury, the deep, deep hatred for those fucking twats, their grey uniforms and their impunity. The cunts: those bloody daddies walking like kings and expecting every single prisoner to submit to their will or suffer the consequences.

The rage was building inside me, a part of me knew it was no use and it would get me into trouble if I let it go. I was behind the blankets in the hope that the thick wool could contain me.

Everything was lost anyway, I could just go and fucking break the guard's balls, and if I had the chance, the daddy's too. There was no fear or inhibition of any kind; I knew I could do it. I knew I was entering the red zone. I could see myself walking the path to pure rage and hatred, when the mind takes off to any other place and the fire takes over.

But there was no use, I also knew there was no use. As well as I knew, somewhere in my mind, that if I kept feeding those thoughts of revenge I would lose control again. I appealed to my logical thinking, the logic that loses all power and strength when emotions are swirling violently in the guts. I pulled the blanket away to give me a reason to control it, getting rid of its ridiculous imaginary protection. I looked at my cellmate, he was sitting on his bed impassible, not knowing or not caring what was going on inside me. He was fiddling with a pen, killing the time. He just lifted his eyes, looked at me for a fraction of a second and went back to his entertainment.

I looked at the window and centred all my mental efforts on it: Focus, focus! The anger was still burning inside and the heat was causing me excruciating pain, but at least it wasn't growing anymore. I was containing it: Focus, Mark, focus.

After a few seconds it lost its driving force and momentum, but I could still feel it throbbing in my guts. It would go off if I didn't reduce the heat more.

Focus. Look at the window, the grey, the bars, that cloud,

whatever the fuck crosses by, but don't fucking stop looking at the window.

I tried to bring a positive thought, or more like a non-violent thought, a simple thing. I thought about Pakistan but that was a mistake. I had lost my opportunity and suddenly I just wanted to kill the fucking twat that got me into that shithole and doomed my brilliant future.

Focus on the window! The voice inside was almost yelling, bringing my attention back to the cell. I just stared at the window for a few more seconds, not trying to change anything in my mind, just containing the rage. A part of me knew not everything was lost, not yet, and even though I could not even believe that myself at that moment, I hold onto that part, the one that was saying: "Look at the window and focus!"

After a while the guts settled, the heat cooled down and I felt I was safe. There was anger still but my mind had won again, everything would be fine as long as I didn't see red.

***

Five years ago, I was on an island resort performing my hypnosis show. Lauren, my wife back then was also my agent and marketer. She would come along with me sometimes in my trips to assist me. I was performing the *HypNaughty* show, a very successful show for adults I started touring with years earlier.

The *HypNaughty* show is not appropriate for prudes. It is fun, but it requires certain mind openness and a sense of humour. I ask some volunteers to get on stage and help me with the show, as in any other hypnosis performance. I must remark that it is naughty but not dirty. However, anyone who stays on stage is going to act with no inhibitions, experiencing a very relaxed state of mind and with no conscious mind judging their movements. This means that they might find themselves acting in a way they probably wouldn't in public. In a hypnosis performance, that is the point! It is what brings laughter and happiness, and I have never had any volunteer leave the stage regretfully or embarrassed, quite the opposite.

What might seem embarrassing for prudes is the sexual content. The difference between my family show and the *HypNaughty* show is that I introduced sexuality into it. I can tell my onstage volunteers that their chair is the sexiest and most attractive thing they have ever seen. Although this is not an explicit sexual command (which I would never give), the subconscious appeals to the primitive mind to act on that chair or around it. With no inhibitions, men and women use their sensuality to seduce the chair in whatever manner they would normally seduce someone, in accordance with their personality and without the barrier of the judgmental conscious mind. This is really funny. I don't say that myself, I can see and hear the laughter from the audience, and I get the positive feedback from my onstage volunteers.

I always film my shows and upload part of them to YouTube. This is something every single person is informed of before they step on stage, and their acceptance is a condition of participation.

It was my first show on that island resort and I was wrapping it up when an American couple approached my wife, Lauren, and asked her to delete any part of the filmed material containing images of their son, who had participated on stage. Lauren told them very politely that it was not possible and that everybody participating in the show did it voluntarily and was aware of being filmed. They have also accepted that the footage will be uploaded to the Internet. The father insisted.

His son had done very naughty things up there and it was imperative we deleted the film's content. My wife insisted too, maintained her stance, and calmly explained the situation to him again.

The father was not going to give up and puffed up his chest, threatening Lauren and this time demanding the original film be destroyed. The situation was becoming too combative and so she decided to call me over to have a chat with the gentleman.

I approached him with my biggest smile, willing to listen to whatever his petition was but also determined to make him understand the situation. Conflict can be solved; it can always be solved in a positive manner if both parties aim to find a solution and not to simply impose their way. As I was approaching this man, as soon as he saw me, he made himself taller by posing in a threatening way with his chest tightened up, fist closed and tense arms, looking down over me as much as his height allowed him. Before I could speak a word he demanded, "Delete the content of that film. My son is on there doing very embarrassing things and I will not allow its uploading to the Internet."

Even though arrogance had been my defence technique for many years, my manipulative strength and the flaw that would get me into many troubles, it was also something I found irritating when exerted upon me, as much as or even more than I would exert it on others. This man's attitude took me back to the Ferrier, the streets of Southeast London and the young offenders detention centre. I could feel the arteries in my neck throbbing and my heart was pumping hard in a way that didn't resemble any romantic trait.

Yet, I kept my cool and I asked him, "How old is your son, sir?"

"Twenty-three years old."

And I could not hold my disappointment anymore, "Fuck off then! Your son is a grown-up man and he participated willingly, plus he had a lot of fun! You have been harassing my wife and creating a problem where there is none. If you excuse us, sir."

I turned around with the anger still bubbling inside, agitating my guts. But as I walked away and the pressure of his presence stopped invading my personal space, I calmed down and sighed. I turned around thinking it was just one show and I had so many recordings, nothing especially funny or remarkable had happened that night on stage, so maybe it was just a matter of forgetting about it and making his family happy. It wasn't that hard.

I walked towards him as he was walking to the exit. I reached him among the crowd and tapped his shoulder gently as I approached his back to call his attention. Then he turned around, hands up in the air, and suddenly jumped backwards yelling, "Do not touch me!"

That did it. It was the tick, the sign, the red button already hidden in my head that no one had been able to reach in many years.

I heard once in a documentary that in the most stable places on Earth, where the tectonic plates have been inactive for hundreds of years, where no seismic activity is ever expected, there is a latent force that, if triggered, would cause the earth to shake so violently it would provoke the most severe, unexpected and destructive earthquake. That is exactly what happened there. I was calm and composed, balanced and feeling that nothing had to be controlled anymore, at least consciously. That effort had not been necessary in so many years. But his arrogance, his threatening attitude, the entrapment with false accusation plus the assumption of aggression he had implied by turning around in that manner, that did it.

My voice was clear, loud, deep, and pulled up from my abdominal cavity, strong and firm, but overall frightening, "You fucking cunt, get out of my sight now! I don't want to fucking see you! Just go fuck off now!"

There was a silence and as I pointed at him with my finger I knew if he didn't move away, if he didn't get out of my sight I had the power to kill him.

Lauren stepped between us and somehow scared, told him, "Sir, please move on, leave this place now. I have been married to this man for two years and have never, ever seen him like this."

I saw red.

Hatred is never a welcomed emotion. We tend to ignore it or avoid it. But in fact, it is an ever-present emotion. Even where there is love there is also the potential for hatred. The more we love, the more capable we are of hatred. It works like that and no one can escape it. This is because hatred is also useful: it can keep you alive in many instances. It can ruin your life too; I should know.

There is no difference between two people when it comes to their feelings. We all experience emotions in one way or another. Some allow themselves to feel more intensely, others are not so intense, and some are condemned to live on the borderline. But we all have them. What marks the difference is what we do with them, and here is where the mind comes in. The mindset we have is going to determine the decisions we make upon feeling an emotion, whether we will be carried along by it, work on it or even dismiss it completely.

When I see red there is no mind, there is only an imperative sense of survival. There is no fear either; no fear of consequences or of death. If we are to find a positive thing about fury engendered by hatred, it is that you cannot be more alive than when you are not scared of death.

In a world where positive thinking is the paradigm to escape depression – being a supporter of positive thinking and dreaming big myself – I want to make clear that walking the path of hatred can also be a starting point. Not to hold on to, but to move on from.

I have not seen red again since that night on the island, and before that moment many years had passed since I last felt the arteries in my neck throbbing. When I actively and consciously took the decision to turn my life around in 1985 when I was released from the young offenders institution, hatred and violence stopped being part of my life, and it faded away as I grew in personal improvement and life success. It was a rocky road and the trip was rough and slow, but steady. When the ride is not smooth, or I should say when the ride is so twisted, we might expect our subconscious mind to jump in to protect us if it feels we face a real threat. That is until we make the right choices required for that trigger response to change where necessary. I honestly think it is such a primitive response; I wouldn't like to lose it completely, were my family in danger of being hurt.

When Mum broke up with Stace the Ace, my sisters and I felt sorry. We liked him so much. Although Mum and him used to argue quite often, home was a safe place to be. We were not scared anymore of Mum going away, or at least we felt secure that we wouldn't be left with a monster if she wasn't home. Today, Stace the Ace remains one of my mum's best friends and they take care of each other, but back then he walked away and, after some other boyfriends, Dave arrived at home one day with his shaved hair, thick neck and solid body, pretending he cared.

Dave was a roof fitter and used to pull buckets of tar up two and three floors; his arms were built and mighty. He came home one day with a smile and some presents for us. I did not like it from the start. I was already a teenager, a very arrogant teenager, and could sense his own haughtiness. But also there was something dark in him. And so, the door was open again to a persecutor. It would be the last time though.

There was nothing I could say, none of my opinions about Mum's boyfriends would be considered. He moved in a few months later. I don't remember when the hatred started to build or whether it initially stemmed from my adolescent arrogance, as it does in those years when feelings are borderline and emotions seem to overpower any other thoughts with an intensity that fills the guts.

Dave was not a partner to my mother; he came in to be the leader of a pack. His despotism and autocracy were pitiless. He had money and would use it to control my mother. He would give my mum some cash to buy food upon request, then he would come back drunk asking her for the money yelling, "What have you done with the money! I gave you lots of money fucking bitch!"

I couldn't forget every time he said "fucking bitch", those words dug deep into my flesh. My mum would say she bought some food. Then he would gather all of us in the living room and start abusing us one by one. We all had our turn, he would threaten us and call us scum, reminding us over and over how we would have nothing without him. Then he would go to the fridge and throw all the food into the rubbish to make his point.

Dave brought back home an inferno. My mother was a lovely woman, soft and tender. It is hard to define which part of her would choose men who fed on her ulcerating body, causing her as much damage as possible to satisfy their needs.

He would get drunk first. He would fill up his huge body with alcohol before spitting his rampage over us. His overbearing attitude and his penchant for beating anyone who crossed his path awoke in me a hatred I did not know I was capable of. A hatred so intense it was painful, so big that it could not fit in me. It felt like the cavities in my body were full of a sticky tar I couldn't get rid of, a tar that was corrosive and would make my skin burn. He drank the money for our Christmas presents and sexually abused my sister's friend. The loathing I felt for this man was surpassing the strength of any feeling I had experienced up until then.

Like many other days, that evening Dave was drunk, and he wanted cigarettes. He took his stanley knife and poked it in my throat, just pressing enough to tense the skin around it.

"Get in the fucking van!"

I moved slowly, stretching my neck as much as I could to avoid the blade. I got into the driver's seat and he stumbled his way to the other side. I was shaking and pondering whether to run at that instant. But I knew that even if I escaped from him then, he would be home waiting for me. Again, he put the knife against my jugular and forced me to drive him to the fuel station.

While he was calling for cigarettes from the van to the girl behind the counter, I tried to get her attention with small movements of the head, ever so slightly to avoid the blade in my flesh. But she wouldn't look at me, and I drove back with the steel accidentally digging in my skin, held by a drunk man and with the unavoidable inertia of the van's motion acting upon the knife, helplessly begging for the good fortune to get out of the van alive.

From the bright future, I can say Dave was my nemesis and it was he who proved my mind was strong enough to get where I am now. However, at that time of fear and uncertainty where my life and my family were in constant jeopardy, I could firmly say Dave was the greatest fucking cunt on earth.

Dave wouldn't touch us kids much physically, not with the vehemence he would intrude into my mum's flesh, even though he had no second thoughts about poking a knife against my throat. We knew what he did to Mum. He would be careful not to leave marks, but whenever he forced our mum into the room and locked it, our hearts would shrink and sorrow would darken it, as if the tar Dave had in the back of his van had been poured directly over our open chest.

I cannot say what would have been going on inside my sisters, but I know hatred was building up strongly inside me, heating my blood to an extent that would drive me to my limits; a chemical reaction that only needed a drop of the reactant, just a tiny drop, to explode.

Although he did not care for anyone in my family, his need to give the appearance of an upstanding man was important to him. He would transform into another person outside or at work. Like the guards at the young offenders institution, he would believe himself a man of good.

His business as a roof fitter was successful. Maybe he thought it was a small duty he had to comply with, as I was a teenager learning to be a man but he gave me the chance to work with him for a small sum of money. Every now and then he would take me to work with him for a few coins and I would help him with tar buckets and passing him the tools, eventually fitting tiles myself.

I did not enjoy it in the least. Working with him meant I had to spend time around him. His presence was like an ulcer. I felt sick when he talked to me, every time he commanded me to do something I would feel the imperative to hit him in the head with whatever tool I had at hand. I hated him so much. The hatred was consuming me. Whenever he was around I would feel all my energy racing up into my head, and the pressure was very difficult to control.

It was a grey day like any other day in London. The city wouldn't gift us with sun too often, it was like the clouds wanted to keep it for themselves. Dave had a call to check some roofing issues in Covent Garden flower market and he took me with him. Looking through the van window, I remained in silence all the way to the markets while he faked an interest in my life and made a few disgusting jokes. Once we got there, I followed him up to the roof with a box of tools.

I was up there, standing close to him with some tools in my hand. Dave was squatting, pulling some felt from an old worn-out piece of roof while ranting about the state of the roof, whoever the twat responsible for it was and the fucking noise down in the market place. He was too close to the edge. No closer than any other occasion, he was too close simply because that day I wanted to kill him.

His body was leaning into the void. The murmur of a joyful crowd travelled up to the roof. I was certain the fall would kill him. Someone would yell at the sight of his body falling and the people would spread in shock or fear to let his skull crack on the pavement. I would even conform to the outcome if the fall made him a cripple. For sure, I would hear screams and cries and confused voices asking for help.

I felt the blood pumping hard in my heart. Not the kind of beat that anxiety gives, nor the fear rushing to fly or fight. It was an unyielding beat, firm and strong, a decision maker. The hatred that filled me was pushing out against my muscles and my whole body was tense. My teeth clenched and my eyes brightened. I was only one, two steps away. I just had to kick him in the centre of his back and push him forward with my foot. Then Dave would be gone.

My mind was clear and there was no doubt, no fear, and no hesitation. There was nothing I would be accountable for: the two of us were alone on the roof. No one down in the market aisles was paying us any attention; everything was too busy and too confusing. Accidents happen. My mum would be free, my sisters wouldn't shake in fear any more, and I knew I would go home and sleep well knowing that the man was no more. My body and my mind were ready. Ready to push, ready for the kill. I could even see the irony of the man dying in a bed of fresh flowers that he didn't deserve.

But I didn't kill him. I had a strong mind; a mind that was driven by ambitions of a better life. It worked by itself there, in a deeper part that I could not reach then, not voluntarily. For a fraction of a second it guided the pain away to a greener pasture and the burning hurt faded away enough to stop me from becoming a murderer.

That time passed quick, and the hatred came back, but it was too late and Dave was in a safe spot on the roof, and I wouldn't be a murderer anymore. I had no regrets, but that didn't last long.

Hatred is a strong emotion, it made me see red and lose any fear or regard for whoever was in front of me, especially when he was the cause of such deep sentiment. However, it would probably be an underlying feeling that triggered the hatred, the impotence and frustration of not being able to change a situation, or protect my family and friends.

When I see red the fury builds so solid within me that in the past it has made me hurt others on several occasions. But it also saved my life more than once, and it certainly freed my family from an undeserved curse, wiping Dave clear from our lives, at least for a while.

It might have been a Friday evening. We were all watching a television series in the living room. I was seated on the floor, cross-legged and my back against the couch. My cousin was there too. Mum and two of my sisters were occupying the rest of the seats. We were enjoying ourselves and Mum kept asking my cousin and I whether we would stay for dinner. But we didn't know, we had no plans yet; most likely we would be going out after the TV show was over.

Then we heard the main door slamming open and the familiar stuttering voice coming up the stairs: Dave was home and drunk again.

He was shouting to my mum, "Where is my fucking money, bitch?"

By the time he got to the living room we were all standing and ready to defend ourselves, which was never more than standing upright and tense expecting the worse.

My mum's voice rose up over him with a pretended firm tone almost resembling a plea, "I bought some food, Dave. I told you so! I told you I needed money to buy food!"

"You fucking bitch! What do you do with my money? Where is the food! Can any of you see any food, huh? Can you!"

He looked at us, one by one, abusing us and lifting his fists in the air. My mum stepped ahead timidly and told him the food was in the freezer, where else would it be?

Then he started towards the kitchen on a lower floor. We could hear him swearing and kicking whatever was in his way. Then we all ran to the kitchen to see what was going on. Dave had opened the freezer and was throwing all the food we had for the week through the window onto the street. And that did it.

I don't remember whether I consciously thought about what to do, probably not. The familiarity of my home and everything in it guided me back upstairs and then another floor up.

It had been hanging there since I could remember. I cannot recall the wall naked of it; almost ugly and completely out of place. Maybe it had been there all this time with a purpose I could not have deciphered till then, in a state of mind that scratched insanity. There were two swords crossing over a heraldry shield on the wall, I pulled one of them out and went back to the kitchen. I had had enough.

I went back to the kitchen, sword in hand. I think someone tried to stop me, but it was no use. I was ready for the kill.

The screams around me belonged to another dimension; I could hear them in the far away distance even though they were just there. Dave was unaware that the terrorised wailing in the kitchen wasn't because of him anymore. He turned around yelling something like, "Shut the fuck up" and faced me as I seized the sword up ready to release the first blow. His face changed. His eyes wide open and the mouth twisted in an ugly grimace. He instinctively crossed his arms in front of him to protect his face. Then, once I struck with the first blow, I couldn't stop.

I wasn't thinking about killing him. I wasn't thinking about anything. Suddenly Dave's wailing and crying joined with the crowd. I could hear the word "stop" over and over, but I never stopped. I was seeing red and nothing else. I noticed Dave's supplicant voice and it made me strike harder. He was much stronger than me, and even unarmed I believe he could have found a way to stop me. However, there he was, cornered against the fridge begging me to stop. He was in shock, Dave would never have expected any of us to retaliate against his abuse, and he would never have fathomed that if we did, he would be attacked viciously with an old decorative sword.

There was blood everywhere and I slowed down as my body got tired. Dave took the opportunity to run away. He slipped, crouching to my side with one of his hands covering his head and the other one dangling on his side.

I didn't try to stop him; that was enough. My pulse was racing up and the heat within my body was almost unbearable. I was standing in the middle of the kitchen breathing fast with the sword now lowered against my leg. All my family was around, they all looked at me in disbelief. There was a thick silence where all our breaths seemed to fill the room, giving it a dense atmosphere. Then my cousin said almost whispering, "Fuck, mate", and it felt like we all suddenly awoke from a nightmare at the same time.

My mum suggested I went to the shower. The police didn't take long in knocking at our door. The neighbours had called them when Dave started to throw food through the window, and by the time a police car turned up everything was over. Our next-door neighbour told them about Dave and how he had seen him covered in blood with a very badly wounded arm leaving the house, screaming and running disorientated. They searched for him around the Ferrier and when they found him, he was wandering around like a mad man escaped from an asylum. He was holding his arm tight in place. The policemen called an ambulance and made sure he had medical assistance before coming back to our home.

I came down to the kitchen to meet them. One of them was walking around and taking notes, the other one was talking to Mum. The latter asked me to sit down. I was scared. I realised now what I had done, and even though I would have done it twice without hesitation, I knew the law didn't see it that way. The police had hardly ever protected us from harm at home. It was obvious that I disliked them; it couldn't have been any other way whilst I was a criminal. But my mistrust came from back in the times where my mum had the soul beaten out of her body and they would do nothing to protect her or protect us children.

My mum offered the officers a cup of coffee to which they refused, just shaking their heads. The policeman who had addressed me first sat down in front of me and described the state they found Dave in, trying to leave the Ferrier but not able to find his way out. He was in shock. He had lost a lot of blood and his left arm was just held to his body by damaged bone and a bit of flesh. My mum started crying at this point. I didn't care; I did not care in the least what happened to that cunt. But I was worried about what would happen to me.

The policeman who was taking notes interrupted the narration and told his partner he would go out to take declarations from the neighbours.

The other one nodded and kept talking, "Mark, you almost chopped his arm off. That is a very serious offence. However, we have heard the whole story about what happened. We understand you were defending your family, therefore, we are not pressing charges against you."

My mum started sobbing and suddenly I realised my sisters and cousin were standing behind me at the kitchen door. I felt like a pressure valve was releasing all the accumulated steam behind my back.

The policemen left and the tension disappeared with them. Now we were all a bunch of floppy bodies, too tired to do anything else. But there was a difference: Dave was gone and we were safe now. We didn't hear a word about him for almost two years. Then one day he was back.

I had spent some days away with my mates, sleeping in smelly couches and sniffing glue. I came back home in the afternoon and as I walked into our living room I saw him seated on our couch drinking a beer with Mum. I thought it was a bad dream, I couldn't believe he was there. I looked at my mum and interrogated her with a simple gesture, and she took me to the kitchen, "He has changed."

No, he hadn't changed in the least and thank goodness my

mum did not put up with him for very long this second time. Still, the time he was there, although the hatred had lost intensity – it had almost turned into a sort of indifference – I avoided him like the plague. Then, one day, he was gone forever. I never asked where.

As I write these words, I feel the need to reiterate how important a strong mind is. As much as I saw red, there was always a point of coherence and logic brightening some place back there in my mind, which would keep me sane to an extent. I did not kill Dave when I could. I could have drawn the sword through his guts; it was easy, he was drunk, slow and stunned, and I had the power and the energy to do it. Yet, I didn't.

I feel compelled to talk about the importance of building that strong mind, either by holding to your ambitions or making the great effort sometimes in trusting yourself and that you have the potential to do great positive things. And, of course acting upon it! It is a job in itself.

You have to look for that feeble coherence among all the thoughts of hatred and follow it to the extent one is able to in any given situation, at any stage in life. Sometimes it will be a small action or inaction that doesn't change the outcome greatly, but other times it will make a huge difference. And the more the mind is used in this way, the easier it becomes.

However, my story is not going to resonate with everybody living a situation as bad as I lived. I felt different all along, because I wanted it to be different. I did not conform as I saw others do. It is a personal choice that allows the change.

My sister Ali had pretty much the same life that I had, maybe easier in the sense that she grew up at home and wasn't institutionalised at a very young age, as I was. However, she is doing life in prison. She saw red, as I did when I grabbed the sword from that old shield on the wall, but she did not hear the voice whispering, "Stop now, please". A part of me could hear it, it didn't make me stop, but it allowed me certain control or to slow down my actions. Ali was completely deafened by rage.

She was at her friend's place. A rival gang of girls showed up and threatened to kill her friend. They'd had some troubles before and these girls were looking for revenge. The rival gang arrived with a car, raced inside the driveway and almost crashed it against the house wall. Her friend came out yelling at them and then one of the girls jumped out of the car and over to my sister's friend attacking her violently. Ali saw from inside the house that they were armed and did not think twice. She grabbed a knife from the kitchen and defended her friend with fury and resolution.

She would have been dismissed with a self-defence verdict, had she stabbed the other woman once or twice. But in that instant, for Ali there was only red to be seen: I should know. She stabbed her victim over seven times, and so she enjoys freedom no more.

Hatred can do such bad things, but can also save you. I wouldn't like to encourage you to feed this emotion, but know that it has its place and a reason to exist. Thus, we should not ignore it or repress it, at least while we don't hurt others. Understand it; anger makes us move ahead if perceived correctly. It is your brain telling you that something must be done about it. It is up to you to pick the right choice.

If I can give you one advantage of losing it to the extent of seeing nothing but rage and acting with it, it is that, paradoxically, this frenzy once helped me gain the respect of a whole tribe of skinheads and made me the only person on the Ferrier estate who could walk freely in a suit without being harassed by thugs.

It would have been about the time Dave was at home, that I became a skinhead with the whole gang. We didn't know what a skinhead was, we had no concept of the ideology behind it, nor did we care about it. It was just a matter of toughness and who would be able to perpetrate the worst violence, therefore becoming the most feared.

We wanted to be feared, that was our concept of respect and power, and so we became part of that ruthless tribe. Adolescence doesn't give you much of a sense of commitment to anything, even less when the sense of belonging is atrophied and there is a perpetual lack of love at home, or any place we moved around for that matter. Not long after, I would end up in a young offender's institution, where a major change in my attitude would occur.

I encountered a skinhead gang later on in life, and not in the best or most peaceful of situations, as no one would possibly conceive of dealing with these people. I was on my way to becoming an honest person. Once I left the young offenders institution, I was determined to change my life and follow the steps that would lead me to a successful life, which back then was the same as now: love, travels and financial freedom.

But it is very hard to erase over eighteen years of violence, misconduct and crime, and even when I tried to be honest, I would end up interacting with those that weren't. I would say I had a hierarchy that determined who I would consider honest or upon whom I would exert my honesty.

I can see how this profaned what the word honesty signifies, and doesn't align with the concept of integrity, to which it is tied. But it was as much as I had at that moment, and although it is certain that wherever you are in life you can move to a better place and achieve whatever you want, it is also true that there are obstacles in the way. They are not easy to jump over, and you'll have to work out the way to the next milestone: you won't be able to fly straight to the finish line (if there is a finish line at all!).

I was working in a fuel station doing the night shift. My new sense of honesty would allow me to find a job to produce money for my life expenses. However, in the same instance, I could not see anything wrong in letting my family and friends inside the shop at night to do the grocery shopping free of charge. In fact, I would be very consistent in how I would see that as good behaviour, as I was helping others.

However, on one occasion, I let in one of my workmates. She had a crush on me and I won't deny I liked that very much .

One night she brought her brother along. She started to kiss me at the counter and invited me to take her to the back, in the storeroom. I knew straight away what she was planning, of course I knew, I had a very well-trained delinquent mind. I told her I would not let her steal the money from the cash register. She offered me half the loot, and yet I could not do it. That would have been for personal benefit, and an unlawful way of getting money. My selective integrity was not yet as good as it should have been, but I knew I was on my way.

Around this time, I met a couple that became very dear to me. They have helped me in a few instances, and even though they were aware of my past, they never treated me as if that past existed at all and trusted me.

I had been known for stealing cars, over and over, as well as destroying more than a couple of vehicles, and yet they were confident they could leave theirs with me for a couple of days while they were away. I had a great sense of duty towards them and I reassured them I would take care of that car as if it were my own flesh.

I drove it home after work and parked it there. That same night the radio went missing. Someone had stolen it, and I knew who it was. Ferrier estate was a small town, and I had learnt how to tell who was responsible for every crime. That one had Nate's signature.

I was furious and I felt the fire building up within my guts. I was about to explode. That was my friends' car and my friends' radio, and I would not tolerate anyone menacing their property, not under my care anyway. I grabbed an iron bar I found in the driveway and went to Nate's house.

As I arrived I yelled at the entrance, "Nate! Fucking get out here right now, you fucking cunt!"

His father answered me from the top floor window, "What the fuck do you want? Nate is not here, he's at Lenny's!"

Lenny was the skinhead's leader. I knew who he was and I had met him personally because he was dating my sister Ali. I knew what he was capable of, and that he was the most feared person for miles around. No one messed with Lenny unless they were willing to suffer a terrible death. But I did not care, I held onto my iron bar and went to Lenny's house. There was nothing else in my head but a purpose: making Nate pay. Very dear friends had trusted me, and no one would mess with me while I was protecting their property.

I know I would never have seen red had that radio belonged to me. I would probably have gotten very pissed off, of course, but nothing like that. It was the animal rage protecting my pack, the only attitude that can possibly protect effectively, as it is fearless and would not stop at any threat.

I banged the door shouting. Two thugs came out and told me to fuck off. Then one slammed the door in my face. I did not bail then, I had only one purpose and I knew Nate was inside. I banged the door with the side of my fist again till they opened.

This time it was Lenny, the skinhead leader, who stood in front of me with at least ten of his thugs covering his back, "What the fuck do you want?"

"Where is Nate?" I snapped. "I know he's fucking here. Tell him to come out."

He called Nate to the door and I immediately grabbed him by the t-shirt and dragged him outside. I was in a total rage, holding him by the collar and lifting the iron bar ready to hit his head, while I screamed at him about the radio.

I was about to hit him when Lenny took the iron bar from me and told me to fuck off. I would not move for a few seconds. I didn't get what I had come for. I was standing in front of Lenny with a now much larger group of skinheads behind, maybe ten or more.

It wasn't fear that made me move away. I could have died there, belted to death by those men, but that didn't even cross my mind till days later. It was the realisation that I was not going to get close enough to Nate to hit him, nor would I get the radio back, that made me retreat. There was no use.

I didn't go home that night but the next day. When I arrived the next evening, Mum told me that Lenny had been to the house to get me with thirty or more skinheads. She was awfully worried. As Ali's boyfriend, she knew Lenny too, and she knew what that gang was capable of. By no means would the blood ties with my sister protect me if I had pissed him off enough.

But Lenny hadn't been there to hurt me at all. It turned out I had been the only one in history with enough balls to threaten anyone in his house, or so he said. Since that moment I would be respected without question by most of the crooks in the Ferrier as the most dangerous thugs in the area protected me. That allowed me to do something that, even though it seemed very simple it was not and could have risked my life: walking through the estate wearing a suit. That was one of my first steps to a brighter future. A change of image.

Chapter 7

The Ferrier

I was in the TV room and thought how funny it was that our ancestors went to the hassle of dividing time into fractions of minutes and seconds to give us a sense of advance and progress. They gave us a sense of control, as if we could decide the cycles of the Earth around the sun, and then align it to our own life, measuring it in terms of numbers. As if time really mattered inside the YOI.

There, in the TV room, the numbers were already lost. Dates expressed in numbers are so difficult to remember. What sticks in the mind are the events, although they might mix incoherently and then reorder themselves according to the emotions they produced in us.

I was cold, but within those walls coldness was more an inner mental state of numbness than an external condition. I was listening to the whispered conversation of two inmates sitting by my side. I wasn't sure if I was bored or feeling sick, my stomach couldn't distinguish the difference any more. I decided to isolate myself in that social time. I crossed my arms and sunk my chin into my chest, as if hiding my whole head between my shoulders.

There was this simple punishment the guards particularly

enjoyed. They would leave the TV screen on an empty channel, forcing us to watch a twitching of horizontal lines in all shades of grey with a fuzzy background noise. It was a nonsense torture that would drive us crazy, and surely provoke a fight after a short while.

Sometime before, on another dateless and hourless day in the YOI, one of the young kids protested about the grey screen. One of the guards walked up to him and punched him straight in the face. No warning given. Then he said, "Well, now you'll also see stars."

Inmates didn't usually laugh if the perpetrator was a guard, the cruellest would put on a dirty smile that was almost a grimace. But the guard's laughter thundered in the TV room.

When they stopped, we all stayed there pretending we were watching something, just killing the time, some whispering travelling slowly among the rows of chairs until the guards got tired and sent us back to our cells.

With my head sunk between my shoulders I hoped for a TV show, whatever would make me forget about whether I was sick or bored, sad or desperate.

One of the guards shouted behind me, "Silence!" The two inmates to my side stopped talking and sat down very straight, moving their eyeballs as far back as they could to check whether a blow was coming for them from behind. It didn't. The guard walked away and towards the screen and pressed one button on the device. He turned the volume up and I listened for the first time to a melody that would become the soundtrack to some of my life-long memories and of many others in the UK. They were broadcasting the first episode of Eastenders.

I lifted my eyes with the chin still stuck to my chest, and I sighed imperceptibly to the sight of credits on the screen. Someone sneezed on the other side of the room and then one of the daddies yelled, "Shut the fuck up!"

A reply came back, "You shut up, fucking cunt!"

Then a chain of insults started from one row to the other. One of the guards hit the back of a chair with a cudgel, but except for the boy who was sitting there, no one else noticed.

A short and unexpected silence, the result of a synchronicity mistake between the cursing and abusing, left room for a whinging voice who obviously never expected to be heard among the defamations, "I just want to watch this thing!"

Everybody stopped for a second to see where it came from and I felt glad that no one could identify the speaker, because his tone had already sentenced him to a great deal of suffering the moment he walked out. The buzz was restored and the guards started to lose their patience, if they had any.

Another guard started to hit the chair legs on the outside row with the cudgel, but before any of them dug their weapons into the flesh one of the daddies stood up and yelled, "You all shut the fuck up now!"

Silence fell like a blanket covering all of us at once, including guards, who just came back to their positions. I guess they weren't in the mood for a riot and were too tired to make us suffer their violence. It was an uneasy peace, but enough to allow our minds to wander senselessly into a TV series.

The melody and the credits were already gone. There was a bit of a buzz in the scenario being played out on screen, possibly a murder. When fiction is mimicking life as a drama but the audience watching has gone through a tougher life with no such melodramatic parade, it does not appeal to them. I wasn't amused but it was enough for the confused turmoil of my guts to rest, nothing else to think about for forty minutes.

I was an Eastender myself, at least in the geographical sense of it. After a while I couldn't help but smile timidly inside. Somehow it was comforting to see naive fiction about the infamous Southeast London; nest of crime and a no-go area, they said. The concrete jungle: my home.

***

The Ferrier Estate was named after opera singer Kathleen Ferrier. It was a utopia and was said to be a social experiment. Planned in the early seventies as a solution to the great problem public housing had become, the Ferrier Estate was a dreamland that would be the home of over three thousand people.

The first occupants moved in during 1971, and by the end of 1975 all the blocks had been built and all houses occupied, plus a number of shops to supply the big concrete neighbourhood and its inhabitants. It was said that one could cross the Ferrier without touching the ground, just by walking along the entangled pathways that its balconies and myriad of concrete levels formed.

There were green open areas; it was designed with a community purpose. The children would play safely on the great open spaces and the adults would watch them from their balconies whilst socialising with their neighbours. It was the perfect place to build a strong and peaceful community.

A great and strong community was indeed created, but the architecture and isolation of the grey blocks, with its labyrinth of never-ending corridors, soon lost their light to poverty and overpopulation, stigmatising the Ferrier as one of the most dangerous estates in the UK.

We moved into what they called a maisonette with four bedrooms, three floors, a bathroom and a toilet. Mum was with Dave then and it was a great improvement on what we'd had. The Ferrier was simply a concrete box, with long, poorly lit walkways and a thousand and one corners to wait for a prey. I was already savvy enough about crime to discern this advantage.

The inside walls were as drab as the outside. The dull green of the grass breaking out from the pavement cracks was not bright enough to add colour. As I look back then and I reimagine myself as a teenager, I could not think of a better place to grow up: a labyrinth, a maze of alleys and balconies, corridors at different levels, spacious areas to feel the freedom and strong wide columns to hide behind. It was a perfect jungle to play in.

Yet a perfect jungle to die in too, to feel the violence of those whose souls blend so well with the hard and sombre masonry. In the Ferrier, the same corner could be a castle for a young child and a dwelling for a drug addict at the same time of the day.

The Ferrier was as hard as it has been depicted so many times by the press. Even if many Ferrier dwellers defend its integrity to the death, talking about a real community, the good people that lived there, one thing cannot be denied: safety was not a thing within its concreted borders.

However, it is true that a paradox reigns in places like the Ferrier, a human touch of compassion that is unavoidable even in the worst places. There was something good that happened within the confines of that social experiment. Those hunks of cement, enclosing life and isolating it from the rest of the world – not only by a physical border but by a barrier of prejudice – would also gather within it a kindness that would shine brightest among the darkness. Unfortunately, I happened not to shine so much in those days.

As I walked home one night accompanied by one of my sisters, we heard two men talking and looking over one of the many concrete walls that characterised the estate. He was clearly saying, "Do you think he's dead?" The other shadow shrugged and they walked quickly to a car without noticing our presence, or maybe just sparing us out of carelessness.

My sister held my arm tight as she knew what I would do next. I shook it off gently and walked around the wall. A man was lying on the floor, his throat wide open in a clean cut and his head resting dead in a pool of blood. I walked back to where my sister was waiting and we went home.

The press will always paint the Ferrier as the most obscure of places, a nest of criminals and ruthless people. Just to declare oneself a Ferrier inhabitant would give one the classification of inferior social status and condition your interlocutor to perceive you as scum. And yet there was a part that was opposed to the burglars, the half-dead addict staring at the void in front of them, the pools of blood that threatened to scare children at night, the violence parading the streets as royalty, and the despair of poverty in far too many of the homes half-hidden in a maze of never-ending walkways. There was a great camaraderie.

Upon my decision to change, and as soon as I had the chance, I was determined to get my mother out of that shithole. I was able to pay her rent on a nice flat in a better area, because she deserved better, and she moved there upon my insistence.

Mum couldn't handle it. She was in a nicer and safer place, but she told me it was "cold" and stayed only for a couple of months before she moved back to the concrete block. As she said, friendship was in the Ferrier. Where scum exists in the form of delinquency, and fear and roughness gets stuck in the walls, humans rise to prove their commitment to life and to kindness. The Ferrier Estate was not a shithole for those who inhabited it, at least not all the time. It was a place with a community who helped each other. Where the struggles are greater, so is the kindness. Even looking at myself, the worst version I could be back then, I wouldn't think twice if I had to defend my loved ones and those who were part of my community. I always did so even if my methods weren't exactly honourable.

I grew up in a shit hole. I was a mindless delinquent. I used weapons to threaten and hurt people, stole many things and smuggled many others. I was addicted to all sorts of drugs and destroyed property over and over. And yet, because of all that, I can demonstrate that wherever you are, you can still learn good values. In the most unexpected places we will find goodness. Values and kindness are not exclusive to successful people. Economic status does not determine kindness, and ironically, generosity is greater where less is to be found.

The Ferrier Estate is no more now. Its deterioration did not start as a result of the crime, but rather the crime came as a result of a neglectful government administration. I am not trying to blame anyone or make others responsible for my own actions or for those committed by my gang. Nor do I blame the environment or the government that let the Ferrier down.

Maybe it simply didn't calculate for future costs, regarding people as mere numbers and not as real lives with real stories. But I cannot deny that the places you choose to inhabit, whenever you can choose as an adult, have an influence on your life and sometimes you have to walk away from what is most dear to you in order to change and pursue a better life.

Chapter 8

Glue in a Concrete Jungle

Every Friday a guard would set up a table in the TV room, almost bare of goods. We would be given some money upon complying with certain work duties. On the table rested a few things we could buy, like paper and pens to write letters, chewing gum and toothpaste (we were only provided with powder to wash our teeth).

We'd just have enough to cover very basic needs; paper and envelopes were very precious. Confined in the YOI your heart yearns for love even though you cannot bring yourself to soften and recognise it openly. Consequently, you keep it safe deep inside and minimise your enthusiasm when a letter is delivered to your cell.

Sometimes we just killed the bright in our eyes with a forlorn gesture, because the more we had alive in our souls the more they had to take from it. It wasn't about being mocked, it was about keeping the letter safe from the cruelty and not revealing you had an asset they could rip from you. Destroying your dignity wasn't enough for them. The guards and too many inmates were hungry for power and respect, and no one within those walls could understand respect in a form other than fear. So it was imperative not to show the letters mattered.

The hunger caused by the excess of plain food – deprived of

vitamins or any other nutrients for that matter – would make the need for a cigarette even more obnoxious, and that bare table on Fridays could hardly supply all of us. Some of the inmates had gained the favour of the guards due to good behaviour, where the favour was simply to be allowed to do some tasks outside relatively unsupervised. They were known as the trustees. That was gold for us, as they would also become our trustee, our link with the outside world and the smugglers we needed to get extra cigarettes.

I was clear of most addictions and drugs with which I had corrupted my body in the past, but I would sniff in the fumes of others smokers with urgency and delight if I had no cigarettes myself. I did not have a girlfriend, but my ex-girlfriend was kind enough to love me all the way through my imprisonment. She would throw a pack of smokes over the brick wall that delimited our freedom. The trustee would keep a couple of them as payment and I would enjoy the tar and nicotine drowning my lungs with every draw, breathing in not only to deceive my stomach, but also to imagine my ex-girlfriend, her scent impregnated in the cigarette. If the smell wasn't there, at least the memory of it had gone through the plastic. I was taking it in with my lips and sucking it through the filter.

It was cold outside and I was enjoying a cigarette with some other inmates when we were called to duty. I put out my cigarette carefully and kept the rest in my pocket. It was February and icy cold. We were not given any more clothing than a shirt and a thick woollen jumper.

I walked outside in a line with another three inmates and a guard leading the party. We were taken to the south wing of the building, where the Chief's office and the Doctor's ward were located. The windows were wider and taller there, with no bars on them, as if they had more right to the sunlight. On the floor under the windowsill, there were three buckets and a grey old rag hanging on the edge of each. We were to wash the windows that day.

The water was freezing and five minutes through the task my fingers were swollen and red. I could hardly feel them. One of my inmates was ticked off violently and told to stop shivering. I looked at him, his hand shaking and not even able to grab the rag. I felt his pain as I could hardly feel whether I was holding the rag myself. I surely had the intention but I could not feel anything below my wrist. It took just an hour to finish the task, which made me think it wasn't too bad after all, as I had not lost any fingers to frostbite.

As we entered the building I could feel the deriding warmth of the heating, which was so weak you could only feel it in contrast after exposure to polar temperatures, and my hands had been. They were so raw that as I tried to hold them closer to one of the wall heaters the heat felt like needles stabbing the flesh. Rather than providing any kind of relief it caused such pain that I contented myself with rubbing them against my trousers.

After a while I started to feel the blood rushing back to my fingers and the pain fading. Suddenly, I appreciated the early mornings milk runs in East London for the first time, the skin stuck to the glass and the grumpy milkmen asking us to hurry up. It came to me like a sweet memory. Whatever the conditions I had living on the outside, they were outside and now I would recall the memory with nostalgia and realise my freezing hands weren't so painful when I wasn't between those obscene walls.

***

The concrete jungle was the perfect place for a teenager and his mischief. Three mighty blocks of grey cement enclosing a small city of more than three thousand dwellers, the Ferrier had already delivered its results as a social experiment. In the eighties the estate was considered one of the most proliferating nests of crime in England. Regarded in other parts of London as a frightening place to go, many people wouldn't dare to step in it.

I would not be honest if I took only the romantic part of living in the Ferrier and told you about its strong sense of community, because I was part of the reason for its infamous name. But it wouldn't be fair not to acknowledge that the Ferrier was loved by most of its inhabitants, and the sense of community and care you would get there had no precedent in other more privileged London suburbs. The architecture created a microenvironment where people set their own rules, which might not have been based in integrity or kindness but those virtues would flourish in the good hearts sharing the same space.

Poverty was present and dense: lack of money and need was all over. It could be seen in the long corridors, the walls and the weeds growing out of the concrete cracks on the pavement. There was also some prosperity, small business would thrive as the structure forced its population to become secluded and confined to its limits. For outsiders, the Ferrier would feel like a rat cage they would not like to step into. For us, this enclosure was so familiar that it gave us a strong sense of safety and belonging.

Chapter 9

Food Stamps, Ham Sandwiches, and Small Jobs

I was in a constant fight with my fate. The children's home didn't do any good for my attitude, indeed it reinforced my bad ways. Also, as I grew older I became more aware of the poverty I was experiencing. My arrogance grew too, in order to cover for the shame and embarrassment that my clothing gave me. Whilst in the children's home, among the obscene hardship of children with no parenting figures, my threadbare clothes weren't a big issue. But I was a teenager like any other now, and wearing unbranded outfits from the charity store was a consistent punch to my dignity. I needed money and soon.

My appearance made it clear that my family status was embarrassing, but worst of all were the food stamps. Food stamps pushed me down beneath my own soles, my confidence smashed by the obviousness of my dirt poverty.

I couldn't bear the looks of others while I was redeeming my food stamps in the school canteen. They were like an evil token that drew me down to where no self-esteem was left. I was a man, and they were the sign of slackness, a family not provided for. Even if it wasn't yet my responsibility, I already had the feeling of not complying with my minimal contribution to the world and my family as a man.

I cannot accurately describe how insignificant a piece of paper stamped by the government made me feel. So small and nothing; I had no pride left. If other kids mocked me because of the food stamps, my heart would shrink and be pushed down into my stomach, a humiliation that I could only express with aggressiveness to the external world. And even masking the nothingness I felt with hostility wasn't enough to summon an ounce of dignity.

I started to sell my food stamps for half their value and then I used my manipulative skills to get the rest ing value from the canteen staff in its equivalent of food or drink. It was double the work of exchanging the food stamps directly, but it did two things for me: it saved me from the embarrassment and it encouraged my entrepreneurial spirit.

Where the children's home had failed to straighten out my behaviour, in a new attempt to achieve the unachievable, social workers and teachers talked my mum into enrolling me in the army cadets, assuming an extra dose of authority would do it. It didn't. Eventually, I was kicked out of there, as nothing can be done about a kid who doesn't respect any authority but his own.

But the cadets gave me three things: good friends who brought me valuable experiences, a source of money that would start me on my entrepreneurial path – not completely honest, but a start – and a healthy care of my appearance which I still value very much to this day.

Within the realm of institutionalised groups, rules, uniforms and duty, the cadets were probably one of the best places to meet peers and have fun. I don't regret my time there and I believe belonging to them helped me in my future endeavours. Not a thought I would hold at any moment during the two years I met them once a week, but the friends I made and how they led to my first experience overseas – a dream come true – is something I must be grateful for.

Following military rules, it was obvious that our uniforms must be impeccable. I was taught to iron shirts and trousers in a thorough manner, respecting the formal creases and erasing even the smallest and imperceptible wrinkle. I mastered this skill very quickly, as quick as I learnt to appreciate it. Whilst we would learn to make ourselves invisible among the bushes in camp practices, I discovered a better means of camouflage that would protect me from the shame and embarrassment of poverty, through my new ironing skills. If I could care enough for my pieces of clothing, washing them carefully and pressing them thoroughly, my appearance would not give away my privation. Moreover, I also realised soon enough how much a healthy look would do for my manipulative skills.

Whilst the initial gain of a well-pressed shirt accounted for an improvement in my mischief, it also gave me the pride that led me later on to a healthier and orderly life. Throughout our life we are consistently learning skills, and none of them are irrelevant, even when it seems too petty or trivial to grant it any extra thought. Ironing is a basic skill that helped lift my self-esteem, improved the results of my entrepreneurial activities, fed a healthy pride and sense of belonging, and also got me more than a good job.

And then there was the money. There is something that would grant immediate success when offered in a group of teenagers: food. While I was in the cadets, before our weekly meeting, I would go to Tesco and buy ham and bread rolls, make sandwiches and sell them to my mates. It was a good start and the system was cleaner and smoother than selling food stamps, as I would not lose money in the transaction. I enjoyed that. I really liked the sense of touching cash that was a product of my honest actions. And with that feeling in mind, I found myself another job.

I got a job washing dishes in a restaurant. I also started to help my grandad, who let me work for him in his cleaning company. Whilst the dishwasher job wasn't of vital importance to me and my reliability was quite dubious, I tried to do my best for my grandad and keep myself clean, never messing up with my responsibilities. I also vowed – using my double standards integrity – never to steal from his clients which was an easy thing to do when we were left alone in the middle of the night cleaning big offices in London.

I had another job delivering milk in the mornings. I would wake up at three in the morning and load the milk-van. It was so cold that my hands would get stuck to the bottle glass. It wouldn't have been such hard work if it weren't winter and I probably would have enjoyed it in spring and summer, as it was easy money and it didn't require much skill.

For a teenager, to keep a job is not so easy, especially for a teenager like me. I was too busy spending time with the guys and there were faster ways to make money, although not honest. In addition to my poor accountability, a large part of my money would be dedicated to drugs which didn't contribute to my labour reliability in the least.

There was a hierarchy in the use of drugs. Smokes were a must and a forever addiction. Marijuana was probably the always present and resourceful back up for our highs. The most devastating drug for me came in the form of a presumably harmless substance sold in any regular store: glue.

Chapter 10

The Gang

Regular children in regular neighbourhoods, attending average schools, have groups of friends. In the Ferrier, they were gangs in their full meaning. Although we would call each other friends, and to the best of our knowledge we would treat each other as such, there wasn't the sense of team spirit a cohesive group of non-delinquent friends would enjoy. We shared and we supported each other in a way – we never dobbed. This was a tacit agreement. We dealt with our own consequences, should we unfortunately get caught.

Even though I was part of a gang and had very dubious morals, I somehow liked the idea of earning money honestly – at least part of it. Sometimes I would try to make things right, but I would always end up being drawn to the dark side of mischief and crime. I could feel a part of me that was yearning for well-earned money, but it wasn't well developed yet, and I had this other side that would succumb to the ease of stealing under the immunity of my youth.

All of us in the gang knew we were untouchable. And if we weren't, if we were to suffer any consequences, we had all lived hard enough in our own homes to dismiss them as just a pain or an obnoxious deal. There was nothing that could really dig in our conscience or add anything more to the suffering we were already used to.

I was indeed the least violent guy in the gang, even when I could see red and had the potential, I never liked violence for the sake of it. Since primary school, I carried a knife with me. I only used it a couple of times as self-defence and never to initiate a conflict.

I despised bullies, although I would walk with them and many were my own friends. I guess we were all escaping from something. Dave was around then and home was not home anymore for me. I dreaded to see him about; the streets were far more comforting than any place around my own family at that moment.

Richie was part of the gang. He grew up with me, our mums were very good friends. He was so volatile. He would snap at nothing or randomly punch a passer-by in the stomach with no motive. It was like he had to pull something out and had no morals in place to filter his actions. A problem in his legs forced him to walk with calipers when he was young. Rather than developing any sort of empathy in him, disability had the opposite affect. He would conceal any sense of weakness with an absolute lack of mercy or commiseration.

Simon was as cruel as Richie, but he would go further, inflicting abuse on animals. It always seems viler to attack an innocent creature. Animals are considered inferior beings to human intelligence – an assumption not always accurate, of course – and whoever hurts an animal for plain satisfaction shows a lack of the most basic compassion.

Kevin was my best friend. He was a big guy, as attractive as he was aggressive. Kevin was calmer than the others, he wouldn't snap as quickly and his reasons were more personal – although not excusable. He was still a very dangerous person to be around and if you said the wrong thing to him you put your safety in serious jeopardy.

The same applied to Brett, we used to marvel at his ability to ride his bike in a wheelie for a whole mile. Raised in a rich family and with all material needs covered, he was a great bully and one had to walk on eggshells around him to avoid personal harm.

Vince was a great kid who probably wanted what we all did in the end: belonging. He was the son of a working couple and both parents spent most of their time away from home, leaving Vince with a generous money allowance. Initially, he would share his money with us, spending it on arcade games but later on it would cost him his life as he succumbed to a drug addiction.

Mick was as tough and aggressive as any of the others. He was the son of a single mum who would use us as involuntary voyeurs for her own pleasure. She would dress up in front of us in her tiny underwear whilst Mick would lower his head and walk out of the living room.

They all had a common ground: violence.

Although I was also riding the same wave, I always knew I was different at some point. I did not have the need they possessed to hurt people at random. I would defend myself from any aggression without hesitation, but I could see no use in doling out free violence for the sake of personal satisfaction. It had to be induced for me to retaliate. Aggressiveness can be easily induced when one has been suffering it for a very long time. Too often, it emerges from your subconscious and acts for you when there is really no other means of communication known to solve conflicts. Even when the conscious mind first becomes aware of this, its resistance might not be strong enough to counteract the inertia that pushes violent actions.

For years, even back then in my teens, I had seen my mum beaten consistently by her partners. Although when Tommy left we all enjoyed some peace at home with Stace the Ace and another very good guy called David, she would still go out with men who didn't care much about us. Violence at home would be present in all its strains over time: in the form of physical, psychological and emotional pain, and also plain indifference and neglect.

I remember the Irish guy. He wasn't aggressive, but his apathy and negligence towards us were another kind of violence. When I think of him I think of fish fingers; a small bag of fish fingers, in a bare freezer waiting for us, as children, to make a meal of them. The time with him at home, occupying the place as head of the family, brings back memories of hunger.

Curiously it also gives me a warm feeling, like a lukewarm current of water over the naked feet, so nice and gentle: that of my neighbours' kindness. They used to feed us every now and then with a proper meal and that would make our day.

The Irish left our house in the most unexpected way. We were all watching TV and we heard a big explosion. It was a time of IRA terrorist attacks and London was suffering the burning of bombs on a constant basis. My mum jumped, startled off the couch and asked, "What was that?"

The Irish guy just shrugged calmly on his armchair replying, "It sounded like a bomb."

My mum got so suspicious about his attitude that she kicked him out of the house assuming he was one of the terrorists.

We'll never know whether he was a terrorist, but he was off and away, and out of sight. Unfortunately, mum met Dave not long after, and the fish fingers seemed a feast in comparison to what we lived through with him.

Those were my wandering years. I hated school and never actually attended if I could help it, and once in secondary school I could mostly help it every day. I would wander the streets for days, sleeping on friends' couches or even mattresses laid on a corner in the street. It didn't really matter. Half the time, I would be thinking about where to find money and working out the means to get it.

I learnt how to keep my hands clean when it came to burglary. I would drive the car and manipulate the rest of the gang into doing the dirty work. It wasn't difficult to convince them, as they were more than willing to perpetuate any sort of crime. They lacked the ethics and enjoyed it. We made a good team, for great or small mischief and our rapport would excel even without verbal communication.

There was one thing we would do without any sort of planning. We probably didn't see it as a crime, more as plain fun with minor damage to others. We would invite some girls for dinner in a restaurant and enjoy as much food and beverage as we pleased, with no restrictions. Then all of us guys would stand up and walk towards the door, to the girls' astonishment. They wouldn't know what was going on. As we got closer to the entry, we would yell, "RUN!" and leave the premises and the bill behind.

Yet, I still had a part of me that valued money earned honestly. It was developed enough to urge me to work, although not as dutifully as I should. I would sell non-stolen goods whenever I could get them. The job washing dishes was in a pizza restaurant. I wasn't the most reliable worker, of course. There is an apathy that develops as a result of the lifestyle you choose or find yourself dumped in. Although, it wouldn't be fair to say that as a child I chose to grow up in a home that was "homeless", seeing my mum beaten almost to death over and over. Neither was the abuse inflicted upon us in the children's home my conscious election.

I guess I had a choice in whether to use school as a door to that life of success and travel I was craving. But I hated it. It was all about authority, being told what to think, and obedience.

However, there was one subject I not only liked but loved. Even though I would be an asshole and misbehave on a consistent basis during the class, I would attend nonetheless to learn: English. In fact, maybe I suspected it would be the only subject useful to my future, and indeed it was, as later in life books would become a door to new possibilities. If I hadn't learnt the reading comprehension needed to grasp the meaning of words and the love to get attached to them, I would never have been a self-taught hypnotist or anything else for that matter.

Chapter 11

I Pushed Her

In one way or another, all the boys in our gang – and the girls who would often come along with us – suffered our fair share of abandonment and brutality as young kids. When I look back and try to be objective about our lives, I view my own as the toughest of all. I do not say that with a sense of pride or relative superiority over them, but as a confirmation of how ambition, a strong desire to achieve it, the right mindset and the willingness to change can lead you to a better place regardless of the difficulties.

I don't pretend it was easy to transform the violent attitude that I had highly developed in my first years of life. It is not my intention to present myself as a successful person with only a mildly turbulent past so as not to scare prudes or to avoid being judged. That wouldn't do justice to my story or prove how much change is possible. Of all the things I did wrong – and I have a never-ending list – there was one that sunk so deep in my heart that I learnt it in just one blow. It would drive me nuts and get me into trouble whenever I saw my friends behaving in this loathsome manner: violence against a woman. As always, and to my own shame, I did not learn this lesson theoretically.

She was my first serious girlfriend and we were both about fifteen. It wasn't a healthy relationship but it was the only way we knew how to have a relationship. One day I was arguing with her, we both were quite fiery. Although our gang was all male, we would hang out with girls who would be as much trouble as us. And she was no exception.

I pushed her. I lost it and pushed her. I did not think about that, it was a normal thing to do. I had seen it so often, over and over: at home, in the street, my mate's parents, my own mates. Fortunately my mum was present to intervene, putting a halt to the altercation and my aggression.

She walked towards me with a firm step, straight back and high head. I was not used to seeing my mum with such determination. She was a lovely woman, fun and bubbly, but feeble. Not since I was little had she ever exerted her authority enough to overpower my arrogance. Not often anyway.

I knew she loved me, but as she walked towards me I also knew in my heart that I had done something terrible, something that awoke her hatred, something that was making my chest tight as she came closer. She stopped in front of me and looked me in the eye, "Mark, after you've seen what I've gone through. I am so disappointed."

She walked away, shaking her head with the saddest look on her face. It felt like an evil claw squeezing my heart so hard it was going to break. I could steal from others, use my manipulating skills for vile purposes, abuse and insult whoever was in my way if they jeopardised my wrong doings. I was more prone to crime than to good – honesty had a relative meaning in my vocabulary. But this time I had disappointed my mother, and I suddenly realised why.

So many times I had seen her half dead on the floor, with broken bones, bruised flesh and even resting in a pool of blood. I was her only male child at home, and by pushing my girlfriend I had turned into one of those men. I was like the one who took her love for life and scared her so much she had to run away from her children in order to survive. I was like the one who was seated at that moment on the couch, exerting a power over her that she could not combat. I was like Tommy, and Dave, the man who made me feel the greatest hatred I was capable of.

I never did it again, and since that moment I could never bear anyone acting like that. My mum deserved to be loved and respected, as do all women, and more than anyone, the woman I'd chosen to be with. That realisation came with an awful feeling of guilt and shame, the recognition of myself as the monster I did not want to be.

It wouldn't be the first time I would feel like that, over and over, along the years. But it was necessary. No personal change can be achieved without this trigger. It is up to us to decide whether we are willing to accept our mistakes – regardless of the pain they bring – and move beyond guilt and shame to be a better person. Or to deny our wrongdoings with cheap excuses, hurting others, as we were hurt.

Chapter 12

Sacred Island

In the turmoil of peer pressure, delinquency, arrogance and a fight for survival, I found a place where the time would stop and I could sense the goodness in me. It was just temporal and I carelessly left it behind, but it planted a seed that eventually broke free from the tar in my heart and mind and would later contribute to my success. Like my gypsy family, the dojo became a sacred place for me, a place of love, belonging and identity.

I found the dojo by chance. I was running after Kevin. He would turn around and go backwards every now and then, waving his arms up and down with both middle fingers pointing to the sky. It was his triumph dance. I would laugh at it every time. As I opened my mouth to release a guffaw, the cold air got me in the back of my throat and made me cough, slowing me down.

A flagrant laugh escaped from Kevin's mouth. He kept running fast. No one was following us. Not any more. That fat cunt from the service station couldn't even walk four steps without puffing out his last breath.

I recovered and sped up to catch Kevin. I saw him turning the corner and followed, to find myself crashing into a young woman. We both fell on the floor, and she rose up against me, "Son of a bitch!"

I was quick enough to avoid her backpack hitting my head. She had good reflexes; that I could tell. I heard Kevin laughing louder. He was pointing at me mockingly. Then he shouted to the young woman, "Hey bitch! Get fucked!" while still running. By then, I had caught up with him and now we were both running together.

Adrenaline was rushing up and down my body. No one was after us. The guy at the servo would have called the police, but they had better things to do than chase a pair of kids for some cigarettes. I could feel the euphoria pumping in my blood, it made me feel powerful. I didn't want it to stop, but my lungs disagreed.

Kevin's energy was also dwindling. He made a last turn into an alley and stopped behind a metallic rubbish bin, leaning forward with his hands on his knees and puffing between laughs. I let my body slump to recover from the physical effort. Kevin was a big bloke, with powerful legs and mighty hands. I was more equipped for breakouts; my body was lean and agile.

I punched him gently on the shoulder and he lost his balance falling onto the wall. We both laughed. Then I pulled out of my pocket a sealed cigarette pack and offer him one.

"What did you get?" I asked.

Kevin felt his jacket pocket and pulled out a half-naked doll. He held it on his flat palm and we both stared at it curiously. It was a woman in a red bikini. Her tits were huge, bigger than her head and pointing upwards. The largest piece of clothing was a headpiece with tropical fruit on it.

I pointed at it with my finger and then pushed it gently, her head, tits and ass started to wiggle.

I looked at Kevin, "What the fuck is that?"

We burst out laughing, a deep belly laugh that hurt in the ribs.

Kevin managed to say something, "I have no fucking idea! I grabbed it from the counter when that fat cunt started yelling at us."

We had been wandering the dull streets for hours, when we passed by the servo. We had no need to talk to each other to know what was going through our heads. Kevin walked in first, and went straight to the fridges to grab a soda. I came in after, heading to the counter.

I managed to get the fat guy behind the counter out into the aisle with my gift of the gab. We knew the cigarettes would be behind it. As he moved out, I quickly positioned myself behind him and grabbed a pack of cigarettes while I signalled to Kevin with my head.

The fat guy wasn't stupid, but was slow enough for us to snatch a few things. He saw Kevin on the convex safety mirror and I moved fast avoiding his grip. Next thing we were running in the street, the fat guy cursing us from a distance.

I opened the cigarette pack and offered Kevin one. The sexy doll turned out to be a lighter, so we giggled as the flame came out of its fruity head. Kevin pulled two sodas and five chocolate bars from his jacket.

"Didn't you get any cigarettes?" I asked.

"Sorry, mate, that fat cunt was too quick. He saw me in the mirror."

I shrugged and took one of the sodas. We left the alley and went out into the open street chewing a chocolate-caramel bar.

As we walked down the street, Kevin kept harrassing whoever dared to give him a bad look. He would pull his middle finger out with a grimace on his face, then just keep walking and laughing loudly. Even when he didn't intend it, his laugh sounded vicious.

I didn't like Kevin's attitude in the least. I used to feel uncomfortable when any of the gang bullied other people. I was up and ready to defend myself, and for sure I would beat the hell out of anyone while protecting what I thought mine. But the unwarranted abuse they enjoyed didn't amuse me in the least. Yet, I would go with it, and maintain my tough attitude in front of everybody, regardless of how it felt inside. Peer pressure is all an adolescent can count on, after all. We were only fourteen, but Kevin had already had a growth spurt and our attitude could be quite scary. Kids have the power to terrorise because there is an expectation of innocence and anything different is simply grotesque and frightening.

As we walked further and grew tired, the adrenaline and our arrogance wore off. Our shoulders started to drop, and our attitude lacked drive. Boredom was gripping us again. I put my hands in my pockets, looking languidly at the shop windows. Kevin asked me for another smoke and giggled as he lit it with the fruit-hat lady.

There was an open door, in an old red brick building. Inside, the silence was only broken by some synchronised voices sharply pronouncing monosyllabic words. As we passed by, the street seemed to halt and the voices entered my ears loud and clear. I stopped there, frozen, hypnotised. The voices echoed in my head and I was drawn inside.

"Hey Mark! Where are you going?" asked Kevin.

I didn't concede an answer or look at him, I just moved my hand inwards prompting him to follow me.

It was a small hall with cracked plaster walls and many informative posters covering them. It smelt damp. The floor was covered in a bluish mat, and standing on it, were ten kids all organised by height and dressed in white outfits with yellow, green and white belts. Our presence clearly distracted the students, who turned their heads curiously towards us.

Kevin shook his body uncomfortably, "Let's get the fuck out of here, Mark."

I punched him gently on the arm, as if to persuade him to be patient. I wanted to know more, unsure about what exactly, but I wanted to know more about whatever they were doing.

Then a short, strongly built man, with a deep voice pointed in our direction with his chin. It sounded like a gentle thunder, "Take off your shoes if you want to join us."

Kevin and I didn't know what to do. He shrugged and said, "Fuck it," then turned around and left the hall.

I felt embarrassed. It wasn't the humiliation of being poor, or holding food stamps, or the shame of not having good clothes.

It was a disgrace that came from somewhere inside, an uncomfortable place, yet it felt like a place of honour. It hit me like a sharp pain in my stomach, a punch of unworthiness.

Maybe I did know that feeling, maybe it was like the guilt of a four-year-old breaking his sister's only doll, but I didn't remember it. It didn't feel like being naked, it wasn't a personal shame, it went deeper. I had intruded into something sacred and I felt out of place within.

The man spoke again firmly, "Boy, take off the shoes and join the back line. Now."

I obeyed. Quickly. Without any hesitation I took my shoes off and walked slowly towards them. He had a commanding voice, but somehow it didn't force obedience. It was an authority so full of confidence that it would never be questioned. Powerful by itself, it had no need for fear or punishment.

I joined the group. I was very uncomfortable. I didn't have a uniform. In those moments, I wouldn't dedicate a millisecond to introspection or noticing how contradictory it was that I *wanted* to wear an imposed outfit. I just felt a strong desire to belong to the group, and the uniform would make me one of them.

I had no idea what I was doing. As I was sent to the back line, I stood side by side with two big guys, tall, lean and several years older than me. They weren't paying me any attention, but following a choreography of fast movements and vocal cues. I observed them for a few seconds before I decided to try myself. And then it all fell into place.

The movements were incredibly easy. My body would respond

neatly, as if every command to my motor system were already stored in some part of my brain, and I just had to recall them by trying them once.

I caught the short man observing me. I didn't like being watched, but he wasn't wary or suspicious; unexpectedly it made me feel proud.

The class came to an end and I whispered to the big guys in the back line,"Hey, what's the name of that guy, the teacher?"

Both gave me a threatening look. I could sense their fury; I had done something really offensive. The most curious thing was I knew it. The instant the words came out of my mouth I knew I had been highly disrespectful.

I would have sworn it wasn't my intention, because it wasn't. My mind was clear and the exercise had breathed fresh air into my core. I felt optimistic and sort of "clean". It was as though, inside that hall, among those kids in white pyjamas, the haughtiness of the Cheshire Cat had no place, it had been pushed away. And yet my rushing mouth had exposed the attitude I had been sporting a while earlier with Kevin.

I lowered my head and muttered an inaudible apology. Then one of the big guys gave me a friendly pat on the shoulder and moved away. I didn't know what to do, so I stayed there looking at everybody moving around, grabbing bags that had been leaning on the wall. Some parents came to pick up the younger ones. And suddenly I felt out of place again.

I looked for my shoes and rushed towards them trying to escape the unpleasant feeling of personal displacement.

As I was tying the laces, the teacher came to me.

"Hi, I am your sensei. What's your name?"

"Mark."

"Ok, Mark, will I see you next week?"

I nodded, not daring to look him in the eyes. Then I rushed out of the hall as a group of little ballerinas walked into the community hall giggling and jumping.

The sensei's name was Brian. I came back the following week. This time I dragged Kevin with me, who admittedly, wasn't very keen until he found a bad use for karate. It was my first real contact with martial arts and it was a love affair. The only other time I had felt such excitement at trying a new activity was when I tried to hypnotise Scott in the children's home.

Back then I couldn't make any link between karate and hypnosis, nor why I was a natural at that martial art. Years later it became clear: karate is ninety per cent mind, ten per cent physical strength. Once you understand that, you never question it when you see a little girl breaking a brick in two and a strong, grown man breaking his knuckles attempting the same.

I told Mum I wanted to go to karate. I guess for her that sounded like the sweetest melody. It was a guided activity where I would be supervised and, moreover, I would have to accept the sensei's authority if I wanted to stay in the dojo.

She made a great effort to gather enough money to buy me a uniform, and I took the biggest pride in wearing it. Mum also tried her best to keep up with the fees, but abundance at home was as abstract as the noun itself. Sometimes, we just couldn't afford it, and showing up at the dojo when I couldn't dutifully pay my debt hurt my pride and my heart.

Sensei Brian was an incredible man. His heart was placed as firmly in his chest as his were feet on the tatami: strong and balanced. There were not many adults I respected during those years, and Sensei Brian was the one I respected the most. I would never question his authority and causing him trouble would bring me a mix of guilt and grief that went beyond disgrace and shame. It would be dishonour for degrading a sacred place.

Kevin wasn't as keen as me for the dojo, but he decided to join the training sessions, although he didn't last long. He learned to enjoy it and although he would not possess the same reverence for the sensei and the dojo as I did, he too would change his ways once we crossed the threshold of the community hall.

When things went well and money allowed us, we would follow a routine that soon became a ritual. Kevin and I would walk to the community hall together and on our way we would buy a soda and a Mars Bar. We would buy them, *not* steal them. That ritual was part and parcel of our belonging to the dojo, and thus it must be respected.

The times things weren't easy, I would miss the training. Sensei Brian would insist on me coming back for karate lessons regardless. I was to pay him in the future but on many occasions the future would never come.

I was an excellent student; my skills were exceptional. The rate at which I was improving was simply outstanding. I gained flexibility and speed in record time, and soon I had no difficulty in following the older students in their routines. At one stage I became invincible at the dojo, including beating opponents double my size and weight. I was beating black belts when I was just a yellow belt. I was a natural as Sensei Brian put it.

Training with Sensei Brian was a tough business and exhausting, but the energy that place transferred into me was the push needed for my skinny body to bear the physical conditioning. Hundreds of push-ups on our knuckles at the end of a training session would make my body tremble under the effort; my hair soaked in sweat. It was painful and my joints and muscles would ache for hours and days afterwards. Sometimes I couldn't even move the day after a session and my legs and ribs were bruised and sore on a constant basis. I believe I broke fingers and toes on many occasions, but never bothered enough to worry about them because of the fear of being told to stop the training.

No physical pain would stop me from going back to the dojo. I was diligent with my training and I even made a dojo out of our living room. I would train at home for hours. It was a time I would enjoy deeply but my sisters would dread. Sensei Brian wasn't at my home-made dojo exerting his authority and good judgment, so I was still the same uncontrollable kid. I would use my sisters to practice locks and kicks. Only Ali would retaliate and I must admit I would enjoy having a fair opponent at home.

Mum resolved to disband my home practice and placed the couches back where they belonged, destroying my dojo. She would insist on me training at the community centre, more to stop my sisters' wailing and my fights with Ali than to encourage me in a healthy activity. But she was short of money more often than not, and every time I was further behind with my fees.

My pride and shame at not being able to cover the debt were as broad as the range of my karate abilities. Sometimes I wouldn't appear for weeks, too embarrassed to take Sensei Brian's time without paying him. It wasn't fair. I dreaded those days. Among other things and beyond the enjoyment and the much-needed discipline, the dojo was my sacred land. It felt like being myself, without all the shit that insisted on burying me when I was outside. There was no pretentious Mark and no need for survival. I felt protected and respected, and in exchange I would protect and respect everyone there. Stepping inside the dojo would instantly cause a shift in my mind.

Life outside was no different though. Once the training was over I would go with the gang to fill up a trolley at Tesco and run straight out with no contemplation. I would do it wearing my gi, cheering our canniness by insulting any passer-by and viciously laughing at Tesco staff.

The dojo and its sensei resonated with the part of me that knew for certain my life was destined to go far beyond the eastern suburbs of a polluted London; that bit of dreamy common sense that would drive me one day in the right direction. That sacred land was a breath of fresh air among the piles of sticky tar, and even though I couldn't know then, it planted a seed that grew ever so slowly, but nonetheless firmly, and with strong roots.

Chapter 13

Glue

In response to the inability of institutionalised education and the children's home to have any affect on my behaviour, it was recommended I attend a highly regarded boarding school. Mum, teachers and social workers agreed that it would be in my best interests to be secluded again. This time, I would be sent to a good school with high expectations of my academic and behavioural compliance. Fortunately for me, the highly reputed boarding school principal didn't have such expectation upon reviewing my school and psychological records and rejected my application.

I had already been expelled from two schools and suspended on so many occasions no one bothered to keep count anymore. Today, as a father, I can empathise with the feeling of desperation and helplessness of the adults who cared for me, even if their care was timid or just the result of an obligation. No one knew what to do with me. The army cadets were the next proposal to try and straighten me out.

As I mentioned before, the cadets gave me three great things: friendship, entrepreneurial skills and an interest in self-care. It was also a fantastic place to learn life skills and survival techniques, which would have aligned with my character traits if it weren't for a small detail: the core of a cadet group was institutionalisation.

I wasn't born to be told what to do. However, I did manage two years as a cadet. My last day with them, I was summoned to the office quarters, as I had been many other times. I hadn't done anything especially wrong in the last week, just my average display of defiant behaviour. My brigade supervisor escorted me to the main office as if I were a prisoner. He walked behind me avoiding conversation and looking away if I looked at him. I didn't bother asking why I was being taken to the office; to be dragged before authority without being given a reason was a way of life by then. I knew there would always be a reason, but sometimes there were so many that I wasn't certain what it would be that time.

The captain of the cadets was standing in the middle of the office talking to a senior cadet. When he saw me coming in with my supervisor, he dismissed the other boy. I wasn't invited to sit down or given any explanation; he didn't even greet me. He just beckoned me with a head movement and I didn't move from where I was. *Fuck him, what the fuck does he want?*

Then he spoke, "I won't waste my time as you have wasted ours, Mark. You are out. Give your uniform to your supervisor and don't come back. Your presence here is pointless. You'll never amount to anything."

I remember how I didn't care at that very moment. How his words had no effect on me. I shrugged and murmured, "Ok, fuck you all". Then walked out, lit a cigarette and left.

I wandered the streets for a while, with one hand in my pocket and the other with a cigarette, looking at the floor and walking with the fast pace that anger prompts. I was pretending I didn't care, and probably a part of me didn't. But, again I had been rejected and expelled. The Captain's last words thundered in my head, "You'll never amount to anything." Fuck him!

It wasn't the first time I had heard those words, and it wouldn't be the last time: the violent teacher whom I defeated with a cheeky smile; Tommy who didn't have anything nice to say but beat our souls out whenever he got the chance; Dave who would add "Fucking cunt" to the end of the sentence; my cousin's dad, an army man, would never get tired of saying it in a resolute tone and carelessly, as if I should never expect better words from anyone.

"You'll never amount to anything."

I turned a corner and saw Kevin talking to two girls at a bus stop. I threw the cigarette butt on the floor and went to meet them. Fuck the cadets. Fuck everybody.

Nevertheless, my time with the cadets was quite profitable. I would make good money from my sandwich trade. I always sold everything, never had stock left or wasted, and I would make around twenty pounds each time, which I would use to cover my expenses and invest back in my sandwich business.

Then there was the job at the pizza restaurant washing dishes and my grandad's business. At school, every now and then I was still selling the goods my Jamaican friend would gift me. I was managing to put some cash in my pockets in an honest way. But that didn't stop me from stealing with the gang, especially when that cash was more easily gotten and the stolen items offered better revenue after sale than my honest businesses.

I would spend the money very unwisely, mainly on cigarettes and marijuana, and the money would disappear twice as fast as it landed in my pockets. The gang was on the same wavelength. Each of us would invest in drugs till the very last cent, every time more expensive, and it was ruining us. Unfortunately, we found a drug that was fairly cheap and perfectly legal. It couldn't get better than glue.

We would get the glue in general stores. One can would do for four of us and we would all have a bag of glue each from just one can. Then we would just sit and sniff it and sniff it until we were all completely fucked out of our heads.

It was fast and simple, also cheap and highly accessible. When the local store we frequented realised the amount of daily sales they were achieving in cans of glue, they doubled stock and always made sure they had some available for us and any other glue sniffer that was desperate for a fix.

We wouldn't always buy it. Stealing was not a problem for us. Sometimes it was easier to steal the glue itself than the items we'd sell to buy the glue. It would depend on our mood and inspiration for doing things right, which was quite feeble in general and almost nonexistent in the case of drug use.

We used to sniff glue every single day, once or twice. We would get a can of glue and a plastic bag and take turns. The fumes would evaporate very fast so we had to be quick and keep the bag tightly closed between sniffs and rolling. It was a very quick high and it didn't last much, but oh, it felt so good then.

Sometimes we would fight for the last sniff, when there was hardly anything to breathe in, in a clumsy tug of war with the plastic bag. If the bag opened even a bit for too long, which would be a fraction of a second, the fumes were gone and with it the chance of another sniff. Then a burst of uncoordinated voices and the dumb violence of inept brains would break out amongst us, but with no serious consequences.

It was also around that time that I started to get caught for several crimes. I hated to go inside houses and steal stuff. I would be the driver, ready for the get away.

Sometimes there was no need to go inside, the electricity boxes functioned with coins in those days, so we just had to locate them, break them open during the night and take the money. I would sell stolen jewellery, clothing, small white goods and even booze. But there was something I actually enjoyed stealing very, very much – cars.

In most cases, I would steal cars out of need, as a mean of transport. These crimes were the ones that landed me in court more often. I was a minor, in a sense almost untouchable. Worst-case scenario I would spend a weekend in a young offenders institution, and then back home. But when the conditions of living outside prison are not much better than inside, a couple of days locked up doesn't teach you to appreciate the value of freedom.

I was summoned to court several times during my teens. I don't remember attending all of them, only the occasions when I felt like it or when I thought I had no option and feared the worst consequences, maybe. This time it was in Bexley Magistrates Court. I took the bus to Bexley.

It was a familiar building and unfortunately, it would take on further significance in my life not long after. The stairs to the main entrance raised almost three levels alongside a red handrail, but I would usually go in through the door at the rear, where the parking was at ground level.

I walked in and listened to the judge with my arrogant attitude, showing more boredom that I actually felt in an attempt to irritate their authority. They couldn't do much more than push me around, on my way in and out, but I couldn't care less about that mistreatment. I would either get wild within the allowed threshold of the building restrictions or just go with it knowing that I was invincible, and wait for my release, back on the streets.

I spent what I thought was a fucking eternity inside there, and took the bus back to Kidbrooke to meet my mates. I was completely sober and my brain was clear. I hadn't had any glue that day or the day before.

Once off the bus, I walked to a bare building site where I expected to find my friends. I saw four of them behind some bushes. Their eyes were lost in nowhere. They were mumbling, dribbling and laughing idiotically. Two of them were fighting for the plastic bag but their movements were so uncoordinated and clumsy that both fell onto the floor, and the one with the bag rushed to sniff the last bit of glue while the other was abusing him and trying fruitlessly to punch him with a wriggly fist. The other two were just laughing and coughing noisily.

One of them saw me and said, "Hey, fucking Mark! Come here mate!"

He tried to stand up but couldn't. I had never looked at us from that perspective. I had always been one of them, one of the brainless boys literally frying their heads with poison. Suddenly, from the outside, from a sober viewpoint, it didn't look so much fun. In fact, it was pathetic. For the first time it hit me: I was pathetic when I sniffed glue and I was frying my brain to insanity or to its death.

Kevin tried to reach me again and grab my arm. He started to tell me an intelligible story about something that had happened, and suddenly changed to business talk and someplace they had been "having a look at". I nodded and helped him to sit down again. He was having trouble standing and was leaning on me too much.

I looked at all of them with sorrow, they moved like drunken puppets with a cloth tongue. I told them I would find them later; I had something to do. Then I walked off with the firm decision that I would never sniff glue again. And I never did.

Certainly it was the last time I ever sniffed glue, but one doesn't change overnight. Cocaine came after, then heroin and ice. I have seen the last two destroying lives and families, fortunately I never felt attracted by them.

Kevin ended up married with a beautiful and kind woman but he would be very violent with her and couldn't overcome his addiction, which aggravated his abuse. He ended up losing everything he had, wife and kids. Later in life, while battling lung cancer, his body didn't cope with an overdose of ice.

Brett didn't even make it that far. After a long addiction to heroin he could not bear it anymore and blew his own head off with a shotgun.

Vince started to use the money his parents had given him to redeem themselves for their absence during his teenage years on drugs, and he continued later in life spending any money he got on them. I lost track of him as I lost track of Mick, both lost into a life of addiction to hard drugs.

Last time I saw Simon I was leaving the house I was living in with my first wife and my little son. I saw Simon seated in a car with the window open, as I passed by I saw how he had the rubber band around his arm, which once released would instantly fill his body with lethal, highly addictive heroin. I turned my son around; I did not want my kid witnessing that. It was the last time I saw Simon.

During my last trip to England, three years ago, I came across Richie. I waved at him but he didn't recognise me or could hardly recognise any one. I stopped him to ask what he'd been up to since I last saw him. His skin was dry as cardboard and very blotchy, an obvious sign of a heroin addict. No muscle was sticking to his bones any more and his teeth were either missing or too damaged to keep any ivory colour. I don't know whether he is still alive, but I could see then that his heart wouldn't continue beating for much longer.

Chapter 14

No Lives Left

The air in the corridor always felt like a metallic chill on the back of the neck. We would line up in the morning to go the bathroom and have a shower. Each of us had a bar of soap, and powder to brush our teeth. The cell doors would open and we would stand there waiting for the guards to lead us in a line to the bathroom.

That morning, I was more tired than usual. I reluctantly got out of bed and stretched the sheets with care, leaving a perfectly made bunk. I took my toothbrush and the tooth powder, plus the towel. Barry and I stood out of the cell as the doors opened and followed the queue to the toilets. It was my mate's turn to empty the night bucket, so he was carrying it. I dreaded cleaning the night bucket. We both made an effort not to shit in it at night, ever more earnestly if it was our turn to empty it the next morning, but sometimes our austere and hostile diet didn't facilitate our endeavours.

As we arrived at the shower I realised I had forgotten my soap. Unfortunately, one of the guards realised the same thing as I was turning the tap open.

He was the most feared guard in the institution. His body was huge and he had a strong German accent. The big, thick belly that hung out in front of him was not the sort that makes you think of a feeble man of blubber, but of round strength and violent heaviness. Worst of all, he was ruthless.

It was said he had been a soldier in the Nazi army in WWII, and no one had any reason to doubt it, His manners were different to the other guards. His ruthlessness seemed to be even more controlled than his colleagues in an environment where impunity is the norm for those with the right uniform. That was already scary because it made you wonder what he would be capable of if given the chance. He was over sixty, maybe one of those teen soldiers who spied on their own parents in Nazi Germany. He had lost none of the vigour a crooked mind can rely on to commit unforgiveable crimes.

Next thing I knew, I felt the harsh, cold tiles pressing on my back. He had lifted my naked body against the wall. His hand was open and he had placed it under my nose so my head was tilting back. I could feel the power of his arm driving force up to my nose bone.

I suspected that he could kill me with a single movement, shoving my nose bone straight up against my skull and the broken pieces digging into my brain. He bent his elbow and put his disgusting face so close to mine that his foul-smelling breath ran up into my nostrils.

"Little cunt forgot his soap? Fucking shitbag!" he grunted. I felt the tension in his arm, as if he were fighting to control his own body and stop himself from killing me. Then suddenly he released me. I felt my neck lashing back violently, and I slipped down onto the wet floor. He walked away and pushed another inmate in his way, causing him to fall against the wall and starting a chain of hysterical laughter and abusive behaviour.

***

I wasn't scared of death back then, I was so used to it that I didn't even give it a thought. But now that I had a good life to live for everything changed.

The doctor listened to me and without wanting to worry me, said he wanted to make sure everything was ok up there. It was only a routine check. So there I was, seated on a chair pretending to be relaxed and smiling to the little girl who was jumping around and playing with a doll whilst her mother tried to keep her still.

They would call my name and then I would go into the tube. The doctor said that if they repeated the process and did a second MRI, it meant that they had found something. That wasn't what worried me, because something inside was telling me that they would do a second MRI. I had no doubt about that. Only in the YOI, when I had felt death breathing on me, had I feared it for a fraction of a second – back when the German lump almost killed me for a bar of soap. But this time, death was terrifying, nothing external was threatening me, it was growing inside me.

In 2004, I had already been in Australia two years. I had left a life back in London. One that insisted on dragging me over and over into a past I did not want any more. I was walking a fine line all the time, a tight rope that divided two worlds: the one I came from and the one I wanted to live in.

I would love to say that they were compatible and that I could keep my friendships and sustain the love I had for all the people and places I had lived in and with. I would love to say that it doesn't matter what the circumstances are, it is the people and who they are deep inside that is important. But the reality is that we create an environment that leads to one thing or another, and with our actions and attitude we shape it to fit into a specific category.

Unfortunately, on the side of that line where my past resided, the circumstances were shaped by negativity, violence and ruthlessness. I ended up realising that I did not resonate with that anymore, and that would never resonate with me unless I chose to stay there.

People and places that did not support the successful life I wanted could not come to the other side of the line with me. Neither could I waste my time reassuring people I was still there for them. I am a loyal friend, but I am also exigent with the loyalty I receive in return. Little by little, people started dropping out of my life, and when certain that we didn't need each other anymore, I found it easy to wipe clean my history and make room for the good to come.

I thought I would die that year. I seriously saw the end of my life. I looked back and saw all the times I had been about to die and didn't even care, but the myriad of emotions I was feeling at that moment told me how scared I was this time.

I had been teasing death for so long, before I turned my life around, before I could even see what life was worth. I was careless with that precious gift. Back then, survival was just a matter of animal instinct, and somehow I always managed to keep myself alive, despite my reckless attitude, despite my disregard for my own physical integrity. I did not fear death because I believed myself invincible. But that was back then, when I had no sense of future, a concrete future. Before I became a father and a husband.

I sat down in the resting area waiting for the nurse to call my name. I don't particularly complain about any sort of pain. I had been in many difficult situations and suffered pain that would threaten my health – even my life – many times before . So I wasn't the kind of person who runs to the doctor with an earache. But this time was different. I sensed there was something really wrong. I am not prone to headaches and I had one for over nine days. Something was happening inside my body, something I could not ignore.

The wait was long, and I passed over the pages of a magazine without even reading a word or realising that it was upside down. I decided I would not say anything to my family till I knew for certain whether there was something to worry about, and at the same time I knew I would be telling them very soon. So many times I had defied death and deceived it, and now she would catch me from inside. She had gripped my brain and I wondered if she would let go as she had done in the past.

There is a reason to be alive. Many support the idea of a purpose in life, a motive for us to be in this world. I agree with that. I thought about myself, and the steps I had taken in this world, and concluded I must have had a purpose, otherwise, why would I still be breathing. Thinking about that – even though it did not release the worry of it all coming to an end soon – made me realise that at least I had complied well enough with whatever my mission had been. How else could I have beaten death so many times?

The first time it happened I couldn't have been aware of what was going on or whether there was a danger. I remember the pain and see now that I was very lucky I didn't lose my eye. I was five, and as was my ritual, I had run away from home to roam the streets. I would probably have been playing with other kids, wild and free and completely careless, as any five-year-old boy would be, with the handicap that there were no one to supervise my actions.

My mother thought I was playing with my tin box and my animal cards upstairs in my room, and when a neighbour brought me home covered in blood and half unconscious she screamed and paNateed, needing even more assistance than I did.

I remember the car very clearly. I didn't see it until the moment the wing mirror hit me in the face. I must have run into it at just the right time to get out of it alive. Cars in those days were made of heavy steel and as it was speeding down the street I stepped right in front of it. The wing mirror hit my face opening a deep cut on my eye. I didn't faint but I was stunned. I felt someone lifting me and running somewhere. Next thing I heard my mother screaming and from there, despite the blood and the pain, all the attention was for me.

Waiting for a death sentence in the clinic, I couldn't help but smile at my little self, enjoying the attention of doctors and nurses for a while, with no concept of death, life or danger whatsoever. Only delighted and surprised by what a bit of blood could do for me.

This episode was repeated years later in a similar manner. I was thirteen and I got a skateboard for Christmas. Even though I always knew I had a strong mind, it would not free me of the mindless attitude of a teenager. Moreover, maybe the strength I had was detrimental to my safety, magnifying my adolescent stupidity. I would say my life and all my mistakes are proof of it.

I dived down a steep street with my skateboard. I was approaching the street that crossed it and I knew instantly I had to stop. Unfortunately, I didn't know how to stop and also I couldn't. I hadn't seen the car speeding through when I jumped off the skateboard. As I rolled down towards the side on the pavement I saw my board rolling down between the wheels of the car.

I stood up, bruised, with burns and small lacerations all over my body, and lifted my hand in the air giving the driver a finger and a good string of insults. I was happy to be alive, but obviously I was happier about the story I was about to tell my friends.

A door opened at the end of a corridor and a nurse came out with a clipboard and called my name. It was my turn. I smiled at him as he led me inside the room. There was a small cubicle, cold and dark with some electronic equipment and three screens. On one of the walls there was another door and a big window.

The nurse asked me to empty my pockets and led me to the next area. It was a cold place even though the temperature was nice. It was the coolness of antiseptic and white steel. He asked me to lie down on the machine and asked whether I suffered from claustrophobia. I shook my head and pretended to be calm.

"Please stay very, very still," he said.

Then he left the room and the upper part of the MRI started to move towards my head. The noise was numbing and it hurt the soul somehow. It was metallic and icy, a vibration my senses didn't like, the opposite of love and warmth. Nevertheless, the science that could condemn my life may at the same time aid my recovery.

I didn't want to think, and yet I thought about how I was being scanned inside a huge roll, like a sausage. Humour is always a good way to soothe the heart. Then it came to me. There was that time that I not only miraculously survived thanks to the power of adrenaline, but also saved people from injury and their property from damage. It was a danger that I had created myself, yes, but still I managed to make it right.

Teenage brains have an amazing ability to develop and create complex imagery for absurd ideas which lead to nowhere, but when presented against the reasoning of "why not" – and with no regard to the consequences – compel the perpetrator to carry them out for the sake of it.

With this disposition, myself and a mate were riding on my bike to nowhere in particular with no other purpose than to kill time. We were up on a hill in a place that had become in a tacit manner a dirt course for bikes. We saw a concrete roller sitting at the top of the hill and in unison we marvelled at the idea of pushing it down the hill. There were no second thoughts or doubts. So we did it.

People down the hill heard the thunder of the concrete roller travelling in their direction and the screams started. There were some cars parked in the roller's path and someone tried to jump in his car and move it out of the way, but another man forced him out of the vehicle and off the roller's trajectory. At that moment my friend and I grasped what had happened. More accurately, we realised the magnitude of what we had just done. We shit ourselves.

Enlightenment comes with a delay in such young and drug-addled brains, I must admit. We both started down the hill running as fast as we could to stop the concrete roller. It didn't even occur to us that there was no human way we could hold a tonne of compressed cement in a cylinder rolling downhill, but that didn't matter.

Fortunately my adrenaline was stronger than my logic. As I reached the roller I threw myself on the floor face up in front of it, and just as it was about to smash me, I lifted it with my feet and diverted it with my legs to one side. The inertia, the blessed laws of physics and my mindless attitude saved not only my life but also a lot of damage. The roller changed direction and stopped a few metres from us. My heart was pumping hard and I heard my friend say, "Fuck, mate!" Then we just walked up the hill, took the bike and rode away, ignoring the commotion we had caused among the people around us.

The metallic sound, like that of an evil tuning fork, stopped and the machine moved its cylindered piece back. The nurse opened the door and helped me out of the room.

 "Please wait outside. We'll come out with the results for your doctor soon."

I knew it. I would be back there, I could tell. I was so certain. I had intended to make a real effort to be positive, I wanted to keep the hope, but something inside was telling me that I was going to see the black lady of death far too close again, and this time it could be the last time.

The German guard with his Nazi past could have killed me back then in the YOI, for a bar of soap. He didn't need any more reasons. Neither was there any sort of logic for the crook who put his gun against my cheek while demanding the money I owed him. I could not even remember whether I owed him the money, whether I had spent it carelessly or he just felt like bullying me for a bunch of fake t-shirts I was trading from him.

It was the Cheshire cat smile. It got me into more than enough trouble as I grew older. I pissed him off so much. It was just for a few quid but showing my arrogance did it. I don't think I conceived dying at that moment, not even with a gun against my cheek. My story could not end in suburban London. No way.

I could not be scared of broken glass slowly cutting through my skin in a pub, hands about to be chopped off or knives presented in my face, because I was somehow certain that the end wasn't anywhere close. Maybe I also had a lucky star.

On two occasions, I smashed a car. The first time, I was completely drunk and craving a cigarette. I got some friends from the party we were at and we stole a car belonging to a party guest. But who cared back then? I drove mindlessly, in my style, and crashed it against a parked car. We bounced backwards and forwards hitting four more cars in our trajectory. What was left of the vehicle was an accordion of metal and broken glass. Somehow no one was seriously injured, or if we were, we were too drunk to actually feel it. In any case, we just took the car as far as we could drive it. I recall I left it in a park. Then we all ran off.

The second time I drove a car against a wall it was my boss's. He had lent me a brand new car as a reward for my good results at work. I worked in real estate several times during my twenties, and always became the best seller everywhere I went. So in good faith and as an incentive, my boss lent me a fancy car to drive around. Again I got drunk, again I smashed a car, and again I walked away unharmed, leaving a mass of unrecognisable metal and glass.

I heard the door in the corridor opening again, and saw the nurse with the clipboard. My name was called for the second time. I dreaded hearing my worst fears confirmed.

"Does it mean you're weak to give up, maybe not, but it does mean that you're weak if you don't try and try again."

Mark Anthony

Top: The children's 'home' Erith Lodge, apparently now an old peoples home, picture taken on my re visit to the UK in 2010, the playroom where I first hypnotised Scott bottom right, my bedroom for a while, top third from right.
Bottom: The Ferrier Estate aka the Concrete Jungle, home for many years where a great camaraderie was formed between many who lived there, and many memories made, both good and bad.

Top: The Ferrier Estate. Where the walk-throughs built to make it easier to access other parts of the Ferrier then became run-throughs after a mugging, a hiding, to get away from the Police.
Bottom: The Ferrier Estate shops which once were bustling with paying customers, then became just another place to thieve for some, junkies, teenagers and people just trying to feed their hungry loved ones.

> When things at school were becoming way out of control, and the Mindless Delinquent began to show his true colours.

BEXLEY LONDON BOROUGH
EDUCATION DEPARTMENT

O.E.S. BALL, B.A.
Headmaster

Telephone: 01-300 5865

Hurstmere School,
Hurst Road,
Sidcup.
DA15 9AW

4th November, 1981.

Mrs. Colella,
90, Halcot Avenue,
BEXLEYHEATH.
Kent.

Dear Mrs. Colella,

   Marc Colella

I regret to inform you that your son misbehaved today as follows :-

1. Failure to comply with instruction of Deputy Headmaster.
2. Wearing of ear-rings in school.
3. Refusal to accept authority of the School.
4. Leaving the premises without permission.

As this is not the first occasion, a suspension from School of ten days has been authorised by the Chairman of the Governors. He will be expected to return on Thursday, 19th November, 1981 at 08.45 hrs and must report to me at my study.

In the meantime I would be glad if you would telephone my Secretary to arrange an appointment to discuss your son's future in this school.

Yours sincerely,

J. V. WOODWARD

> And then the letters from school would become letters from the probation department.

INNER LONDON PROBATION AND AFTER-CARE SERVICE

122-130 POWIS STREET, WOOLWICH, S.E.18
Telephone 01-855 5691/4

Mr. Mark Colella,
14 Homero Square,
Ferrier Estate,
Kidbrooke, SE3.

Your ref.:

Our ref.:
SRH/PM

8th May, 1984.

Dear Mr. Colella,

We have been asked to prepare a social enquiry report about you for the Croydon Crown Court in connection with your forthcoming appearance there, should you be pleading guilty and willing for a report to be made. The purpose of this report is so that the Judge will have some information about you which will help decide what sentence to impose and this would save both you and the Court time and inconvenience.

If, however, you are pleading Not Guilty or if you are pleading Guilty and do not want a report to be made, we naturally do not want to trouble you further. It would be helpful if you would let us know by 15th May. If we have not heard from you by then, we will not be contacting you again.

Many thanks,

Yours sincerely,

Mrs. S.H. Hills
Supervising Secretary.

Top: Some of my grades started off quite well in my new school, I enjoyed English and didn't mind Maths, but deteriorated very quickly, finally leading to being expelled from yet another school.

Bottom: The letters home with the words "I regret to inform you" were becoming more and more expected in our mailbox.

199

Top: And the school report begins to show where things began to get even worse, my attendance record was 20 days out of 114, my failure to comply to authority was getting worse.

Bottom: And yet another letter home to discuss Mark's future 'education'.

HURSTMERE SCHOOL,
Hurst Road,
SIDCUP, Kent.
DA15 9AW.

21st July 1981

Dear Mrs Cooper

...4... Year Form Movements.

We have recently reviewed the standard of work of your son ...Mark... of form ...4BS... and we are of the opinion that it would be advisable for him to move to a new form.

The change of form will take place on ...8th Sept. 81. and the new form will be ...4CU......

Yours sincerely,

Head of Year.

Headmaster.

Top: My Cheshire Cat Smile was getting me into more and more trouble, my attitude towards teachers and instructions lead to being put down a class.

Bottom: My attitude towards school and what I felt it 'wasn't' teaching me begins showing more and more in my school reports.

Top: My second home at the time, with more regular visits than I could count, Bexleyheath Magistrates Court, eventually to become the start of a 'Short, Sharp, Shock'.
Bottom: The Young Offenders Institute, a place where somebody decides through 'their own choices' which path they're going to take from that moment on.

At home on the Ferrier Estate, cooking was something that I learnt very early, and to this day I still love to cook.

Top: Me as a teenager, visiting Mum at a caravan park where she loved to holiday, my niece Lou Lou enjoying uncle Mark's attention.

Bottom: At home on the Ferrier Estate with my sisters first born Jamesy, the apple of my eye back then.

"Dress for success, and if you think you can't afford to, you can't afford not to."

Mark Anthony

Chapter 15

Not Everything Lost

Visits were scarce and brief. I cannot recall the frequency, as the time within those walls had a strange constancy: sometimes fast but somehow slow. While living in that moment it seemed very slow, terribly slow. But once it was night you could look back, see that nothing really was done and that, in fact, the time passed quickly.

I couldn't be bothered counting the days because I didn't really care. I wanted to be out, but my dreams had all vanished. Suddenly, I just had the same life waiting at the end of my sentence. That bloody judge, he was supposed to give me a weekend in detention, not three fucking months.

I was lying on my bed when one of the guards came to the cell and announced that I had a visitor. I calculated that two more weeks had passed since my mum and Leah came to see me. It felt longer than a week, and it would not be Saturday, so I worked out it was Sunday.

I followed the guard, walking with my body somehow crunched and hands in my pockets, wondering if Leah would be there today. I knew she wouldn't, but it was nice of her to visit me and write all those letters. I thought I might have her again, just for a while, and not only in my imagination.

I walked in the room where tables were now placed in a strategic arrangement to emulate privacy but guaranteeing none. We would sit down at one side of the table and wouldn't be allowed to move. Our loved ones would be on the other side.

I saw Mum smiling at me and waving enthusiastically. I was very glad to see her but I couldn't figure out her bright eyes and happy attitude as I walked towards her. It seemed to be out of place. It was like a rainbow in a grey room, and not in a good sense because it was far too colourful. It was more of a nuisance than a sign of hope.

I sat down and she started talking fast before I could say a thing.

"Mark, I called the company, that one you signed for before you were sentenced. They are going to wait for you!"

Who, how? Wait for me. For what? What was she talking about?

She kept on going, ever so excited, "Once you are out, you have the job and your passport is all ready, because you did that before, didn't you?"

I looked at her in disbelief. She erased the smile from her face. She looked worried now.

"But Mark, aren't you happy to hear the news? You'll be off to Pakistan very soon."

Her face changed again and her lips broadened beautifully. She almost couldn't fit the smile on her face. She looked so beautiful, and I must have been looking absolutely dumb. I had disposed of any speck of hope about going to Pakistan. I could never have guessed, not in my wildest dreams that a big company would bother to keep open a position for a ratbag like me. Especially with all those other posh and readily obedient candidates. I was in fucking jail, for goodness sake, and yet the opportunity was out there waiting for me.

I felt a smile drawing slowly and reluctantly in my mouth, because the muscles of my face were so untrained for a sincere smile from the heart. I jumped over the table and hugged my mother. I was going to Pakistan.

Chapter 16

Cleaning Products in the Middle East

My experience in France never killed my ambition to go overseas. In fact, it reinforced the feeling that I could manage anywhere anyhow. Once I recovered from the shock, it all became an adventure left behind. However, my bravery was touched in a wise way, since I started to consider safety as a relatively important trait in my travels. Although I still had a fairly reckless perception of security. A sense of security or a sense of moving in the right direction towards a better future was important. And the job waiting for me after my sentence in the YOI was all that: exciting destinations and honest money too.

As soon as I was released I met with the company agent that gave me the job to arrange my contract. I was sent to Pakistan straight away; my heart full of hope, ambition and, moreover, an immense sense of freedom.

I worked as a door-to-door salesman selling cleaning products. We would work with a partner and travel to different countries of the Middle East. Language was not the huge barrier I had expected it to be, as everything was about demonstrating the efficacy of our products. I would smile to the head of the household and pour some of the product on a surface in the house, mainly the kitchen, always the greasiest area of a bench or table. Then, I would do my magic and wipe the area clean.

It was almost like a performance, a magician's show. And I styled my most dramatic gestures doing the demonstration. The surprise on the faces of my audience made me expect applause on more than one occasion.

No one ever clapped my performance, but it was real fun. I was a very successful salesman. My Cheshire cat smile and manipulative skills were as much at work here as they were in the past – just channeled in a better direction. However, a criminal mind doesn't just stop working and cease to exist.

I don't know why I did it. It was stupid and I didn't need to. But still I did it. That week I was partnered with a huge American bloke, he used to wear a lot of gold jewellery and would leave it on the night table before going to sleep. All the sellers would share rooms whenever we travelled around. I was sharing a room with him as well as the working hours, and I grabbed one of his rings. I put it inside my sock and kept it behind the toilet cistern, hidden so no one could see it, and planning to recover it later.

As I said, I cannot even think why I would do that. It was pretty stupid. I was so resolved to be clear of my past and never commit a crime again, and yet I could not help it when the thought of having that ring took over my mind, in what seemed a harmless obsession. I was a magpie; I had always liked bright things and jewellery.

My work colleague reported his ring had been stolen, and both the manager and the leader of our group entered the rooms and searched thoroughly for it, with amazing expertise. They found the ring in the toilet cistern and accused me of the robbery. I denied it over and over. I did it, I was the thief but I defended my innocence, which was simply as silly an act as the robbery itself. The shock when they found the ring belonged to me. And, let's face it, there was no other possible option: I was guilty.

They dragged me to their office and forced me violently down onto a chair . We were in the United Arab Emirates. One was holding me down with his hand on my shoulder standing beside me. The one who spoke sat down in front of me.

"You have committed a robbery. Here, under the law of our land, the punishment is to chop off your hands."

Before hearing those words, I was confident I could use my gift of the gab to spare me any sort of punishment. However, as I heard those words, I gulped down all my arrogance and stayed silent.

"You have two options, you either quit the job and we send you immediately back to England, or we report you to the authorities and leave them to exert their punishment upon you."

I very much appreciated my hands. The word 'immediately' was more than accurate. In a few hours I was flying back from Dubai to London, and never thought about that company again.

Chapter 17

Canada

It would not be my first time abroad. The travel bug was a biting creature that would come with me everywhere, and bother my brain with constant dreams of going away. It wasn't an escape from an unpleasant reality or a trick of the mind to avoid the present, nor a defensive mechanism to soothe the emotions. It was just my nature, something within me.

My father was a trumpeter travelling around Europe with a circus. I felt very close to the gypsies, even deep in their poverty they could not stop their longing for travel. It was in their blood and somehow it was in mine. My first trip abroad was not a pleasant one though. I was just five and we went to visit my father in Italy. He would reject me as his son. I would feel lost in a world of words I could not understand and unwanted in the heart I yearned to have a place in.

Before the YOI, I had also been to Canada, visiting a friend I met in the cadets. His name was Billy. Billy was part of a group of cadets participating in a cultural exchange. His group ended up in London and we clicked as soon as we met. We became good friends and I dreaded his departure, but promised we would visit him.

A year later my mum was in a relationship with David, a nice man who treated us fairly. He was a welcome change from her previous partners and probably similar in traits to Stace the Ace, whom we still have feelings for. Mum and David were talking about a better life, somewhere else what about Canada? David would go there first and see how things worked and whether there was a good chance for all of us. I was still in contact with Billy by letter and both families thought it was a fantastic idea for me and David to travel together and stay at their home.

It was resolved; we would fly to Canada then. My mum bought new trainers for me. They were the first new shoes I had ever had, not from a charity store or inherited from a cousin or friend, but brand new shoes. I was thirteen and had never had brand new shoes. My toes were squashed and deformed, as if they belonged to an inept ballerina who never got her pointe right. It was the result of wearing shoes two sizes too small for my feet. I would buy them from other kids, and bear the pain of toenails digging in my skin or breaking far too close to their root as long as I could wear decent and beautiful shoes.

The trainers my mum gave me were awful, terribly ugly, with bright blue and yellow that would never have been considered a good combination or have any aesthetical harmony if it weren't because it was the eighties. And yet I could not help but love them. It was my first experience smelling new shoes and still today, whenever I buy a pair of trainers and open the box, my mind flies back to that day I left the UK for Canada with David. The scent of new leather mixed with rubber and the cardboard of the box, still brings that sense of gratefulness I felt for those awful, ugly shoes. I knew mum would have made a real effort to gather the money for them, and that meant a lot to me.

Billy's family was all heart. Rich in love but not much to offer in material things. They had virtually nothing. But despite their lack, their generosity was overwhelming.

They lived in a house so small that it didn't even allow for a toilet, which was a cubicle outside. I can only fathom that if hell had a smell, the scent of that toilet must have been as breathable as Beelzebub's sulphurous home. The stench was such that it would sneak into your pores and not just your respiratory system. David and me had to hold ourselves from spewing every time we were in there.

Yet, we could not complain, it would have been a terrible thing to do. Their hospitality was staggering and everything – except the toilet - however small, old, scarce or broken was so amazingly bestowed on us that we loved every minute with them.

The third day of our stay, we came back to their home after a stroll with Billy around town to find that his father had acquired a portable toilet for us so we did not have to use the outside sewer. I don't think I have to say more about their generosity and the sort of people they were. I loved that family, their unselfishness and kindness is an example of what money cannot buy.

We spent a few weeks with them and David and Billy's dad talked a lot about migration, work and whether there would be a chance for my family to come to Canada. Billy's dad offered to sponsor us, and then a handshake settled a new beginning for the two families.

We came back to London and started to get ready for the migration. Everything was very exciting at times, whilst other moments we were just living the life we always had with no expectations. I would talk to Billy or receive a letter, then we would move things on, and prepare for the travel, and David and Mum would be so excited. But then a few days would pass and everything reverted to the same East Londoner routine.

We went on like that for a few months, sorting things out slowly with sudden spurs of hope. Although we were putting all our hopes in the move, the efforts wouldn't always be consistent and sometimes everything seemed too disorganised.

Then, one day we received a phone call from Billy and the dream was over. His dad had had a heart attack and was not considered viable to help with our visas any more as he wasn't healthy enough to work and ensure the minimal support legally required to be an eligible sponsor.

I felt so badly for Billy. I remembered all the kindness that was poured over us. The dreadful toilet and its stench were just a mere anecdote that highlighted their generosity. I felt so much for his father but we all felt so bad for our shattered dream. It broke our hearts.

Maybe we all knew somehow. Maybe all the preparation in slow motion, the spurs of excitement fading after a couple of days, were in truth an effort to keep alive a dream that deep inside no one really thought would happen. Mum and David started to drift apart after the bad news and eventually split up. And in this "no man's land" appeared Dave who eventually came to settle in our home, as devastating as the plague.

I went back to Canada twice more later in life but I did not see Billy again. The idea of going overseas would always be present in my head, as a beautiful dream that always materialised and eventually had a good ending, although its beauty was never guaranteed. My travels weren't over after our return from Canada, some of then were painful and all of them experiences that strengthened my mind and soul. But there was one journey about which I can only say I'm just glad that I arrived home safe and sound.

Chapter 18

Left High and Dry

My father's sister and my mum were close friends. We would regard her as my aunty despite the paternity issue still being unresolved. She was married to an English man and stayed in the UK when my father went back to Italy with my older brother. Her first marriage was to a Sicilian man and they had a son my age.

It was the end of the academic year and holidays were around the corner. My aunty told Mum that my cousin had to fly to Sicily to visit his father during the next holidays, but we were fourteen back then and she didn't like the idea of him travelling on his own. So she offered to pay for my flight to Sicily to accompany him.

My mum thought it was a good idea and I thought it was a fantastic idea; a holiday with my cousin in Italy would be fun. My aunty said she only had enough money at that time to send us there, but that she would buy the return fare later. As she had to pay for both of us it was too much money to find at once, but she reassured us she would be in a position to buy the return tickets in a few days.

We didn't have any reason not to trust her. We were close family and had a very good relationship. So arrangements were made and I travelled with my cousin to Sicily to enjoy the Italian sun.

The holidays lived up to my expectations. Summer in London is not a real summer once you have been introduced to the Mediterranean sun. I had a great time and enjoyed being with my cousin and his family until the time of our departure to the UK arrived.

I was preparing my suitcase when one of my cousin's Italian aunties came into the room and told me there was a problem. My cousin's father summoned us to explain that we had no tickets to travel back to London. We were both shocked, but innocently expected the adults to solve the problem easily as neither of us belonged in that place. We were minors and had to get back to our homes somehow.

However, the problem went far beyond what we assumed the adults could resolve and was in fact related to a matter of revenge. My cousin was the negotiable part of a nasty interchange and bribery between his father and my aunty. And I turned out to be at the centre of the revenge, the object and subject of it.

My aunty had prepared the situation in a premeditated plan to force her ex-husband to spend extra amounts of money by sending me with her son, in the belief that he would never lead two minors under his responsibility astray. The problem was that my Sicilian uncle was not the sort that would allow such blackmail. And I learned soon enough that they couldn't care less about me.

I was shaking; I didn't know what to do. I was sure my mother wouldn't have the money to pay for a flight for me, and the anxiety pressed my chest in as I wondered what was going to happen to me.

Then we were summoned once more, this time to the family dining room. I was used to street criminals, but they sat me down with my cousin in a real mafia meeting. I am not exaggerating or attempting to be romantic with this description, nor embellishing the truth. Around fifteen men were seated at the table. My cousin and I were told to stand at one end. The men of the family started to discuss our fate as if we weren't there. Sometimes one would speak in a voice loud and clear, and the assertion would be followed by a muttering of deep male voices and heads nodding till someone would call to order hitting the table. We would just stand there and wonder whether we would be sentenced to anything worse than wandering like strays around the island with no one to feed us or give us shelter.

They deliberated for some time. Maybe it was only a matter minutes, but in my head hours passed before the verdict sank deep in my stomach. They would pay for my cousin's flight back to London, as he was part of the family, but they would not pay mine, neither would they maintain me any more as the holidays were over. So I would have to find my own way from their house and back to England myself.

There are different types of fear, although they might feel the same in the body. There is the fear that follows a bad decision: it comes right at the moment when you realise that you fucked up and suddenly want to stop it. It was the fear I felt when I rushed down the hill to stop the cement roller from smashing cars and injuring people. A fear full of adrenaline that doesn't actually let you feel it till it is over and it slides off your body, making you conscious of its nature but already giving you the relief that it is over.

I knew another fear: every time my mother was away and Tommy would come in banging the door, every time I was unprotected as a child. But because I was in my own home somehow that sense of property and shelter would comfort a part of me enough to survive it.

But the fear I was experiencing there in Sicily was different. There was no adrenaline rushing to my head giving me a possible solution, there was nothing like home to pull close around me and there was no one that could possibly give me a sense of belonging or support. I was standing alone, in a different country, with nowhere to go, thousands of miles away from my mum, without a penny and absolutely clueless about what I could do to solve and save the situation.

I called Mum. I could hear her sobs from the other side of the line. She had no money to pay for my trip back to England. I looked around searching for something to grab, an object, an idea, a something that could assist me with a problem I could not possibly solve by myself. I was helpless. I could not imagine how things could get worse. I didn't need to imagine, the situation revealed itself in the most difficult and frightening manner.

I am not sure how many days had passed since my cousin departed and I was left alone in the hostile territory of men that despised my presence. I was no more than a burden, the intention of a woman to bribe and jeopardise their family. I was the personification of their hatred. Finally my mum called me saying that my aunty did not have the money to pay for my ticket back but she had forced her to pay at least part of it.

My aunt agreed to pay for my trip as far as Paris and I would travel there by train after taking the ferry from Sicily to the mainland first. From Paris, my mum had paid for the train ticket that would take me to London. The instructions were to get to Paris train station and ask at the counter for a ticket to London that would be in an envelope under my name. I sighed in relief but was still scared by the uncertainty of my travels.

The women in my cousin's Italian family were a bit more concerned about my safety and wellbeing than the men who had just deliberated my fate and then ignored my presence after my cousin had left. The Italian aunties packed some food for me for the trip and I was dropped off at the station with no ceremonial farewell.

A ferry took me to the mainland, where I caught a train to Paris. Endless hours passed by before I got to Paris Central Station. I had been travelling almost a full day and my stomach was so empty that it rumbled painfully.

I was exhausted. I walked to the main counter and asked the lady behind it for my train ticket to London. I explained the best I could with not a word of French in my vocabulary about an envelope with my name on it. It had to be there, Mark Anthony Colella. Sure, she must have it somewhere, in a drawer or on a desk behind her. Yes, sure, Mark Anthony Colella! I wrote my name on a piece of paper and pointed at it with my finger insistently.

There was no envelope for me to pick up. I was shocked. With a stuttering voice I repeated once more, "Mark Anthony Colella", ever so slowly, pronouncing every syllable with a wide-open mouth. It had to be there; they must have something with my name on it. There was a ticket for me to London there, behind the counter, they were wrong! There was a ticket to London for me and it was there!

I started to raise my voice nervously, every time speaking louder and faster. My lips trembling uncontrollably as my heart accelerated to a heavy beat that felt like a punch in the ribs but from the inside. The officer at the other side of the counter kept talking in French and shaking his head: "No ticket". The lady was getting impatient and angry, gesticulating a cross with her arms and nodding firmly: "No ticket".

There was no ticket to London. I walked back defeated with watery eyes and shaky hands. I was a stray in a foreign country. A place I had never been before, with a language I had never been exposed to. Suddenly I wished I were in Sicily, rather than in that cold station with an obscure air. The music of voices walking around me was strange, guttural and deep; I couldn't grasp any meaning.

It was getting dark. I was hungry and cold. Not daring to move from the station, I sat down on a bench staring at the void in front of me. I cried. I sobbed till my chest hurt. The noise of the surroundings entered my head as if I were deep underwater, distorted and far away. I was paralysed and my senses were numb. Then, the little sense of awareness that was left after the shock, warned me about two men blatantly watching me from one of the big columns holding up the station's dome. I feared the worst; I had nowhere to run.

I decided to make a move when my bladder reminded me I hadn't emptied it in over ten hours, and very unwisely entered the public toilets. Both men watched me closely and followed behind me. As I was urinating they positioned themselves one on each side of me. The panic command of my body cancelled out any other physiological need. With a sudden move I grabbed my travel bag and ran to the door, slammed it open and ran as fast as I could outside the station.

I don't know whether they followed me, got tired of chasing me, or just thought I wasn't worth the effort. But I escaped from whatever it was they wanted from me, which based on my extensive experience with abuse of all kinds and my street smarts, I knew it wasn't anything good.

I don't have a memory of my first time in Paris, the city of lovers. I have no memories of what happened during my time there. I can just remember myself wandering an unknown city, surrounded by voices I could not understand, shivering at night and walking restlessly with no destination. I don't even remember thinking at all. Everything was blank.

Of all things, this was probably the scariest situation I had lived in, because I couldn't even hold on to the familiarity of the territory. There was absolutely nothing I could grab to make me feel a bit safer. I was desolate.

I would walk up and down like a ghost, maybe hoping that someone would find me. Then one day my feet took me back to the station. It wasn't a voluntary action, I just happened to end up there. As I looked at the clock and recognised it, I remembered the two men cornering me in the toilet and I feared entering that space.

I noticed I was crying; maybe I had been crying all that time, however long my stay in Paris had been up until that moment. I came back to my senses and realised that if there was any way I was going to find my way home it would be from that place I was so reluctant to enter.

I dragged my feet to the information counter and again asked for an envelope with my name. This time it was there, waiting for me! A feeling of warmth and hope filled my body and I managed to smile broadly. As I held my ticket to London I became completely alert, studying everything around me, it wasn't about protecting myself but about protecting the train ticket. It was my pass to safety.

A few hours later I was on my way home, sitting in a tourist carriage, dirty and exhausted, with an empty stomach from several days of starvation. But I was on my way home. I fell asleep.

No one was waiting for me at the station. No one knew where I was and they weren't expecting me to arrive on that train. I made my way home from there, and as I crossed the door my mum threw herself into my arms crying desperately. I had been missing four days and Interpol was looking for me.

Chapter 19

Back to Canada

Back in London I made a commitment to myself to guard my integrity and honesty, but it didn't work that well. Not all the time. Somehow, I would become mixed up with people who didn't align with my new commitment. For instance, when I got a job in a real estate agency, a perfectly honest activity in which I had no need to deceive anyone. There I could use my manipulation skills in a positive way.

I very soon become the best salesman in the office. I was good at making friends in and outside the office, so I got people to like me easily and this translated into more sales. Yet I would sell houses to clients whose honesty was not their best trait, if they possessed that trait at all.

It seemed like all my attempts at integrity and a new life were being sabotaged somehow as I kept attracting criminals and deceivers. However, from my perspective I was completely clean, as I wasn't the perpetrator, I simply happened to be in the space they occupied. They were contributing to my fortune and financial success- even though not a very high success – and I was glad the money I was putting in my pockets was clean. It might not have been completely unblemished as it went through my hands to the vendor of the property, but my commission was the fruit of an honest and perfectly legal activity.

On one occasion I made a great sale. It was a big mansion in the south of London. The gentleman buying the property was about to give me the initial payment in order to hold it for subsequent purchase. He drove me around several strange places, stopped in all of them for a few minutes and then presented me with a bunch of money in a plastic bag. At one of the stops, one of his companions pulled the car into an abandoned industrial area, in the middle of nowhere, by the wall of a ruined building. Then he jumped out of the car and started to touch the wall in a specific area, as if he were selecting a brick. When he found the right one he pulled it out, then a couple of bricks more. From behind them, he produced a black garbage bag packed with several thick wads of cash.

I revelled in the fact that by the time the money got into my bank account it was clean, and thus I was absolved of any dishonest activity.

But before I became a real estate agent back in London, I still had to make another incursion to a foreign country. After the good experiences I had during my Middle East adventures – with the exception of the threat to chop off my hands – and with such great memories of my previous trip there, I decided I had to go back to Canada and start over.

I started a small business from home selling licensed marketing products. It didn't last long but it helped me save enough money to go overseas and I was proud to save one hundred percent honest money, for once.

I talked my cousin into travelling with me, and two of our

female friends applauded the plan and joined us. Soon enough we had all gathered enough money to pay for the tickets and buy a van to travel around Canada.

We would travel around the country doing seasonal work and eventually choose a place to settle and find a more permanent job. At least that was our plan. It is a fact of life for successful people that hardly anything ever goes as planned. But, even though in the moment everything unexpected is a nuisance and far too often has a painful resolution, in the end, and with hindsight, we see that our plan wasn't that good and things pan out for the greatest good regardless of our initial expectations.

I knew one day I would live overseas, and this was my third opportunity, so I was very enthusiastic about the trip. We landed in Halifax. Our van arrived two weeks later, and as soon as we got it, we took off to explore the country.

My cousin, the two girls and I agreed to find a good spot and make it our base to start the search for work. We had enough money to travel and buy the van, but we could only afford to eat white bread and some undressed pasta. A caravan park became our base camp. We were enjoying our time of freedom so much, even if it was scarce of proper food. We were young, very optimistic about the future and having a great time.

But soon enough, things turned around the other way for me for a while. Suddenly, I was alone again in a foreign country with no money. My ability to make friends contributed to both my bad and good fortune.

It wasn't long before I had made some Canadian friends, including a gorgeous girl who was the daughter of the caravan park owners and happened to be as fond of me as I was of her. We started dating. I was falling in love with her.

Unfortunately so was my cousin, who didn't like it in the least that we were enjoying each other's company. Next thing I knew, we were yelling at each other, I could shout louder than him, sure I could, but the harm was already done and he had won. His jealousy led him to tell all the bad stories about my past to my girlfriend's parents and she was kept from me as if I were a disease, banned from even talking to me. In addition and to ensure my now ex-girlfriend's safety, I was kicked out of the caravan park. And when I turned around to search for my travelling party, there was no one to be found. Without me knowing, my cousin and our two friends had packed the van and left, leaving me behind.

This time I was more resourceful than when I was abandoned in Paris, but no one could take away from my chest the fury I was feeling. Loyalty is so important. Loyalty has a great value for me. Funnily enough, that value so important for good relationships and success in life, a great value for all people of good, was strongly developed because of my criminal mind.

It would have another name. It would be born out of the shame that being a dobber would bring me; it would come out of the pride of not being considered as weak or a prick. Even when the ends were not so much born of integrity, the means were part of this value. Part of it came from my sense of responsibility towards my family: never to let your loved ones down. Ever. I would never talk to my cousin again.

My interpersonal skills would get me out of the dire straits. As I started to look for a job in order to survive in Canada, one of the friends I had made during my short stay there asked me to go with him back to Montreal, where he lived. His parents had a restaurant and they had asked him to go back to his home city as they were planning a holiday to Greece and needed him to take charge of the business in the meantime.

My friend offered me work and shelter in his house. We drove his car from Halifax to French Canada. By the time we arrived in Montreal his parents were already in Greece. I started working immediately in the kitchen.

The arrangement went well for a few months. I helped him as much as needed for some cash and a bed, and we had fun together. I met a lot of people in Montreal and soon I started dating a girl. I was pleased with the situation and enjoying myself very much. Until my friend's parents came back from Greece.

My friend's parents didn't like me in the least. To be fair, it was dislike at first sight for both them and me. His father wouldn't stop nagging me during work hours and following me everywhere in the restaurant, and I couldn't bear his presence. He would be behind my shoulder all day, checking every one of my movements and his eyes would never leave me whenever I was handling money. He was obnoxious and more often than not, very rude.

Even back then, I was a calm person with composure; it was part of my nature and very useful if I wanted to manipulate people. But my patience was quite limited if someone were trying to overpower me or exert any sort of authority over me, especially if the reasons were unjustified. I was doing a good job. I had done a good job in their absence and never caused any trouble. However, I was being treated as a criminal with every step I took, I couldn't even work properly with that man literally over me most of the time.

One day I lost it. I was tidying some plates while he stuck to my back, obnoxiously looking over my shoulder at what I was doing. I turned around and snapped at him, "Would you fuck off? That's enough!" then I walked away.

I lost my job, my shelter and my friend in a few seconds.

Chapter 20

Loyalty

Fortunately, another friend I made in Montreal told me of a pizza restaurant on the other side of town where he could get me a job. By then my visa had expired and I was staying in Canada illegally, but I did not want to leave, so I quickly accepted.

There is a law that says that we attract what we are. I do not believe that rule to be completely accurate, but it is certain that I kept attracting what I was and what I was trying to stop being – a criminal. It might have been my attitude, the way I moved among criminal minds. Still today I can recognise them easily and even though I reject firmly that company, I don't feel uncomfortable and cannot avoid certain familiarity. I know how to deal with people who are immersed in a delinquent world. Thus, it was fairly easy for me to deal with my boss, who far from being a regular restaurant owner turned out, allegedly, to be an underworld figure dealing in drugs.

Anyone could see that the restaurant where I was working was not a regular hospitality business. People moved through tables in a weird manner, food was not important. Whispers, concealing hands dragging small parcels on the table, suspicious eyes and a woman under the tablecloth enlivening a guest's dinner, were the dining landscape.

Overall, I was pretending to serve people who were pretending they were being served. At some tables the tension was so thick it could be cut with a knife; in others serious matters were being dealt with in a low tone and volume. Prostitutes demonstrating their skills in the open or squatting under a table were a regular sight.

Among those characters and in that environment, the skills that made me valuable weren't my hospitality skills, but my discretion. Also, my boss seemed to be fond of me and trust me. I liked the job, I felt relatively comfortable among those people. My boss appreciated me, my boss's hard-nosed wife loved me like a son, my manager was a lovely woman who cared for me, I moved to a more serious relationship with the girl I was dating and I was making more friends. I was having a good time working there.

Unfortunately, the same jealousy that had left me alone and without travel pals or money a few months prior hit me again. One of the pizza delivery guys was very keen on making my girlfriend his partner. However, his feelings for her were not reciprocated. He made me responsible for his failure in the realm of love and romanticism. He discovered I was an illegal immigrant and dobbed me in to the Department of Immigration.

I was serving tables. One of two men sitting at a table signalled me with his hand to come over. I came to their table and he asked me whether I could change the TV channel.

I nodded, "Of course, sir. Which channel would you like to watch?"

Then they both stood up and the other man said, "Mr. Colella, you have to come with us."

I was puzzled. They identified themselves as immigration officers and said that they just had to make sure it was me who they were after by listening to my British accent. I left the restaurant with them and in no time I was back in a cell again.

The hearing in front of the magistrate happened almost immediately. But it turned out that the hearing was not about me at all. I was an illegal immigrant and there was not much to deal with in the courtroom. They would deport me, period. However the magistrate was very inquisitive about my work arrangements and the restaurant I was illegally employed in, and overall, the person who was my employer.

The moment I realised the main cause of my presence in the courtroom wasn't my guilt, the tension I had accumulated during my wait in the cell escaped in a silent sigh. I was in trouble again, and I wouldn't get away with it, but it made a difference in me knowing that all the court theatrics weren't about to drive me back to a London jail. I was trying my best to keep my records clean and my person as far away from prison as possible. I had had my dose already.

I was aware of who my boss was and I was not surprised by the reasons for that hearing. The nature of the hearing uncovered itself quickly. I was unimportant to them, however my presence and my illegal situation gave them a rare opportunity to get hold of my boss.

The magistrate named him and enquired, "Is this the man who contracted you?"

I replied, "That is his name, yes."

The magistrate affirmed with a resolute tone, "Therefore, he knew you didn't have your documents in order and could not work in Canada. But regardless of this knowledge and against the law he employed you."

I replied firmly, "No, he did not know any of that. I never told him."

I was lying, he did know.

The magistrate asked me the same question a few more times, pressuring me to give him the answer he was expecting and needing, every time his voice more inquisitive and threatening. I didn't budge. It wasn't really that I was aware of the magnitude of the impact my words could have. It was a matter of loyalty and pride as a result of my past. I wasn't a grass or a dobber.

I learned later on, they were after a legal breach in order to get to my boss by any possible means. Unexpectedly, my fortuitous position as his illegal employee, was offering them the chance to imprison one of the biggest drug dealers in the area.

I stood firm before the magistrate, holding onto that criminal pact I was used to, which I still maintain now in my years of honesty and integrity. It resembles loyalty and to me it is loyalty. I knew my boss had done the wrong thing employing me and he did know I was an illegal, but he was helping me and as I said, I am not a grass or a dobber. I was the one committing an illegal act and I would carry the consequences on my own without involving anyone else. That was a gang pact.

It doesn't really matter where that loyal value came from. It was built with strong foundations and it developed into a part of my personality today. Whilst the reasons might not have been very noble, it is a good value that I still promote.

When you move in an environment of legality and honesty, maybe a bit of dobbing might seem like the right thing to do to avoid greater damage or to teach a lesson. I don't agree so much with that. Teaching lessons and lecturing are not a good way to move in a world of crime, neither is advisable. Also, the lesson would backfire and would be taught to you for being a dobber, maybe costing you your life.

It is not the fear that makes you keep that pseudo-loyalty, it is the responsibility you have for yourself and your own actions. In the gang, there was a tacit agreement when a crime was perpetrated, if someone was caught, they would pay for their own consequences. There was no sharing of consequences even if a crime wasn't committed to its completion by a single person or without accomplices. The moment you were caught it became your problem.

When I decided to write a book, I envisioned a motivational book to show people that it can be done. Wherever you came from: it can be done. I decided to be open. Sugarcoating any part of my life was not an option. I help people on a daily basis with weight loss and quitting smoking. I can do that because I have gone through it myself and I can relate to them. I was overweight when I was released from the YOI and a smoker since I was five. I also help people with anxiety and depression, and of course I am very familiar with those too.

But all those handicaps, that basically most of the western population suffer, are measured by their symptoms and their impact on our health. Therefore they are mostly perceived as something we suffer passively, regardless of how the problem was created. Thinking about my book and as a hypnotherapist, I concluded that being overweight, struggling with addictions, anxieties and depression are a result of other causes we carry within our subconscious.

These are not usually revealed, however, and can vary from one individual to the next. The reality is that we approach them publicly only as a burden that we suffer, and we tell the story of how we overcame it with positive thinking, effort, endurance and intention. All of these are good values that anyone can appreciate at first sight. But I wondered if that might give the impression that people who overcome those types of problems had those qualities to begin with: a balanced person with a calm past, or a past only marked by an overweight-bullying problem, for instance.

It clicked in my mind that many people that have lived or are living in a social strata most average citizens would not like to step in, would not feel represented by that idea. How trivial does the problem of being overweight feel to a woman who is suffering domestic violence? How can being overweight even be a worry when your next decision could kill you or your children?

I thought of a father who had lost everything, his family, wife, children, job, money and status to an addiction, and wanders lost and virtually homeless. Is smoking his main problem? What about a hopeless twenty-year-old that every adult around has given up on and predicted would become a criminal?

These people would not care about weight loss or stopping smoking, they wouldn't even consider trying to solve their anxieties, as their worries are far beyond the spectrum of health or beauty. Their needs are survival skills, and everything else seems like a whimsical wish only for people who have no serious problems.

Allow me to downplay weight loss and an addiction to tobacco for a second. Years back, if someone had told me their weight was jeopardising their lives, while I was starving with my sisters at home and suffering the burns of a scabies treatment, it would have seemed a relatively minor complaint. More so as I felt the cannon of a gun on my sinus and a knife slowly digging into my throat.

Even when I was in the worst of situations, I did know deep inside I could get out. But the time to tell others they also can get out came when I was completely out and on my path towards my higher goals.

I write this book to reach those who don't believe in themselves and are living extreme hardship, in consistent physical danger or who think they are driven irremediably to a life of crime. In order to do so, I have to convey who I was, without guilt and just from a neutral observer's point of view because it is in the past, because I have compassion enough to understand I could not do better back then, and because without this compassion – which is different to being self-indulgent – I wouldn't be here.

I felt it was time to share my perspective on these points, when we talk about loyalty. Loyalty is only a value when it is used to its full and honourable weight, not to hurt other people. It is not an apology. No matter who you are, or were, as long as you have the will to change into a better you, it is possible – regardless of the time it takes. It is also important not to get stuck in previous wrongdoings and to feel guilty and indulge in self-pity, using them as an excuse to stay where you are and avoid the work necessary to make a better life.

It was Miranda, my wife, who brought the argument over the value of loyalty to my attention. I was telling her a story about how, when I was sixteen, I stole a car from two brothers in South London who were infamous for their vile crimes.

She said, "Well, that is not showing much loyalty, is it? You risked your friend's life and never put yourself out there accepting your responsibility."

That is technically right: there was our loyalty agreement. It was my friend who broke it, but my action – or inaction – was less than honorable, and I put his life at risk.

We had both stolen a car. It belonged to two of the most infamous villains in South London before we made it ours. We took it to my friend's garage, painted it, and changed the entire exterior until it was unrecognisable. However, we did not touch the interior.

We drove it for a few months until we got tired of it, and then we exchanged it for another one with a guy who collected cars. It was a Jaguar and it flew. No police car could match us, they just couldn't catch us. We forgot about the villain's car and enjoyed our new old Jaguar. It might have lost some of its exterior sex appeal, but had an amazing engine that sounded like glory and made us fly through London streets.

One day someone banged on our home front door violently. Two big thugs forced the door open before anyone could answer. They scared my mum to death yelling and demanding where I was. Even before my mum could give them an answer, one of the thugs stomped up the stairs and got into my room.

He grabbed me by the neck and started shouting in my face, "Fucking cunt! It's you who stole our car!"

"Get fucked!" I said. "It wasn't me!"

The thug kept yelling and spat on me, "We've got your fucking friend in our boot. You are fucking going to give me a thousand pounds now, or he'll be dead before tomorrow!"

I got rid of his grip and told him to fuck off. He wasn't my friend and I had no idea what he was talking about, I told him. They left the house.

Miranda was shocked, because I did nothing about it. I did not say I was responsible for stealing the car; I did not try to save my friend's life in any manner. That couldn't be me, the man she loved. But things don't work like that. I obviously did not have one thousand pounds and my friend's parents were rich, so I wasn't that worried about his life.

But the main point was the loyalty. In a world of good values learnt with integrity and where other people shared them in the same measure, loyalty to my friend and telling the truth might have solved the problem. But then we would have to assume that a South London villian would share those values, which is most unlikely and quite naive.

However, the point was that my friend had dobbed on me. The brothers had recognised the car in the street, as we did not change the interior, and then enquired to its current owner, who obviously told them about my friend. He was pretty easy to locate being the son of a London multimillionaire. It wasn't that easy to find me, to do so, my friend had to tell them who I was and where I lived. He broke the loyalty code, a criminal code, but it was there. He also put my whole family in danger, to gain nothing. I can acknowledge now that he was scared to death, but that wasn't relevant back then.

Does that make me a bad person? Well, the point of this book is to show you that I wasn't that great either. In fact, I was a fucking shitbag . But I am no more, and I have been helping people for many years now. I do good to many, making them laugh and helping them to heal and move forward.

Back in the courtrooms in Montreal, the judge kept insisting my boss was aware of my illegal situation in the country and therefore had committed a crime. I kept insisting that was not the truth, standing firm with my first answer, which I repeated over and over.

Eventually they let me go, holding my passport and telling me to get ready as in three days I would be leaving the country and going back to England.

I went back to the restaurant, as I was dragged from there and I felt I had to at least offer an explanation. When I arrived my boss was seated at a table with two of his men. They were waiting for me.

"So the judge asked you several times whether I knew you were illegal," he said.

"Yes he did," I replied.

"And you said every time I didn't."

I nodded.

"Good, son, very good. You didn't grass. You didn't tell them anything." He was nodding slowly and I felt his satisfaction and pride.

After a short silence he spoke again, "I have talked to my wife. She might be able to help and you may be able to stay in

Canada."

His wife was the madam of the most visited brothel in the city, and in the short time between the court hearing ending and me getting back to the restaurant, they had thought to sponsor me as a waiter in the brothel so I could get a visa extension.

I was very grateful. Unfortunately, the next day I got notice that she wasn't allowed to sponsor me as I had already been charged, and the proceedings for my deportation had already started and nothing could be done about that. Then my boss called me and asked me if I would drive a truck down to the border of Canada and the US for him. It was an easy job and he would pay me well, so I accepted.

As I was entering the kitchen to get ready for my shift – as if life was still continuing there – I wasn't really caring about the deportation but thinking about the job driving the truck when the manager grabbed me by the arm, took me to the rear door and outside in the back alley.

"Please, Mark, do not take that job. Do not drive that truck. It's going to be packed with drugs, please do not do it!"

The truck I was meant to drive had been packed with cocaine hidden in the tyres. I must admit that it didn't impress me much and my decision wasn't the result of a sudden excess of honesty, I had simply decided that after the YOI I wouldn't be involved in illegal actions, at least as much as I could avoid it.

With that in mind, I went back into the restaurant and told my boss I had changed my mind. He just nodded and said, "It's ok kid ", and we said farewell in a friendly manner that very moment.

Two days later I was back in London. But there was another trip to Canada in the near future.

Chapter 21

Across the Sea

I was back in London and working in a real estate agency when I met Ciara. There was another real estate office in front of mine, and I had noticed an interesting young woman working there. I used some of my lunch breaks to cross the road and talk to her. She was petite and very nice, I fancied her quite a lot. The day I asked her out, I had already spent several weeks pondering whether to ask her out for a drink to get to know her better. I felt confident enough she would like my company, but when I offered her dinner one evening she told me she wasn't very interested.

Instead of accepting my invite, she proposed something else. There was this other girl, her workmate, whom I had paid little attention to but would like to go out with me for sure. I found it a strange proposal at first and then I thought why not? After all, I had made up my mind to go out that evening and I had no reason to think she wouldn't be good company.

That was how I met my first wife. She was fun and smart and I had to admit I was quite physically attracted to her too. That date was just the first of many. We moved in together soon after and married. It was the beginning of a long relationship, great adventures and two beautiful children.

Those first ten years with Ciara were full of excitement, and not always welcome adventures, I must say. Slowly and by chance, I entered the world of electronics and computing. It was a discreet and unexpected enterprise, which developed into a profitable business. But it also saw the dark side of finances.

Although we were settled in London and working hard to build a strong and secure home, I never discarded my idea to move overseas. It had been present since I was a kid and during all that hectic time my sights were still aimed somewhere beyond the borders of my London life and across the seas. An unfortunate financial fail persuaded Ciara to join me in my big dream and the desire of a new life away from England. It felt so strongly within me, and now my wife was supporting it. I couldn't ignore it anymore.

We talked about Canada as twice I had left a part of my heart behind when I departed that beautiful country. My memories were vivid, and the good moments and the faces of people I had encountered there began to pop up in my head in a utopian dream. We became very enthusiastic about migrating there and visualised a magnificent life among the Canadian wilderness and its cosmopolitan cities. The difficulties I had gone through there bore no weight whatsoever in my remembrance of the country and my good Canadian experiences also outweighed the stresses. I loved it and no complication had ever been great enough to overshadow all the good moments.

We travelled to Canada to explore the territory and check what would be available for us in the new country. It was a delightful trip, and it gave me new memories made in better circumstances.

We arrived in Nova Scotia as I did years before. Our first son was still a baby and I booked a nice, comfortable and spacious room in a hotel in Halifax Harbour. As I entered the room I couldn't help laughing at the memory of the seedy hotel in Montreal where I had to spend a couple of nights after getting kicked out of my first job there, and consequently losing my safe accommodation.

Back then, I had little money to afford any luxury and I found a hotel at a reasonable price. It was run by a big woman with lascivious manners. Her exuberant breasts were almost exposed and her eyes brightened up when she saw me coming in the narrow hall that was the reception. She would lean on the counter making her breasts even more obvious and her voice was extremely sweet. Her attitude made me lean back and widen the personal space. She gave me a key and waved me goodbye with a greasy hand of bright red nail polish.

The room was small, dark and smelly, but the worst part was finding bugs and semen stains covering the sheets. I called the lady to the room only to be sexually harassed instead of receiving new clean sheets. Back then it felt horrible. It wasn't easy to intimidate me, but the feeling of being fresh meat for that huge breasted lady made me prefer the cold of the streets. Now, in a new light, I told Ciara the anecdote and we both laughed.

We had a very good time in Halifax. I explored job opportunities by walking the streets, asking people, searching in newspapers. We also started looking at different places to settle. It seemed the chance was there for us. But in the end, everything came down to a very unpleasant reality. The Canadian immigration department is not a body of forgiveness and permissive attitudes, and my previous illegal stay in the country and subsequent deportation banned me from applying to stay any longer than my holiday visa allowed, let alone settle in Canadian territory. I was simply unwelcome.

We came back to England. My hopes sinking deep from my heart down to my toes and a profound feeling of failure dwelling deep inside. I wanted a better life for my wife and my son, and I had failed at it.

Chapter 22

Down Under

When I first held my son in my arms I cried like a child. It was, without comparison to anything else, the best thing I had ever experienced. My first son. It wasn't only the profound love that flowed between us at first sight, nor the big sense of responsibility and duty that made me stand up straighter, ready to protect him, tall and strong, before any danger that might threaten him. It was also the realisation of one of my biggest dreams, a life accomplishment. I always wanted to be a father. I had been practicing with my nephews for years, and now I was given the role, the real one, for the first time. I was confident I could do it, and I could do it right.

My sister Rose gave me a beautiful present when I was fifteen. It is the romantic version of this story that I remember, and I do so because it is so full of love and it marked me so deeply that any difficulty or raw reality that might taint it with the ordinary colour of daily life, sounds like an unfair representation of it.

She got pregnant very young and no one took responsibility for the paternity of the child. When the baby was born, they both stayed at home with us. I loved my nephew to death. I loved to nurse him and play with him. I was only fifteen, but I already knew that being a father would be my ambition in life, and having the opportunity to take care of my nephew was a gift. Regardless of whatever else was going on in my life at that moment, or how I would behave and my questionable actions outside my home, I always had a pounding sense of protection towards my family. Rose's son was all I needed to grow the love within the walls of a broken home, which was still holding itself together with the strength and bits of care we granted each other.

My nephew is now a grown man and has his own family. We still have a very close and special relationship. I thank my sister for that.

My baby's birth was not only a soul-lifting event, his presence in our lives gave me more strength to follow my dreams. I had already been reading about hypnosis and my interest kept growing, but I really didn't know what to do with it. In the meanwhile, I had to declare a business bankrupt, I had failed to move my family to Canada and I had gone back to being an employee and had to limit my enterprises to small activities. But I knew things would change somehow and at some point soon, the big move was close and then everything would fall into place.

The impossibility of starting over in Canada was a great disappointment. Although I was still looking to a future lived overseas, the experience had drained me enough that I needed a rest from further imagining about some place beyond. Then an opportunity arose for us unexpectedly.

One of my cousins had migrated to Australia and prospered in his life out there. He suggested we should do the same as there were more opportunities and he would be there to help us with our new beginning. I didn't think twice about it. It felt absolutely right in my heart that Australia was the place. It immediately sunk in my core as an ancient knowledge that had always been there. With no shadow of doubt or hesitation, I knew the continent was our new home.

I applied for a visa for my family and we started preparing for the big move to come. I worked very hard to gather enough money for a new start in a new land. Sometimes I would get discouraged as we hardly heard any news about the visa process from the Australian embassy, but then I would remember how my dreams about Pakistan had died the moment I heard the judge's gavel hitting the wooden block, and how the opportunity was still there in a completely unexpected way. I would talk to my wife about our new life. We would both fantasise about a house, nice weather and a great environment for our son. We would sit on the couch with our little boy and tell him fascinating stories about Australia. In my mind it was already happening.

A year passed by and my hopes were fading. I feared we would miss the train to far away land again. Then a letter with an official stamp arrived. It was from the Australian embassy. My family had been granted a visa that allowed us to live and work in Australia indefinitely. The dust settled and I saw a bright future in front of us.

Chapter 23

Cigarettes and Mop Sticks

Two guards took four of us to the officer's canteen. We had to clean the room and were given some rags, buckets and mops. I didn't know the others very well, but it didn't matter at all. You don't get to make friends inside the institution, you just learn to behave in a way that keeps you away from trouble and minimises the abuse.

Barry was sort of my friend during the time we were sharing the cell. It wasn't a lasting friendship; we both knew we wouldn't see each other once we were back on the street. Maybe, if we had ever come across each other in the street in London, we would have just passed by without exchanging a word. Friendship was a valuable thing and quite enjoyable while behind bars, yet it was an asset with an expiry date, and that didn't bother anyone.

On the other hand, it was comforting to know that you could talk to someone about whatever you felt like without fearing any vulnerability later on. It was a matter of fact that once on the outside, we would ignore each other or simply forget about the YOI and anything that happened there for good.

We were mopping the floor at an extremely slow pace. The reason it took so much effort to clean the tiles was a combination of malnutrition, apathy, tiredness and hatred. Under those circumstances it was difficult to produce much energy. The guards knew it, but rather than showing any understanding, it gave them another excuse to verbally abuse us while we attempted to finish the job.

Strangely enough we were very quiet. There was no energy that day to snap back at the guard. Maybe, it was because we didn't know each other well enough to be confident we would be supported or if it would make us vulnerable to retaliation back in the prisoner's wing. This kept us quiet and just mumbling to ourselves with clenched teeth holding our anger.

One of the guards was getting impatient. He was yelling at us incongruously, maybe fed up of our slow pace and narrow achievement in such an easy task. Maybe it was because our silence and resignation didn't allow him an excuse to belt us.

I looked at him and saw the vein in his neck pulsating under the skin, gradually becoming redder. He was ready to vent his frustration at one of us, without any excuse. In fact, he didn't need it because he had immunity.

 The other guard was observing him snapping at us and raising his voice, becoming belligerent and threatening. Sometimes you thought that one guard might stop another in a moment of unreasonable violence because it seemed, by the way they looked at them, that on occasions they recognised someone crossing the line. Sometimes you thought they could see that but only in the other one, never in their own attitude. That would account for a bit of integrity.

But that never happened. When the moment arrived for a good man to stop a bad deed the most that would happen is the potential saviour would arch the eyebrows a bit higher and slightly open his mouth as if to say something, as if to attempt a movement forwards. Then nothing. That fraction of a second was gone. He would exhale a weak sigh disguised with a fake cough or just turn around pretending he wasn't there while the other would go ahead with whatever violence allowed him to release his anger upon the prisoner.

That moment was coming. I could see it. It wasn't against me this time but the pressure was on another boy. I had seen him only a couple of times, I assumed he was one of the new ones. The other two were just looking at the floor and pretending to clean, with that tortoise pace that was driving the guard crazy. Then a third guard came running and puffing into the canteen and told the other two they had to go with him. They needed support in the prisoner's wing. There was a riot and the guards required back up to contain them.

I could see the eyes of the angry guard suddenly brightening. That was all he needed to hear. The other one though seemed quite bored and disappointed with the situation. The newcomer and the fiery one just ran towards the other wing and the guard left behind told us not to move a fucking muscle till they were back. Then he locked us in the canteen.

It was a matter of seconds. We all looked at each other and without uttering a single word we had become a united gang. We all knew what to do.

The canteen had a bar enclosed behind the same iron barriers we had in the cells. At the other side were bottles of spirits and boxes of cigarettes to sell to the guards. We were quick and efficient. Our criminal minds were switched on. We used the mop sticks, putting two together to resemble pliers and then picked the tobacco from behind the bars and very slowly attracted it towards us. We were successful enough to get one pack each.

When the job was done, we went back to pretending we were cleaning the floor and by the time the guards returned, we were in the same position, doing the same thing and in silence. Only this time we had to constrain a triumphant smile, and we had a packet of cigarettes stuck in our underwear.

Chapter 24

A Lit Darkness

The years of my youth before the YOI were like a lit darkness. If you'd looked at them from the outside, crime, drugs and violence would stand out over anything else. You would need to be deep inside to discern any light shining in shy beams through that turmoil of dark grey and black smoke. But the beams were there, feeble sometimes and other times completely subjugated to the strength of the darkness reigning around. But always there.

I believe that is what makes the difference in your future, whether you can appreciate the timid beams of light and use them, or just ignore them and stay in the darkness, comfortable as a victim. I say I knew I was different from my friends and my family and the difference lay in my ability to understand the beams.

I should say that at the start it wasn't conscious, but somehow they would drive my actions. In the beginning, it was only timidly. But after three months in prison, they would drive me more and more powerfully every time, since I had the determination to see the beams of light and ignore the darkness if it pushed me back down.

A lit darkness is paradoxical and not obvious to the eyes that don't want to see. I wanted to see. I had to see. My mind just forced me to. You cannot dream about living overseas and ignore the signs that would lead you there, or maybe you can.

The triad of witches, The Queen Bee, her daughter and Debra, would dream about Barbados, over and over. I would sit down enjoying their coarse and unashamed laughter and I would share the imperative for travel that ran through their gypsy veins. Rescuing those moments from my memory, I see myself understanding as a child that the Queen Bee and her triad would never go to Barbados because they were expecting Barbados to come to them. In their mind the wish of it was granted as far as they could dream of it.

Sometimes it seems like there is a big leap to reach the other shore where dreams become reality, and the most frightening abyss lies in between. Therefore the dream itself is consolation enough, as the fall seems to be too much to bear. The pain is not worth it for some.

But it is! Because pain is not that terrible and it is finite when you achieve what you are after. However, the pain of not trying is always deeper and more excruciating, and it has no end.

When the Circus Came to Town was a book I would read over and over. I didn't know what I was seeing in its pages, or exactly how the book could bring me such peace and the motivation I needed to advance. As much as I hated school and everything it brought me, that book was like my tin box with the animal cards – a token, a part of my soul. It was a beam of light in the darkness.

My nephew was like a beam of light. I would love him as my own son. I would take care of him and that would keep me out of trouble. That little boy saved me so many times without even knowing it, without me realising.

The gypsy women were another beam of light.

There were the owners of the pizza restaurant that forgave my unreliability so many times and kept letting me wash their dishes. Three immigrants from Lebanon that successfully grew their own business and never forgot me. Dino appreciated me the most and helped my incursion in the electronics industry when washing dishes was not necessary any more. Three beams of light that brought me fortune.

Whoever summoned me to court the day that I saw my friends high on glue when I was sober and conscious, that beam of light.

The way out is there for whoever wants to see it. But one just doesn't escape from the past and the way a mind works so easily. Habits crystallise in the subconscious and the conscious mind, and when the latter doesn't allow you to reach the former, it is like walking with your eyes shut believing that the path is clear but crashing every ten metres.

There is no great abyss between our wildest dreams and us. It is not even a big leap into the unknown, and it is not safer to stay on the shore. It is simply uncertain. We'll trip over many, many times, because our mind tends to conform to what feels familiar. In my case the criminal mind kept working for a long time, until I fought it back so hard that it could not keep up with me.

Chapter 25

The Success Group

Deported from Canada and back in London I was disorientated. I had nurtured the idea of staying overseas and my deportation had occurred in less than three days. I hardly had time to say goodbye to my friends and I left a girlfriend back there who I would never see again. I was back home, but I was different and so was everything in London.

Travels change people and places are never the same again. For three weeks or so, I had the feeling of being back in a very familiar home where everything was exactly as I left it. While that might seem nice and comfortable, at the time it was unsettling, because I was back in an environment that did not support my ambitions.

Nevertheless, I started moving quickly. I got a job as a real estate agent and became a top seller. I also contacted Dino, one of the three guys I used to work for washing dishes a few years earlier. Dino had started his own business in computing and invited me to give him a hand.

That was also the time I worked in a petrol station during the night shift. My criminal mind could not yet discern with total clarity that there was no line of honesty or shades of integrity.

You are either honest and have integrity or you are not. Yet, it was enough for my conscience. Somehow I still had my eyes closed. I was making a great effort to do what it takes to stay away from crime, but my mind was too used to acting otherwise. It wasn't an easy thing to do.

Objectively, life was not easier than before. The Ferrier was becoming more dangerous. Although those living within the concrete walls were not aware of it, living in their microhabitat of community support. It's the paradox of the best human virtues surfacing where the worst human behaviour reigns. I had already moved out, but I kept coming back to Kidbrooke and Bexley to catch up with friends and family.

Then I got a job in real estate, and things started to move in a nicer direction.

I liked the job and it gave me enough money to enjoy my free time. I had already gained Lenny's respect and all his skinheads were not to touch me, so I probably became the only guy in the Ferrier able to walk the street in a suit without being hassled by them. Although what a skinhead considers plain hassle could actually be a terrifying experience. I became the top seller in the office and the boss gifted me with an expensive car that it didn't take me long to drive drunk and smash against a wall after a party.

I was doing my best. However, it is hard to get rid of old habits. So much so that they would even chase me. As I said earlier, I had a hierarchy of what honesty and integrity were, and I didn't have a clear idea of whether there were shades of grey.

I was aware of the limits of legality. From my extensive

experience dealing with criminals – and being one myself, I managed to stay out of trouble. Even if my client was buying a house with money produced out of a wall in an industrial area and suspiciously packed in a black rubbish bag. I was doing the clean job, which was enough.

I would visit Dino at his computer store often and I started to learn about software. I found it very interesting and enjoyed it a lot. So, I wondered whether that was a job I could do. One day, searching in the classified section of a newspaper I saw an ad asking for help with computer software. I called the number and a gentle male voice asked me to go to his place and check out his computer. That was how I met Dickie and the beams of light started to shine more strongly.

Dickie was a funny looking fifty-something man. He reminded me of Doc Brown in *Back to the Future*. He was an average-sized build with small round spectacles and crazy, fuzzy white hair. Dickie was a lovely, kind and well-mannered gentleman. I helped him with his computer issue and he asked me to come back a couple more times to assist him.

We got on very well very quickly and he proposed that we meet to discuss other business and opportunities he could make available for me. Dickie was a very wealthy man, a family man living in a big house on one side of London and owning a lodge house at the other end of the city, where I also helped him with some little jobs. I had seen how he dealt with people and felt very attracted to his circle. I understood it was a great opportunity for me to enter into his network and I was keen to hear whatever he had to propose.

Dickie invited me to have lunch in a very fancy and strange restaurant. It was far too expensive and extravagant for a business meeting. Although I found it a bit strange, it didn't raise my suspicion when the waiter very politely addressed him by name and enquired whether he wanted privacy for lunch. Dickie said he did, and we were led to a very elegant booth. The waiter closed the curtains behind him and around us when he left.

We were promptly served a beautiful lunch, and while I found the amount of privacy funny, I had a very good feeling about Dickie. I sincerely enjoyed his company so I wasn't alert when Dickie abruptly changed the discussion from business talk to plain uninhibited sexual conversation.

He was telling me naturally and in a very relaxed manner about his sex life and his homosexuality, openly and with graphic detail about what he did and didn't like.

He was carrying on and on and I thought it was time to stop him, "Hold on Dickie, I'm sorry, but I'm not gay."

To which he responded, "Oh, I know, but I thought you'd like it. You seem the type..."

"Sorry, Dickie, but definitely no."

I was sure about that. I'd had plenty of opportunities to experiment sexually as a teenager and I was not the prudish kind. He shrugged and immediately changed the conversation back again to business matters. There is nothing like honesty and bluntness to make good friends.

Dickie taught me many things. He became my mentor and I met a lot of interesting people through him. He put together a group called the Success Group, which consisted of me, him and several of his friends. We were of different ages and had diverse backgrounds and upbringings but we all had our ambition in common. The group would discuss ways to be successful in our enterprises and the meetings were mostly held in Dickie's lodge house.

Dickie would spend most of the time at his lodge house, which was rented by well-respected people, all professionals, people I liked to be surrounded by. I would drive an hour and a half every week to meet them and we would have very interesting discussions about mindset, success, positive thinking, and other ways of thinking and acting that would lead to success in our enterprises and personal life. We would also party lots, of course.

Dickie was a magnificent host and used to throw quite wild parties. We were living in the eighties, the decade of sexual liberation, and Dickie would consider that the best feature of the decade. I could imagine what that would be like for a man that probably got married to conform to the social expectations of the times and hid part of his life in the darkest of shadows.

Among all the important things the Success Group gave me, there are two that stand out – reading and my name. We would discuss books like Napoleon Hill's *Think and Grow Rich* and the lives and acts of other successful people. I remembered about my interest for the mind, which had always been there, but was overshadowed by the daily troubles and dark environment I was in. My passion for the mind and hypnosis was starting to develop seriously as part of my life, although it would still take a bit longer to flourish as a profession.

My name was also an important and yet very simple step towards the change of life.

One day Dickie told me, "Mark, you need a name that people can remember easily. Colella is too difficult and non-familiar. I changed my name to Mr. Saruman and I can tell you it made a difference in my life and success. You need a name everybody can remember."

And so, I erased Colella from my rubric and from then on I was called Mark Anthony.

I also made good friends while enjoying Dickie as a mentor. Stephen was a man I got on very well with since the first moment we met. He was a lodger in Dickie's house. Dickie was head over heels in love with him, but he was heterosexual and had a girlfriend. Stephen stopped his advances quite quickly. However, just as I did, he enjoyed Dickie's company and conversation and was part of the Success Group too.

At the time and with all the learning I was gathering, my entrepreneurial soul was growing in confidence and when another real estate agent talked me into opening our own business, I saw a bright light in front of me.

We were quite successful straight away, after all I was a top salesman and so was he. Unfortunately, our best asset was the power of manipulation. That was what made us so good at our job. However, while I was finding the good in myself, the path to integrity and moving away from crime, he saw the picture in a very different manner and was going in the opposite direction.

The new business and other enterprises were taking up most of my time and I started to drift off the Success Group. As it turned out it happened to all the others. It had been like a high of great ideas and good intentions, but it faded away slowly. Maybe because we had all learnt as much as we were meant to there. Maybe it was meant to be that way.

I hadn't seen Dickie and Stephen for about two years when I received a phone call from Dickie. I was happy to hear his voice but he seemed very stressed. No wonder after listening to what he had to tell me. It hit me very hard and deep causing me nausea. Even though we had followed different paths, I cared for them and only wished them the best. I had just heard about Stephen's demise and I was about to hear Dickie's side of the story. Both stories were equally dramatic and I felt the tragedy deep in my guts.

Dickie managed to seduce Stephen at one of his parties. I did not know about that, I would have never imagined it to be honest. It was only one night, and Dickie emphasised it was consensual, something I just had to believe because I never saw anything other than hearty and warm treatment in their friendship. But then Dickie got some bad news he ought to share, and the consequences sunk so deep in his soul it made it unbearable for him to carry the guilt.

We were in the eighties and little was known about a disease called AIDS, but enough to warn all affected people about how contagious it was. Dickie received the diagnosis and had the moral obligation to communicate it to whomever he might have passed it to.

Stephen was in his room, still at Dickie's lodge house. I imagined him opening the door with his big smile and a warm greeting. Dickie entered the room and explained his diagnosis to him and the fallout; Stephen could have contracted the disease when they had sex that one time.

I cannot even conceive the terror in Dickie's eyes when he saw what came after. He could not have foreseen such a display of madness and pain upon anyone but himself. He would have expected an angry, sad, or supplicant man staring at him.

Dickie would have been prepared to welcome the violence of Stephen's fists charging against him in pure frustration and impotence. And that would have been all right, because it would have calmed the anguish of guilt eroding his insides by inflicting pain on the flesh.

But Stephen did not react in such ways. He did not even look at Dickie standing there in front of him. Suddenly he became blind and insane, yelling incongruously and backing away from Dickie in frantic steps. Then, in a fraction of a second, he turned around and ran through the window, out into the void.

I heard Dickie's voice breaking on the other end of the line. I could see in my mind his lips trembling and trying to hold the phone in his shaking hand. Everything happened very quickly and he had no time to react and stop him. Stephen's room was on the first floor. A fence of forged iron spikes surrounded the house. His body was pierced through by three of the spikes and Stephen died instantly in his fall.

I put the phone down and firstly tried to swallow the tragedy, and immediately after to forget it and keep going ahead with life. None of those tasks were easy, but grieving is not something I had time for. I never contacted Dickie again after that. AIDS was a dangerous disease back then, we did not know much about it and whoever suffered it was avoided like the plague. Unfair as it is, I did not know any other response I could have had with the emotional and mental resources I had available back then. It is nothing to be proud of, however it is the truth.

Two years later someone knocked on my door. I opened it and I saw Dickie standing in front of me. His stance was frail and consumed by the disease; so skinny and with the life rushing away from him. It shocked me to see the great man that had been my mentor and to whom I had so much to be grateful for looking like that.

He didn't want to take much of my time, but he had come to ask me to go with him. He was going overseas to preach the word of Jesus Christ and he wanted me to accompany him. It was a weird request, it felt awkward and out of place. I was no believer nor was I prone to altruism beyond borders when I was still trying to straighten out my own life. He would have known that. Nothing made sense. I told him kindly that wasn't for me, hugged him and wished him good luck.

Chapter 26

Seeking the Right Herd

I was exceptionally good as a real estate agent. I dare say I was one of the best. I would have made so much money if I had stayed in it, but my business partner made it clear to me that, even though my entrepreneurial spirit could build a leading company, if I kept mingling with people like him – ruthless and dishonest – my ambitions of a better and successful life would always be jeopardised by the deceptive and criminal actions of others.

We had an office in London by the River Thames and we aimed to only sell houses by the river. The money was coming in quickly and in abundance, but it was money that passed through bad hands and I had a partner I could not trust. So I left.

I found another 'success group' and I was delighted with it. I signed up for a company selling homewares and cleaning products. I was very familiar with going to houses in party plan sales mode. That was what I had done in Pakistan and Emirates for a while where they didn't even speak English so I found it very easy to do it on my own turf. I was thrilled not only with the opportunity to run my own business but also with the support I received from the company.

There were monthly meetings in which they would give us selling tips and motivational speeches. I had a likeminded team to belong to again. Moreover, I was surrounded by people with great ambitions in life, just as I had.

I loved the environment and I would save enough money to pay the cost of travel to attend their meetings – sometimes five hours drive from London – but the cost was never too high. The spiritual lift I would get was worth it. I would not give up. I could do it! No difficulties were great enough to stop me. I would listen to the top sellers in the firm sharing their strategies: how to make others understand that they needed our products, how not to falter at rejection, how to see any obstacle as a challenge, any failure as a lesson and any bump on the pathway as a milestone. My mind was thriving. I was happy and content.

Until I found out that sometimes all the enthusiasm they advocated didn't make any sense and it was not transferable to all clients. Enthusiasm was not the only factor that made a person successful, no matter how much they insisted on telling us it did. In doing that, a lack of integrity would again appear in what seemed a perfectly honest business. It turned out to be a well-dressed and innocent-faced opportunity but sometimes with dubious ethics.

I followed all the guidelines I received from the courses, workshops and seminars I attended religiously. I would organise parties to sell my products to my mum's friends and other friends and acquaintances I could convince anyone that my products were absolutely the best and essential for their lives. However, my sales were low. I did not give up or feel discouraged because I had all those people behind me supporting my beliefs and applauding my performance, all in unison: "Come on! No difficulty is too big, don't give up!"

But one day I came to a realisation that demolished the castle of wealth and the great expectations I had built around it. I sold around three hundred pounds of products at one party. It was the first time that I sold anything. I was thrilled, three hundred pounds was a fortune! But then, it turned out that all my hard work gave me a return of only three pounds.

I was furious. That was highly unfair! In a fraction of a second my opinion of those people changed. They were just thieves, plain and straight thieves. My work was worth almost nothing. All the trips around the country I had funded with my money for a training process that directly benefitted them, not me. It was my work that made those three hundred pounds. It was the money I had earned using my skills. I had invested in this company to help me succeed, not to satisfy their greed. I had been deceived.

However, even then I could appreciate the experience I had gained from the whole situation. What really made me pull out of the scheme wasn't the financial aspect of it, but the razor-sharp cut that I felt inside during one of the seminars I attended. It was plain wrong what I heard there – full of judgment and stealth.

I was still brooding over the unfairness of getting only a five per cent share of the sales after all my work but I remained in the scheme because I had invested a lot of time and money into it. Then I attended a meeting and I heard these words while the presenter was encouraging us to introduce our family and friends to the products: "If they don't buy your products they just don't love you enough." I stood up and left the room.

That did it. That was an insult to my family and friends. I was selling products that cost double the rent money for many people in my family. They could barely get to the end of the month without owing money to someone, and the lack of understanding that chatter showed for people's situations was outrageous and indecent.

I felt the anger and frustration building up inside me. There among those smiley faces and bright eyes – as I had been myself not long before – feeding on the fake enthusiasm of someone who was going to take all the efforts of their work and insult people who could not afford their products. I couldn't bear it any more, it was creepy, shabby and indecent. I had to walk away from all that and find a peaceful place. The manipulator had been manipulated. Soon after I laughed at the irony.

Chapter 27

Beta Videotapes, Broken TVs and Another Gypsy

The electronics industry set itself in front of me again. I met a friend who sold video players. Betamax had been introduced in the UK, and although it had been around for several years it wasn't yet the kind of electronic device anyone would have at home.

However, it was the kind of device any one would *want* to have at home. I did not have that vision myself and I started selling them modestly and with not much expectation. I was a bit disheartened after I felt deceived by the homewares company. Although later in life I would agree their teachings about growing a business and the right mindset were not off the mark, at that moment in time I couldn't even think about them, let alone anything I might have learnt from them. It was a matter of pride. I was furious with the lack of ethics they had shown. It wasn't because I believed myself to be better than them. I never get tired of repeating that the journey was long and slow for me, and I had never been an angel. But I had high expectations and that company turned out to be no better than everything I had around in my neighbourhood when it came to morals and ethics.

I started buying a couple of Betamax at a time from my new acquaintance. I would use the money from other jobs or from selling stuff to buy his stock. By then I had so much experience as a salesman that it was very easy for me to work with a new product, which happened to be in great demand. At the start, I would buy the video players as I was selling them, but very soon my friend proposed that I go and sell them at fairs in greater numbers and offered to let me pay him after I had made sales. That was a fantastic opportunity with very low risk, so I took it immediately.

I packed my car with stock and possessing just a folding table and my loquacity, I started to sell them at small town fairs, driving around the countryside. I could not believe how good the business turned out to be. Customers would almost snatch them from my hands. I would always come back home empty-handed, and very often I would return to the town I had just been in to deliver some more Betamax. I was content and feeling successful.

One day I was walking along the street and I saw a little shop which stood out from the others. It was an electronics shop and was almost in ruins, wrecked on the outside and filthy inside, with all the TV screens, video players and tape recorders piled up everywhere and covered in dust. That store couldn't possibly stand out among the rest in that street, if anything it should have been the opposite. I like to think it "called" me, or more scientifically explained, I already had a predisposition in my mind to see such an opportunity and so it was presented in front of me.

I went inside and asked the owner if he was selling Betamax. He just shrugged and said he wasn't selling anything at all and his only interest was to get rid of it. My heartbeat rushed and I felt it pounding in my throat. That wasn't a beam of light anymore, timid and shy in a pool of darkness, that was an open sky with a bright sun shining all over me. I asked him how much he wanted for it and we agreed a price.

It was fortunate that back in those days getting a loan from any bank was a matter of trust and a couple of signed papers. I had nothing to back up my purchase. I simply explained to the bank manager what I needed and what for. I was completely naive when it came to money matters, and to my misfortune it would take me some time to learn.

I just knew about the exchange of money in a sale, cash in my hand and a million ways to spend it incorrectly. I had never had anyone teach me about money. At home money was virtually non-existent and whatever was available was spent straight away. The concepts of saving, spending wisely or even the simplistic process of paying bills, were beyond my understanding. I could not discern whether paying electricity bills was more important than buying flowers for my wife.

But I was good at talking business. I sat in front of the bank manager and pretended I knew what I was doing. But I really didn't. It was just a confidence burst I had which drove me. It was an empty confidence, full of energy and strength but lacking any practical knowledge to give it a firm foundation. It was one thing to carry out the simple trading of goods, another thing entirely to understand the responsibility of making a business work.

A couple of days later I came back to the bank as I had been instructed after the discussion of my loan with the manager, and to my delight he smiled at me and shook my hand firmly, extending a cheque over the table.

The shop was left by the last owner just as I had seen it, a pile of dirt covering heaps of TV screens, many completely broken and most of them malfunctioning. There were so many and the property was so small that I hardly had room to move around. I did not know where to start. It needed a lick of paint, but there were one hundred more repairs that had to be done.

It took me a couple of days to decide what to do with the shop. Finally, I started moving some stock out of the way, placing it in another spot so I could clean the floor and walls in the patches that were becoming free of clutter. It was like playing an arcade game.

While I was working on giving the old shop a facelift, I saw a gypsy man looking inquisitively through the dirty window display. He stared at me through the glass. Then, after a few minutes he walked away. I did not pay much attention, or at least I did not make it obvious I had noticed him. When you have been used to working your way out of trouble for so long, you have that skill for life – noticing everything around you and identifying it as a danger or an asset in your fight for survival.

That night I left the shop quite late. I was exhausted and as I walked to my car I recognised the gypsy coming towards me. He asked me if the TVs and video players in the shop were mine. I said yes.

He said in a broken voice, "I want them. I'll give you three hundred pounds for those you have at the back."

"They don't work," I replied.

"Can you make them look like they are working?"

"Yes, but still they won't work."

"I don't care. Three hundred pounds. I'll come tomorrow morning to pick them up."

I shrugged, entered my car and drove home. A deal was already settled.

The next day, early in the morning, I prepared the devices for him and sure enough he appeared with two more men and picked up all of them. He gave me the three hundred pounds and asked me if I could get more in two days. I said yes, although I had no idea of how or where I would find them.

I managed to get them from other repair shops, and again he came to the shop with two men and picked them up. This took place several times, while I was conditioning the shop and making it suitable for clients. I could not think of any honest use for those goods, and I was certain at some stage in the transactions between my sale and their sale something dodgy was happening, but again it wasn't my hands getting dirty.

I used the money I got from my commercial transactions with the gypsy to paint and decorate the shop as well as buy some stock. My cousin was helping me to accommodate the new stock and attach the security bars at the back window, when we realised that we had the wrong fittings for fixing the bars on.

I paNateed. I had all my new stock in the shop and the back of the building was virtually an invitation for anyone who felt like coming in and taking anything they pleased. I knew it would happen, I knew any cunning passerby would think it, as that is what I would have done years ago with my gang. I had no doubts I would lose everything if we didn't fix the bars at the rear window. I was getting very anxious.

We sorted out a way to cross the bars so no one could come in and I left the shop with a heavy feeling in the pit of my stomach. I didn't sleep much. I knew far too well how my shop would be raided should a gang such as my own pass by.

The next day, I drove to the shop very early and still anxious. I opened the front door and a sigh escaped from my month alleviating the weight I had been carrying with me all night – everything was there. As I walked to the counter and saw the rear window I could not stop a triumphant smile drawing on my mouth. Sure enough, someone had tried to enter during the night, but they were unsuccessful. I smiled because they could have done it. The bars had moved and were collapsing in a way that seemed impossible to shift, but would have left the way clear and open had the criminals realised that they just had to move one of them to the opposite side to free the rest. I thought about karma, and how I must have been doing well on my path to a life of success, as for the first time I clearly saw that it was working in my favour.

With a bit of paint and a nice banner at the front, the electronics and repairs shop was ready to go. I was very excited, but as always enthusiasm by itself doesn't bring action. The first days no one entered through the door, but I was already toughened up from my experience starting other businesses. It didn't discourage me. If anything, I found it horribly tedious waiting behind the counter, so I would take one of the broken Betamax video players left by the previous owner and that the gypsy had not taken, and I would gut it, dismantle it piece by piece and put it in back together. Then one day someone came in and asked me if I could fix his video player. I reassured him I could and he became my second client.

The truth is that I had not the slightest idea of how to fix his video player, and yet I told him it would be ready by the afternoon on the next day. I spent all night awake in the shop trying to sort out how that mechanism functioned, and where the malfunction was. I took one of the old video players from my stock and opened it side by side with my client's. Once both were open, I observed which parts were different. Although they were slightly different models the mechanisms inside were very similar. Maybe one piece was placed in a different part of the base holding them, but aside from that I could find their corresponding parts inside.

I plugged the new one in and turned it on, observing what was activated within the plastic and metal carcass. Then I unplugged it and plugged in the broken one. It would have been much easier to do both at the same time, but I had only one power point free at that moment and I needed the spare one to plug in the stand light I was using. It was an old shop and it was in the early nineties. Ironically, the place was not adapted for too many electronic devices functioning at once.

The next afternoon the video player was repaired and ready to be picked up. By the time I gave it to my client I had already forgotten whatever I had done to fix it, so when the next client came requesting a similar service, I paid more attention.

I learnt hands on. In fact, it was the only way to learn for me. I would tell my clients I could do it even if I had not the remotest idea of how to solve their problem. That was not something they'd question; if they trusted me and I trusted myself, it could be done. Period. And it was always done.

I became proficient at fixing electronic devices and in a few months I had to find someone else to help me because I didn't have the capacity to do it myself with the increase in demand. I contracted an electronics engineer and my mind was freed to think bigger.

Not long after I saw that a bigger shop across the street was closing and I set my mind on opening another store there. I rented that commercial area and left my first employee in charge of the small shop so I could manage the bigger one.

Although I had the right mindset to open and expand a business, and I was gaining confidence as I saw the results, other areas weren't so well developed. I had no concept whatsoever of wise trading. My criminal mind was still active somewhere in my head, and I would accept deals that were not quite honest. I would spend the money I was making in an unproductive way and without care. It was far more important for me to spoil my wife with flowers than pay bills. Soon I had employees and took pride in treating them in the best manner, but this introduced a more complicated accounting activity that I just wasn't prepared to deal with.

My still active criminal mind didn't see anything wrong in accepting some goods from a not very reliable source. However, I had learnt a lot and I was already savvy when it came to business records, keeping all receipts and inventory up-to-date.

Of course, that didn't stop the London police from raiding my shop and taking most of my stock with them. It was a big operation by the British Police throughout London, a big network of electronics trafficking had been exposed and they were looking for the people responsible for the fraud. Apparently, I had been under surveillance for many months before they got a warrant to search my shop. I had all my documents in order and they could not touch me. They had nothing to accuse me of. However, they could take my stock and they did, which was a huge blow with a very negative impact on my business.

Two months later I went to collect my property from the police station. I walked in and they showed me my stock. It was all pulled apart and knowing that they could not prove I was involved in any illegal activity I gave them a Cheshire Cat grin and asked whether they would put everything back together.

The sergeant came up to me and whispered sternly in my ear, "We know it was you. We cannot prove it, but we know you did it, so just take your stuff, fuck off, and if you say anymore we'll make your life hell!."

I brought a couple of my employees along and picked up my stock. That was the last time I got involved in any illicit activity.

"When time is all we have, why waste your time living somebody else's life."

Mark Anthony

BE A LEADER

1) Begin with praise and honest appreciation.
2) Call attention to peoples mistakes indirectly.
3) Talk about your own mistakes before criticising the other person.
4) Ask questions instead of giving direct orders.
5) Let the other person save face.
6) Praise the slightest improvement and praise every improvement. "Hearty in your appreciation and lavish in your praise".
7) Give the other person a fine reputation to live up to.
8) Use encouragement, make the fault seem easy to correct.
9) Make the other person happy about doing the thing you suggest.

- - - - - - - -

1) Don't criticise, condemn or complain.
2) Give honest and sincere appreciation.
3) Arouse in the other person an eager want.
4) Become genuinely interested in other people.
5) Smile.
6) Remember that a persons name, to that person, is the sweetest and most important sound in any language.
7) Be a good listener, encourage others to talk about themselves.
8) Talk in terms of the other persons interest.
9) Make the other person feel important - and do it sincerely.
10) The only way to get the best of an argument is to avoid it.
11) Show respect for the other persons opinions, never say "your wrong".
12) If your wrong admit it quickly and emphatically.
13) Begin in a friendly way.
14) Get the other person saying yes,yes, immediately.
15) Let the other person do a great deal of the talking.
16) Let the other person feel that the idea is his or hers.
17) Try honestly to see thing from the other persons point of view.
18) Be sympathetic with the other persons ideas and desires.
19) Appeal to the nobler motives.
20) Dramatise your ideas.
21) Throw down a challenge.

A list of positive and inspiring words and quotes which I typed many years ago, these were all I had to help me on my road to a better and more successful life. I read them daily, and still read these and similar 'every day' to keep reinforcing them, always setting new dreams and goals.

Top: Me and my nephew Mace, who is now a young married man… How time flies!

Bottom: Me and my sister Rose on her wedding day, where she married a wonderful man Djah who still remains her loving husband after 30 years.

Top: Me and one of my favourite women in my life, My Mum, now in her mid seventies and Mum to five kids, Grandmother to many more.

Bottom: Mum and another of her children, little Bella her loyal friend.

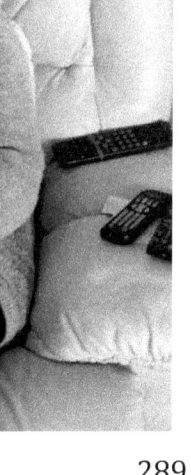

From left to right, Me, Mum, niece Lou Lou and Sylvan on my trip back to the UK 2010.

Me and the man himself, a breath of fresh air in not just Mum's life but ours too, Stace The Ace, one of the most wonderful men to walk the Earth. Mum and Stace are still good friends after 40 years.

Me and my neighbour Steve, a wonderful friend, good Irish family man, and our go to breakfast, dinner or tea man with his lovely wife Eileen who fed us more times than a food truck when fish fingers and bread just didn't cut it. Sadly, Steve passed away a few years ago.

Me and my good friend Paul, who helped me on my arduous path to becoming an entrepreneur by allowing me to sell goods on a sale or return basis, but also my best man at my first marriage.

Chapter 28

Love Letters

The scent brought to my mind her long black hair. Leah's open smile was shining inside me as I breathed in the perfume. It was her second letter and she had scented it with her perfume as she did with the first one. It was such a fresh smell. It would make me feel whole and in a place beyond the bars.

She was tall and slim with big brown eyes. Her Israeli ancestry gave her the dark features. Leah was working as a secretary when I met her in a pub. A beautiful and very sexy woman, I stated my intentions from the first moment I set eyes on her.

As I read the letter I was holding carefully but protectively in my hands, I recalled her walking to the bar and asking for a drink. I struck up a conversation, and we left together that night.

We went out for several months, she was smart and her company used to brighten my day. As she was doing now while I leaned on the wall, seated on the grey wool fabric covering the over used mattress inside the cell. Her perfume – it was her perfume that would take me somewhere else for a fraction of a second. I sniffed with the anxiety of a drug addict, wanting a longer high, battling to inspire the last bit of scent emanating from the mauled paper.

We were together no more. I cannot say she broke my heart or I broke hers, it just seemed that friendship worked better between us. But she would become my girlfriend again while I was lying in my cell, bringing the paper closer and closer to my nose, trying to ignore the ordinary smell of stationary.

I received a letter every second week and I would re-read them every time in my cell. They lifted me up when I was sad, although they couldn't do much about my frustration. That was a whole different matter. I would think about Pakistan then and now that the dream was open for me again, I would allow myself the imagination to take me flying away from the cell every now and then.

Leah would love me while I was inside and I needed it. I missed everybody so much. Never to the point of crying, maybe because that would have jeopardised my image enough to get me punished for no reason – more often that I was already. The tension one lives with in a young offenders institution can break anyone's nerves, and it takes time to rewire them back into a safe place.

Love letters are so important. Leah's letter was making me feel I was still human and lovable, two things that might be taken for granted in the outside world, but that sadly are a luxury in certain places on earth.

Barry stopped playing with a thread that he had pulled from the blanket and mocked me over the letter.

"Why don't you swallow the paper directly?"

I didn't pay him attention and he went back to his petty

entertainment making knots with the thread.

He had some letters of his own, but not from a girlfriend. Once he messed up with me. He took a letter from my hands and I was about to punch him when he handed it back to me with a serious, apologetic look. He knew how much a letter meant. We were friends when we needed one the most and we respected each other for the timebeing, We just needed a dose of humanity and goodness to keep us going in that hell of thick bricks and iron bars.

Leah wrote that she missed me. It might not have been true, but it didn't matter. She had spent some time with my mother having tea and chatting the week earlier, when Mum had been to visit me and told me about Pakistan. Then, I could hear inside my head Leah and Mum talking and laughing, seated at the kitchen table.

Leah was very classy, very well-spoken. Her parents were very posh and straight-laced. It is no wonder they disliked me. I thought about her parents and the day we met. We got on well; I was a nice and polite young man. Then someone told them what I was up to and their opinion changed. I couldn't blame them but at the same time I did not like their falseness and judgment in the least. I still had good within me and I would never have got their daughter into trouble. Suddenly I felt my teeth clenching and exhaling a "Fuck you".

I shook my head. I did not want disturbing thoughts interrupting me and the love affair I was having with the scented paper was too sweet. Leah didn't care. She would drive to the Ferrier with her style and upper-class London accent and sit down with my mum to have a cup of tea. Her letters were sweet in the extreme and she was proficient at writing everything I wanted to hear.

I was arrogant and blunt, and would not think twice about speaking the truth out loud , sharing an opinion or snapping the veracity of a situation in the face of anyone. It got worse inside, where all the inmates seemed to share the same awful traits. She didn't bring that up. Her words were devoted and inspiring: I didn't deserve jail, it was just unfair, she knew me, she knew I was a good man, a good man suffering the injustice of a crooked system.

I leaned my head back on the wall and looked at the ceiling. How nice it was to listen to those words. Maybe they were true? Maybe I was just a victim. I so wanted to hold onto that fantasy, that sweet lie and the capricious nature that pushed me to believe it.

My arrogance agreed with those words, but by now I had been inside long enough and the short, sharp, shock was delivering some realisations. Every time emerging more to the surface where I could not ignore them. I did deserve to be there. I did deserve the sentence that was bestowed on me when the gavel hit the wooden block. But, I also deserved the opportunity that was waiting outside and I was determined not to waste it – not again.

I closed the letter and put it in a safe place under the mattress. Letters were like gold or like weapons that could turn against you. A letter was a treasure of love, and in the wrong hands could cause you to be tormented by any of the bullies around. I wasn't up for any more fights and I probably wouldn't have been so passionate about a letter now that I knew I was almost out and with a passport waiting for me.

But I was exhausted. I was tired of being locked in hell and of all the bullshit around there. It wasn't possible to behave like a decent man and still stay safe, but the being the opposite meant punishment or reprisals.

It was dark out there now, behind the bars. I turned around facing the wall and just seconds later the lights went off and Barry said goodnight.

Chapter 29

Learning to Love

I met Leah when I was 17. She worked in an office as a secretary. My nephew was four years old. I loved when Leah came to visit and Rose asked us to babysit my nephew. It was like having a family of my own. Being a husband and a father was so strong in me that I had no doubt I would be both in the future, and that it would bring me happiness. It was all about love. Finding someone who would accept all the love I had to give and who would love me in return.

I became more aware of what love meant as I grew into and out of relationships. I can see how it is possible for me to drown my partner in love because I have so much to give. And I find it captivating when a woman not only appreciates how much I have to offer them but reciprocates that love.

Leah was that girl; she was very sweet to me. Even though, back then I wasn't quite the partner I intended to be, or maybe I should say, I wasn't as unselfish and generous as I wanted to be. I never learnt about romantic love at home. I had seen how my mother was half killed by the kicks of men who were supposed to protect and support her. I pushed my first girlfriend in front of my mother. I still cannot forget about that, It is not guilt, since guilt is not useful, but it was the realisation of how much wrong I could do to the woman I loved if I replicated what I had lived at home.

I developed my romantic side watching movies – as simple as it sounds. Although the media might not be the best source for this, as it can give a misleading view of the world, it was as much as I had to grab onto. Anything was better than what I used to be presented with at home. Even with Stace the Ace who was so charming and lovely, or David who really loved my mum, her relationships with them were still stormy and short-lived. At no stage did I have the chance to absorb the right way to develop a romantic relationship.

Fortunately, I also had some good input from outside the home. In hindsight, I can see it was a very strong influence, but I didn't realise it back then. Maybe the people who planted the seed in me and created the image of a healthy relationship were my Irish neighbours and Mr. and Mrs. Gilley.

A lovely Irish couple lived next door. They would always have nice meals to share with my sisters and I when Mum went for her weekends away. I never saw them arguing, not once, and I would spend a lot of time at their place playing with their son Steven. He was a couple of years younger than me and we got on very well, but I preferred to hang out with Steve's dad. He was always so much fun to be around, and very much a lovable rogue.

Both families were friends. They always treated my sisters and me in such a loving way. I remember their hospitality, when my mum's Irish boyfriend would leave only frozen fish fingers at home. They would always give us nice warm food and some treats.

I recall the warmth of their generosity as I picture them holding hands. I saw them so often hugging and laughing together. The way they talked to each other was completely different to that of my mum with her partners. My mum was such a lovely lady and so soft-spoken with her children; she would hug us all the time, when she was at home. But it was different with her partners. In her interactions, there was either fear, or anger or just plain stubbornness. There was no harmony or gentle rhythm marking the pace of the relationship; it was like a never-ending storm.

But it wasn't like that with the Irish neighbours, and I saw the same with Mr. and Mrs. Gilley – even more so. I saw they loved each other and although I would not have paid much attention to them as a child, maybe they were the ones that strengthened that will I had to be a family man. Maybe it sank so deep in me because a loving environment can change you. It just catches you even if you are not aware of it.

When I reflect back on the YOI I can recall myself thinking: *This is not what I want for my children.* Not everything was about material success, but about life success. Each person has a purpose or if you want, a desire or a calling. Everyone's is different and I knew mine was to be a family man, and since I knew very well how family should not be, there must have been a better way.

I had to be in the right place to accomplish that dream. I had no idea of how difficult it would be, not the slightest notion of the handicaps I would find in my way. However, the advantage of living a hell at home, being addicted to illegal or toxic substances, facing death many times before even hitting adulthood and surviving psychologically all sorts of abuse is that nothing ahead seems too scary. You know you can live the worst and get over it, you know life experiences can be awful but yet you are still alive and even when the strength fails, there will be another moment where you can move ahead. It is a matter of realising that we always have a choice. Even if it seems like a terrible choice you would rather avoid, you are still choosing something. There is no way around. But the moment you know you have a choice it gives you the power to step forward, even if it is only a little at a time.

I dreamt that Leah and I were like Mr. and Mrs. Gilley just for a moment back then. We were walking home and Mrs. Gilley was gardening behind the concrete walls of her tiny front yard. The gate was open and she called my name and said, "Good afternoon, Mark". I waved at her and she said, "That's a nice girl you are going with Mark." Addressing Leah she said, "Hi I am Mary." Leah smiled and waved and we kept walking.

Mrs. Gilley and her husband had three daughters. They were my second example of romantic love. When we moved to the Ferrier, they occupied the next house and embodied the security and warmth of our previous neighbours.

But Leah and I were not meant to be. It wasn't hard on any of us, we just worked better as friends, that was all. Although, her sweetness did follow me to prison. She became my girlfriend once more during those three months I was secluded. She visited me once with my mum and after I was freed I saw her just a few times.

Relationships grow to a certain point and then fade, but I was not willing to accept that. That wasn't what I had learnt from the romantic movies. That wasn't what I had seen with both my lovely devoted neighbours. I knew deep inside there is that one relationship that never fades. I doubted many times in my own relationships whether my gut feeling was right, and today regardless of my experiences, the turmoil, the storms and the pain, I still know that.

All of my life, I have kept that strong belief that romantic love can be forever. However, the experiences I had during my childhood and my teenage years weren't even close to a healthy relationship . After two broken marriages one can become quite skeptical about it. But then I came back to England to visit my family and I received some bad news that in a strange and touching way would reinforce that belief.

The Gilley's, unfortunately, were not in good health. Mr. Gilley had to be accommodated in a nursing home as he was suffering from dementia, and his wife could hardly take care of herself. I met their daughters and they told me how heartbreaking it was. Yet they smiled while telling me how, when one of them took their mum on the weekly visit to see her husband, both would sit holding hands in silence with the most peaceful look in their eyes, lost in some place that was only for the two of them.

It doesn't matter how confident you are in whatever you believe, if you take the time to look around, you will undoubtedly see it in the outside world happening to other people. This gives you the certainty and the strength to hold on to your dreams and never lose faith in yourself and what you believe, because it shows the chance is out there.

Chapter 30

Migrant

I was married to Ciara for sixteen years. It wasn't long after we met that I proposed. I was working hard to build my business and by the time I owned my second shop I felt confident I could give her a home and a good life. To my delight and joy our first child came soon after. I was living in bliss, exhausted with happiness if that is possible. My business was going well and I opened the third shop. Finally, things seemed to shamelessly shine for me.

However, as good as I was at delighting my wife with flowers and surprises, I still had not learned much about money management. I would mess up my priorities, together with my less than honest business dealings, which led to police taking a great part of my stock. As a result, I incurred great losses that drove me down into a spiral of failures, descending faster and further every time .

Soon I could not pay the rent or any bills at all. Up to that point, I had taken care of my employees as if they were family. I was fair in their treatment and the money side of it, but I couldn't afford the wages any more, and I had to lay them off. It was very hard knowing that I was forcing them into unemployment. Eventually, I declared myself bankrupt and lost all my material possessions.

Finding myself with nothing in my pockets wasn't as scary as one would imagine. I had been there before. I had come from there! Nonetheless, it was a big blow to my ego and my confidence. I dreaded the idea of going back to being an employee but I had no other option as I had to sustain my family. That was more important.

Finding a good job wasn't a difficult task for me. Yet I was so disappointed with life and myself. I never stopped to think about the fairness of our luck deeply; it was what it was. It had always been what it was, even when I could see a brighter future as a young boy, I did not stop to think that I was unlucky or to blame anyone. But I thought I had reached part of that future and that I was on my way up, and suddenly I was heading down again. That felt so disappointing.

That was when the idea of Canada came back to me and I travelled with Ciara and my son to the American continent with no luck at all, unable to stay after my deportation years earlier. My heart was sinking deep down again but now it wasn't just about me. I had a family to maintain and to provide for, I did not want a life of hardship for my child nor did I want to see my wife struggling as I had seen my mum do most of her life.

It was then that my cousin proposed we travel to Australia and we started to gather and complete the documents to apply for a visa. It took a year to get the paperwork. When I got the call from the Australian embassy I saw a new world opening in front of me. It was bright and it was right there for us to explore.

We arrived in Australia in 2002, feeling lost but amazed by the beauty of the East Coast. Certainly, it was a new millennium for us. As soon as we landed and I smelt the air I knew I was in the right place. It is a weird feeling when you recognise your home in a place where you have never been before. I was full of hope and confidence. After all, we were not completely alone in the country, my cousin was there and he had promised to assist my family until we settled, or so I believed. I have said it before, loyalty is not a simple trait, for me it defines the relationship, it is a prime value to respect and to live up to.

My cousin's aunt came to the airport to pick us up. I was surprised as I expected him to do it, but I thought maybe he was busy at that moment. I was still glad to see family around. My cousin's aunt was a lovely lady, and she was very helpful, taking us to the apartment we had rented until we had somewhere to stay more permanently. She helped us with the luggage when she dropped us off, and wished us the best before saying farewell.

As I came into the bare apartment I saw a note from my cousin. "I left some milk and bread in the fridge," it read. And sadly, that was as much help as I ever got from him. We were on our own.

I still visited him, everybody has bad moments, maybe I was rushing to conclusions about him. But entering his house brought me a deep feeling of awkwardness and I understood how unwelcome my family was there just by the looks his wife gave us. My cousin was like a brother to me, but he had failed me. He let me and my family down, as a result I would not see him again.

I never had a problem erasing people from my life, and I believe this is a very good skill, or asset or trait, whatever that would be! I don't feel the need to cling to people who don't contribute anything I consider good to my life. Obviously, my criteria have not always been the best when choosing what was good for me, but loyalty is the starting point to building a relationship and its fault or failing would be the deal breaker for me.

We all fell in love with Queensland. There was no hurry to settle with a job yet as we had been saving for over two years in our quest to move overseas. We took our child to see kangaroos and koalas and enjoyed the theme parks, the beach and the coral reefs. It was a happy time, no stress and breathing in the east coast sun. There was no omen of anything that wasn't exciting and full of success and happiness, we were holding on to that sense of an everlasting holiday so strongly that we did not even allow ourselves to think about the moment we would go back to daily life. A very different daily life than we had before, because there were no family or friends, only the three of us and a whole life to start all over.

I had dreamt all my life about living overseas. It was so stuck in my head since I was a little kid that I never doubted it would happen. As well as being a father and having a lovely wife. Those two things were to be the proof of my success in life, and both included that I was financially independent and free to spend at will. Although I would do the latter even when I did not have the resources due to my total lack of money management.

By the time I arrived in Australia, I had learnt a lot from my mistakes. Even though I still couldn't help being a big spender, I had reordered my priorities and learnt to cover the basic needs before buying presents and flowers for my wife and son. I dreaded not being able to drive an amazing car, to be honest, but the bankruptcy had taught me to live a more modest life. After all, I had already lived with nothing so many times that I knew it wouldn't kill me. Maybe my ego was affected, but I would always manage to feed my family.

The holidays ended and we suddenly found ourselves back to a reality we had ignored the moment we saw a loaf of bread and a bottle of milk in that bare fridge the first day in the apartment – the reality of migration.

A new place full of possibilities, but no anchor whatsoever to hold tight to and start taking strong steps, no family to support us emotionally, no friends to spend good times with, no network to assist us with the job search. It wasn't as hard for me as it was for Ciara. I was used to making friends out of nothing. I could befriend an electricity post if necessary.

She missed her family and friends very much. Once the holiday time was over, that feeling came over her heavy and gloomy. But soon we were too busy. We had gone through so much, we were such a strong couple, and we could make it.

We had already gone through the hardest time of all. Not long before we migrated to Australia she visited the doctor and we were given the news we dreaded to hear. Even though we were expecting it we still did not want it to be true. She had polycystic ovaries and could not conceive anymore. It was a blow for both of us, we wanted a big family, but there was nothing that could be done to change it. She could not conceive or bear any more babies. Now the three of us were about to grow a different baby – a new life from scratch.

Chapter 31

A Cold and Metallic Humming

I found a job at a computer store, but I was very unhappy working as an employee. My heart was craving to start a new enterprise but I did not know anyone and didn't have enough money for a start-up. Ciara was meeting new people at our little boy's school and he was very happy with his new friends. I would go to bed with my mind active, thinking of ideas for a business. There was one that kept flashing in red lights and with sirens, over and over, so insistent it sometimes became annoying.

It was like my soul was shouting at the top of its lungs. I could not ignore it anymore. I decided to find a part time job and start my own business as a hypnotherapist. But it wasn't long before that became insufficient for my soul and ambitions. I wanted to drop my safe job completely and dedicate my life to being a hypnotist.

My wife opened her eyes wide and shook her head slightly. She could not understand why I would reject a full-time job when we needed the money. It was an unnecessary risk to take from her point of view. However, I was in ecstasy because my mind was absolutely aligned with my heart. "I must do it," I told her. Any other option was unviable, the urgency and strength of that call was such that I could not act otherwise. I had to follow.

I was aware of the difficulties that could put us in again. Eventually we reached some stability with my part-time job, she was enjoying her social life with other mums and our boy was happy and glowing. To work full time as a hypnotist and take the risk of a new enterprise would put the family in jeopardy again. It would be like stepping backwards and rejecting what we had achieved. But I could not ignore it. I had a strong feeling that it was going to work. I couldn't *not* try, it simply wasn't an option.

When certainty comes to you from deep in your soul, there is nothing that can stop you. It is a drive so strong that even if you want to block it you just cannot, you are dragged towards the unknown irremediably. You have doubts too. If the situation around you isn't supportive, your conscious mind will find any excuse not to do it. Then a merciless tug of war starts within.

I felt compelled to listen to my wife and her worries. It felt like an unrelenting internal fight. Externally I ended up convincing myself I was doing the right thing for my family. Then the headaches started.

Headaches were rare in my experience. I had never suffered from headaches. And if I ever did they were very mild and brief. This time felt different. The headache wouldn't go away and I would feel it like a frozen drill digging deep in my brain. It was sharp like stinging needles. It would make me frown time and time again, and I could feel the muscles of my face tire from the tension. After nine days, I decided to go to the doctor. Even then I knew I would not leave the clinic feeling relieved with an unimportant diagnosis.

I was so scared. So many times in my life I had been defying death one way or another. I had been through so much pain and fear. I had been masking the fear over and over, with arrogance, with haughtiness, with a Cheshire Cat smile, with violence and with anger. But as I sat in the waiting area of that clinic and saw the nurse standing in the threshold with his clipboard and calling my name again, I knew it was the end. The doctor had told me, "You'll know something is wrong because they will repeat the MRI".

I entered the room again, and this time the cubicle with the technician and the chilling, white metallic tube felt even cooler than before. The nurse repeated the process again, helping me to lay down in the contraption that wasn't anything else but my death sentence. I had no hope. I thought about my child and my wife, my mother and my sister. I thought especially about Ali, who was doing life for murder in prison, would that feel the same as dying, as being gone forever? After all, there was no hope she could ever hold for a different life, could she?

What was going to become of my wife and my son? Maybe it was best if they were back in England, with family support. I had dragged them to Australia following my dreams and now I was going to leave them alone, moving ahead on their own.

And what about all my dreams? There was a part of my brain yelling. I could hear it only in the distance just too far away saying, *No, no, no, this is not the end! It cannot be!* But I was too preoccupied with my own fear and all the possibilities I was losing.

It was like all the negativity I had been holding back for so many years was coming up to the surface, rebuking me, finding the spot I had so earnestly tried to deny it for so long. It was taunting me.

You see! You are nothing and will die soon before you can achieve anything! There was no great destiny for you, you arrogant little shit ! This is all you have been all along. You got this far for nothing, what a stupid waste of time!

Suddenly I was so terribly furious, with life and with myself. I wasn't making it, I had worked so hard to do things right, I had put all my soul into it. I wasn't perfect and I had made so many mistakes, but I straightened up in the end. I had a family and I was finally living overseas. Who would have thought I would make it years back? When I was listening to *Barbados* with the Queen Bee and her sister? When the best place to sleep was a ripped couch with rotten foam coming out, as if it had been gutted over and over, barely surviving on a floor so sticky and full of filth?

I had survived the chill of child abuse, the rawness of sexual abuse, the indignity of authoritarian abuse. And I had done well for my loved ones. However, now I was facing death in such a shameful way. I would be deteriorating slowly, becoming a burden to my family when what I wanted to give them was freedom. I would end up like the guys from my old gang back in London, maybe with a bit more glory but still in a miserable way. I dreaded to imagine myself being bedridden and fed smashed food with a spoon. I could not be a father or a husband anymore. It wasn't fair. It just wasn't fair at all.

I was still staring up at the ceiling. The diabolical tube and its nasty vibration that had been driving all my thoughts of anger and injustice had ceased but I was still paralysed. I saw the nurse put himself in front of my sight leaning over my body, "Are you ok sir? We are done."

His voice brought me back to my senses and the train of negative thoughts started to fade. I was a man of action, always had been. There was no use in letting my mind put me down before my time. My heart was sunken and heavy and I did not cherish any hope, but still there were so many things to do before my death. I had to tell everybody how much I loved them and say goodbye.

I had to wait two weeks before I got the results. After the second MRI I was sent back to the doctors and prescribed some painkillers. I also got some other referral for more tests. The doctor was clear and blunt. I had a tumor in the pituitary gland but more tests had to be done to determine if it was benign. I looked at him, this time my arrogance was gone. I could not feel a shred of pride while I was listening to his words. It was self-pity. All I could feel was self-pity and fear for my family.

There was still that voice, deep down in my mind that was fighting, trying to make me hear it, but I just ignored it. I did not want to listen to it. Maybe it was easier to die, maybe I was just tired of everything. Maybe I had exhausted my energies and I hadn't noticed it until that moment. Maybe I had been so arrogant to think I could make it, but I just couldn't. I had to accept it; I couldn't. Period. I wasn't as good as I thought.

It wasn't the first time I had lost confidence in myself, but it was the first time that I could not solve the situation by thinking, working or acting on it. I could not beat death this time. Cancer is the plague of our times and it had caught me, how could I beat it? There was only one thing to do – the farewell.

Now, when I look back I see what a waste of energy and tears, but at the same time, they were necessary. It was necessary that I died emotionally. It was necessary for me to see the end. It was necessary that things were that way, because when I received the results of the tests, as I held my wife's hand and the doctor smiled at us, a current of light blue electricity, fresh and new, crossed the length of my body from my toes to the top of my head. The tumor was benign. I just needed to keep it in check.

I pressed my wife's hand and she started crying, releasing all the tension of the past few days. I couldn't hold in the tears of joy, now rolling down my cheeks. I was born again.

I wasn't born again in the way I had been many other times. Those times when death kept knocking on my door obnoxiously and capriciously, and I would just dismiss her with a gesture of disdain in my hand and my chin up high. *You fucking idiot, what did you come to do here little miss death ? Go away!*

This time I had been defeated by death and she was the one walking away after seeing me down and humbly accepting her. There was another life for me to build and it would start that very moment. The dust settled again and everything was clear. The voice that had been yelling in the background of my mind, the far away noise that was pushing itself to be heard among all my fears and negative and destructive thoughts, just stepped right to the front and said it: *This is not the end, it is the beginning!*

Chapter 32

The Show Must Go On

The good news didn't keep me from visiting the doctor, being careful with my health and regular checks, but that was a lesser evil. When we left the clinic with the great news we went out to celebrate. It was a splendid night, my wife was radiant and I was full of life.

Our situation wasn't better than before the MRI revealed the tumour, but we had seen such a dark future during the last weeks that everything seemed bright and glowing. So when I told her again I knew what I had to do, this time she nodded and understood. I dropped my job and started to work full time as a hypnotist.

It was the push I needed to dive into my dreams deeply and fearlessly. This time I learnt the lesson as though it was carved in my flesh: any day could be your last. With that motivation, I started to offer hypnotherapy sessions.

I had nowhere to do it but the house we were renting. And to be honest, although I had read every book about hypnotism and the mind that fell into my hands since I left prison, I had just played with whatever I practised on friends. I didn't have the slightest idea of how it would work on a stranger or whether I could really help them at all.

However, I did not let those thoughts stop me. They weren't even that strong. It was like back in the clinic. When the evil humming and low frequency noise of the scan was drilling my head, all my terrors, guilt from the past, thoughts of unworthiness and memories of miserable times came to light only to be erased or at least lose their strength within the border of my skull. My brain had spewed them like acidic bile, and now most of it had been swept away by the voice pounding in my mind with rhythmical insistence: *You can do it Mark, you can do it!*

However, the positive pounding started to fade as the foundations of my relationship with my wife started to crumble.

We weren't enjoying the financial stability we ambitioned. I was spending a good deal of my income investing in my projects. I was also investing a lot of time on reading, studying and marketing my business. The nights were now devoted to my goals and not to my wife. For me it was a necessary sacrifice and it was for the good of my family. No one can expect to plant a seed and grow a fruitful plant if it hasn't been watered regularly and paid the necessary attention. But this theory was true from another perspective for my wife. She would feel that she wasn't being attended with enough care.

The business started to show results. I wrote two books on how to stop smoking and how to lose weight and my workshops were a success. People would seek me out and I was getting results for them. Then one day, I had the chance to step on stage at a charity event and it turned into one of my greatest assets and my biggest success. But it was too late for Ciara and me.

We started snapping at each other not long before my business took off. We were tired. I felt she didn't support me; she would have felt I did not support her. We both were fair in our perceptions, but there wasn't a point of reconciliation in them.

The bitterness brought arguments we hadn't had before and resentments we didn't even know were there. It was bitter and sometimes it felt so was my success. I could not doubt myself, but I was so tempted every time. Every day that passed without a call or a client, or when no response to my advertising efforts was obvious. All around was hard work and I was craving for a bit of peace, an easy path I could walk without tripping over, constantly pulling myself together in the effort to move ahead.

We both could see it was over, yet we both thought we couldn't end it for the sake of our son. So we kept lingering and sidestepping the unavoidable moment. We thought it was the best for him.

In the meantime, success came. I had regular clientele coming to hypnotherapy, but the great breakthrough came with a benefit function for my son's soccer club. I was asked whether I could do a hypnosis show, and I was delighted to do it.

I remembered back in England when I saw Paul McKenna for the first time hypnotising a group of people on stage and thought I wanted to be like him. Almost twenty years had passed, and finally I had the chance to prove my skills on a stage. I was excited and absolutely inspired by the idea. It had been in my head for so long but I could not find a way to get it out, to shape it so it would become a reality. And there was my opportunity, like a gift from nowhere.

My first appearance on stage was in front of three hundred

people. It was good that I knew many of them and there were good friends among the audience. I did not feel any pressure, it was just a matter of having fun. Yet, I would either succeed or fail in front of a big audience.

I couldn't help but go back and retrieve from my memory a very unpleasant moment, while I was working so hard to become a respectable young man. I would accept any honest job I was offered without even considering whether I was suitable for the job and could do it properly. One day I was given a job in a big store. I was contracted as a salesman by a company selling gold-plated jewellery. I had experience in sales, I knew I was good at it and I had learnt in Pakistan and the Middle East how to communicate with people whose language I did not know.

On the premises I felt confident I could do it. However, the first day I found myself beside a pop-up stand, lifting my head to make myself heard over the thirty people who were scrutinising me and waiting for my speech. I couldn't do it.

I started mumbling and I forgot what to say. I didn't think there was a difference between talking to three people or thirty, but sure enough there was. As I was talking, with a broken discourse because I kept forgetting the words, I saw people walking away from my tiny pedestal, and I paNateed. I stopped talking and apologised in a faltering voice, ending the speech abruptly and walking away. That very day I talked to my boss and I quit. I simply couldn't do it.

And there I was now in front of three hundred people, almost ten years later. I had no idea whether I could do it this time, but what I was feeling when I peeked through the curtain from backstage was nothing but excitement and good vibes. There is a fear all showmen experience at a given time before jumping on stage. But it is a challenging fear, a warm terror tickling the gut, a daredevil from your inner child, who is teasing you while giggling. I learnt that terrific and sweet fear that day and it would accompany me to all my shows.

When I went on stage I heard big applause, of course! I was lucky that my first audience was already inclined to like my show and kind enough that they would readily welcome even the worst performance if that were the case. But it wasn't. I asked for some volunteers and I did a show of no more than twenty minutes. It was easy, I didn't push my skills as a hypnotist, I played safe and I heard laughter throughout. I laughed a lot myself and as I left the stage I could hear applause and cheering. That was when I knew that was the job which would make me infinitely happy.

I decided to pour all my efforts into that avenue – hypnosis on stage. It wasn't an easy path but I had never experienced an easy path before, so it didn't discourage me. I would travel three hours to a country town to find that I had only three people in the audience, who just happened to be there because they were the only customers at that time in the pub. Sometimes I would perform for only ten people, which made it very difficult as half of them had to be my volunteers and then the audience was considerably reduced. Hypnosis is a show that cannot work without the audience, they are essential, the core of the performance. They are the performers!

Disappointments came one after another, in and out of home. Driving for miles to cancel a show left me gutted, tired and furious. Being away for so long wasn't helping to heal my relationship with my wife, as tension was building at home. But I sought refuge in my hypnosis, learning, reading and practising new things. Creativity was an escape and if I heard the laughter and applause only once every six times in a show, that would feed my soul enough to keep moving ahead.

I was about to break up my marriage for good when the unexpected happened. After almost ten years and losing hope, right when our relationship was hanging by a fine thread bearing so much tension it was about to snap, my wife told me she was expecting.

It was the right surprise at the wrong time. I couldn't help but feel excited about being a dad again, but at the same time I was highly confused. It wasn't the right time. It wasn't even the right person anymore.

Everything was lost and we both knew it, but neither of us could stop it. Somehow there was no excuse to end it. We had a life together, a beautiful son and a beautiful baby that had just brought a truce for us. We weren't happy together but we did as much as we could to pretend we were, and overall we both loved our children and that superseded any other sentiment between the two of us.

Although my emotional life was spiralling down, my mind was sparking with ideas that fuelled my zest for life. The most productive one turned out to be a very simple thought I had been nurturing for months.

I had been performing a family show for quite a long time now and on several occasions some friends had asked whether a show for adults only would be possible. I knew exactly what they wanted – sex. No one told me explicitly that what they were asking for was sexuality, but I had no doubt that was the way I had to go. Thus, I created 'Mark Anthony's HypNaughty Show'.

I had to experiment for a bit as I knew a freed subconscious stimulated with anything related to sexuality could be a bit difficult to handle on stage, and I was very firm in my purpose to keep the show funny and pleasant but nothing that could embarrass anyone, so 'good, clean adult fun' was a must. I needed to find the balance so I could offer a naughty show but never ever dirty or offensive.

And I did it. It caused a great wave of criticism from other stage hypnotists and even got me expelled from some of their circles. Critics still berate me every now and then, and certainly there will always be prudes who will dread my show, but over the years 'Mark Anthony's HypNaughty Show' has proved to be a successful tool in my career. The overwhelmingly good feedback I consistently get from audiences and participants make it worth it. All the pettiness of my detractors is nothing more than a small nuisance easy to ignore.

I was becoming very successful with my hypnosis shows – mainly with the HypNaughty show – and I was practicing hypnotherapy regularly. I was a full-time hypnotist and that was everything I wanted to be in my professional life. Every time I stepped on a stage, joy would rush up from my feet to make my heart pump strongly, in a calm and powerful beat that flowed through my body with new blood, all over again, every time I heard the laughter and the applause.

But not even our baby could stop us from drifting apart. I hardly saw my wife and I tried to avoid her as much as I tried to see my children and spend time with them. Then one day I received an email. It was from a random person. Apparently, someone who was in the audience of my last show in a country town two hundred miles away. She introduced herself and said that she was very impressed and interested in my work, that maybe she could meet me one day to have a coffee and learn more about hypnosis. I wasn't in the mood for fans to be honest, and I dismissed her politely with another email. But she kept insisting.

After three emails enquiring about my profession and me, I was intrigued. She had described herself and assured me she had been in the front row of my show and I should have recognised her. Out of curiosity I looked at the video of the show – I was already recording my performances. I could not recall anyone with the features she was describing and neither could I find anyone like that in any of the video footage from that show. I forgot about the matter.

However, she contacted me again. She told me once more she would be in my town and would like to meet me. Eventually I accepted. I saw nothing wrong with it and I must admit I was very curious about her and her insistence. The moment I accepted her proposal the tone of the emails changed.

I am not going to defend myself, I knew I was married and yet, I could not help but feel flattered by her emails. She got very flirty with me and I hadn't had that feeling of being wanted for ages. I don't even think it was a matter of weakness, but opportunity. I had spent too many years pretending I loved my wife when it was over. We couldn't find the way to stop the spiral we were falling in over and over. Neither of us wanted to be with the other, but neither of us could find a way out. Or so I thought. Because my wife had found her way, ruthless and unfair, but she found it.

I started to fantasise about meeting this new woman who had some affection for me. I was feeling the thrill of the courtship, but at the same time was aware of my status as a married man and I did not let it drive me in any way. I contented myself with tasting the sweetness of a non-existent relationship with someone who was practically a ghost. And who in fact proved to be a ghost. It was only during those moments when I sat at the computer. There was no infidelity, I didn't even know if I dared to meet her. I had my family, I had my children, and anyway, I was on my way to succeeding as a hypnotist. There was no need for me to walk into another personal relationship or even the possibility of it.

Although it was a nice feeling and it gave me moments of excitement, I was devoted to my career. The audience was growing and the money was coming with more ease after all the struggles. Then one day I had a performance in my own town. I was confident it would be a good one, but I had no idea about the surprise that was waiting for me that night.

My wife told me she would attend the show with some friends. It wasn't usual and something inside was telling me there was something strange about the situation, like a red light popping up in my chest. I couldn't determine what it was and I didn't pay much attention to it. I had to get ready for the show and I had no time for her at that moment, nor to get distracted with a sixth sense prompting me to be alert.

The show went very well, it was a full house and we had fun. I was very tired after it ended though. While I was on stage the energy would fill me up and emanate from my pores, coming from nowhere, but as soon as I stepped off stage it would drain and bring me back to the reality of my family instabilty. It got worse that very night.

My wife was waiting for me at the end of the show. She was escorted by a couple of her friends. She didn't say a thing. She was carrying two big plastic bags filled to the top. She walked towards me and dropped them down at my feet. Then she handed me a bunch of printed papers and told me, "There you go, I want a divorce. Don't come back home. You don't live there anymore."

It felt like ice rushing through my guts and trapping them in its sharp coldness. My heart seemed to stop and the sudden tension in my neck almost strangled me. It was hard to breath. The papers were the printed emails I had been exchanging with that woman I didn't know. A woman I would never know because it was all the result of an entrapment conspired by my wife.

She walked away with her friends in triumphant procession and I was left behind astonished and shivering, petrified like a bronze statue in a Russian winter.

That night a friend of mine offered me shelter. His son was away travelling and I could sleep on his bed. There was a cat in the room, which belonged to the young man. The cat was as infested with fleas as the mattress I slept on. I spent all night scratching and cursing. It was like a bad joke. So many times I had voluntarily slept on mattresses like that in my youth, escaping from home, not wanting to go back, enjoying the hospitality of anyone who would allow me to sleep in their house of filth. I never felt the itch of the bed bugs crawling on me then like I did that night. Because it wasn't that time anymore. I had grown out of that life, I was out, how could I possibly be back to being homeless and bitten by parasites.

She kept almost everything, and I didn't care. But she kept me from seeing my children and my heart was in pieces. She would text me cancelling my visits to the children, telling me they had to go away only hours before I was going to see them. I was rapidly sinking into a darkness I had not known before, because this time I had nothing or no one to hold onto.

My family in Australia had become my enemy. She made sure

no one in our circle would talk to me again. She told everybody who would listen, that she caught me in a hotel room with another woman, she also made sure I could not get close to my children at school. I was like the plague for anyone that was once close to me. It was an unfair choice of punishment. I was broken in all senses. I lost all faith in life and myself.

Sometimes I would just sit and feel sorry for my bad luck, asking myself what was my worth if I couldn't even hold a family together, I could not even get close to my children. That would burn inside as if someone were literally pulling me apart, pulling my intestines out slow and delightfully. That was the image I had of my then ex-wife. I hated her. I hated her for doing that to me. I hated her for depriving my sons of their father.

There was only one thing that would make my heart beat. It was like a pacemaker that kept my hopes alive just enough to avoid the abyss down below my feet. I kept performing. I just had to put one foot on stage and force myself to forget everything that was behind the curtain. I taught myself to fake a sincere smile and to exert the greatest of enthusiasm for my audience. My laughter was a true laughter as I let my audience bypass my sadness and make me happy, even if it was for only a short while.

Then, once the performance was over I would huddle in my car and allow the desperation to drown me in pure sadness.

But 'the show must go on'. That was my therapy. Every time I would get the rush of energy up to my head more strongly. I was doing something right. I was making people happy, forgetting any problems they had for a while – as I was doing myself – giving them the happiness that puts the body in motion and moving forward. My mind was thriving on this feedback, more so than my ego. Every time I had a show the reward for a good performance was the same – the vibes of other people's contentment. And every time I stepped on stage, the depression had less room to push me down.

I was anticipating every show as if it were the most addictive of drugs. It lifted me, it gave me such a healthy high, and it was a win-win for everyone. I started to recover the confidence in myself. I realised I was in the right place and at the right moment to make my dreams come true. I never felt so strongly that Australia was my opportunity to clear my past and start again.

All those years behind had been a rehearsal, and my unfortunate relationship with my ex-wife was the summit of years of mistakes. Only thinking about my children drove me to the madness of a deep depression. Then I resolved that the only thing I could do was to numb my heart to the bribery and the spite of my ex-wife who was keeping me from seeing them, and just wait for the moment when I could reunite with them.

My spirit was coming back on track, but not so much the finances. I still had to maintain a family and keep myself in a different house and that was becoming unviable. I could hardly manage to find accommodation for myself. Also, I had to maintain a little office that I was renting for my hypnotherapy sessions. But, I was feeling optimistic anyway and my heart went a step beyond in exploring happiness when I met my second wife.

Chapter 33

Karma

This could not be more awkward or unexpected for my ex-wife. I met her imaginary lover. The one she used to trick me and force me out of our home. She did indeed exist, but no one could have known.

The show in the country town many months before, had indeed a lady in the audience. She was exactly how the woman in the emails described herself. The image my wife had created – a tall woman with long brown hair – actually existed and she did indeed want a session with me after watching my show. She contacted me several months after the performance enquiring about a session. She would be travelling to my city in the near future and could meet with me then. I called her and arranged the session in my office.

We never had a hypnotherapy session as a change in her plans during her visit meant she didn't have time for it in the end. But we still met up. We had exchanged several formal emails and I was curious about her on a personal level. An interest I would discover we shared when I saw her.

She walked into my office with a firm step, wearing a skirt and blouse. I thought she was beautiful and I liked her movements, the attitude in her steps. We both felt attracted to each other at first sight and shared a nice afternoon over several cups of coffee. It was short and certainly intense. But she had to go and I was left behind with the taste of sweet honey on my lips and nothing else to hold on to.

I did not see her for a while, however we started having conversations on the phone very often, and one day there was something else between us.

I was hurt and still sort of numb to any new love entering my life. I felt suspicious of everything and wasn't sure, but I could not ignore it any more. I was falling for her, and she for me. Her name was Lauren, and her feelings towards me were the same. I was shaking when we decided to venture on a relationship.

I asked her to move with me to nowhere, because I had no home or any permanent place to stay. Despite this and to my delight she accepted. I was concerned and feeling self-conscious because I could not give her all she deserved, but the faith she put in me meant the world. She had a house in a town a few hundred miles away, so she decided to put it up for sale and come live with me on the Gold Coast.

I had nothing to offer her. I was ruined after the separation and subsequent divorce. I was still recovering my self-confidence and picking up the pieces of my heart from the floor every night, gluing them together the best I could. But every time I was prevented from seeing my children it would fall again and crash onto the floor, like a delicate porcelain teapot. The pieces were so small that I foresaw it would never be the same no matter how many times I stacked them all back together.

Yet, I learned to numb my pain more successfully every time in order to move ahead. It was necessary if I wanted to go to a different place. Once the ground I was stepping on was firm enough, then I could solve it. But I was walking in quicksand and every time I received a call or a message from my ex-wife with threats about my children, I would sink deeper and deeper.

Lauren handed me a strong rope to grab on to and, although she could not pull me out and solve my family problems or help me see my children, she was holding it firm for me to climb up.

My new love jumped on board with my projects. She was good at marketing and we soon became a great team, not only personally but professionally. She acted as my agent, marketer and admin support, while I was completely focused on the creative part and our relationship. This greatly helped me to bypass the sadness of being separated from my children and move forward quicker.

The beginning was hard. The depression I had fallen in during the early months had slowed down my career and I had lost momentum. It was like starting again, but this time I knew what I had to offer and how.

We had no money to pay rent and we couldn't find anything suitable at that moment, so for three months we lived in my little office in a shopping centre. It wasn't adapted for living and we were not allowed to reside there, but we would sneak in when the mall was closing. I would pretend to close the front door of my office and walk outside, wait for the security guard to do the routine check, and then I would come back in with Lauren through the back door that was right behind my office.

We only had a kitchenette and we would use the public toilets.

Most of our property was stored in our car and every now and then a friend would offer us their house to have a shower. In the meantime, we would use a small towel and the sink in my office to wash. Very early in the morning we would leave the office, sneaking out through the back door and coming back in through the main one. Many times, we came across the cleaning staff who would look at us with a half smile as if to say, "We know you aren't supposed to be here," but they were always kind enough not to uncover us, I always got on very well with them all.

After a few months, we found a place to stay and then things started to move forward quicker. Lauren worked very hard marketing my product and I devoted myself to my professional goals. The emotional support I had from her gave me so much strength to keep pushing forward. I would try my best not to fall for my ex-wife's bribery and blackmail with my sons, and every time I would tell myself the chance to see my children would come.

That was a tough task. I would feel the scratch in the guts stinging, then breathe deeply and repeat to myself, *keep going*. Fighting my ex-wife only caused more resentment and reduced the chances of seeing my sons. I would just wait and build something big for them, for when they came to me, even if I had to wait until their adulthood.

The HypNaughty show took off in a way I did not expect. I was sure of its success when I created it, but the response of the audience was overwhelming. It was also very controversial. Many of my hypnotist colleagues did not view it favourably, and in fact, it kept me from participating in some courses and reunions. I was highly disappointed by that. It was a great idea, something that I have proven over and over, with thousands of people from the audience declaring it a great show and hilariously funny. But what annoyed me was that the same ones who criticised me were the same ones who tried to steal my idea. That was plain low.

Suddenly we were rocketing up. We bought a black van and new audiovisual equipment for the shows and starting touring the east coast, travelling further every time. Lauren's marketing was highly effective and I did not have to depend any more on the lame marketing skills of country town pub owners, or rock up to a show with only ten people in the audience. Those times were over, I felt there was no going back and my career could only go up from there.

Then the cruise ship opportunity arrived. That was a dream come true. I could do the job I loved the most and travel the world. I was euphoric, I felt like a five-year-old, holding my tin box full of animals. Hypnosis was part of my soul, a token that gave me life. And travelling – what would the Queen Bee think if she knew? I would go to Barbados.

I married Lauren and we had two beautiful girls. I was still sad inside for my eldest children. By then, many years had passed, too many, without hearing from them aside from whatever I could get from old friends.

There was one time when an old friend told me she noticed that my young son was in the same class as her daughter. My heart jumped out of my chest. He was close. He was physically close to me! I started shaking in hope and fear, because maybe I could see him or maybe I couldn't, or maybe because he would not recognise me. He would already be five years old. My friend arranged for me to go to school and accompany her to pick up her daughter so I could see him.

All that time I had been trying to contact my eldest son and writing to my boys, but I never knew whether they had received my letters, or the messages I would leave every week on their home phone, as they had to go through my ex-wife. Later in life I would discover my suspicions were unfortunately spot on and they both thought I had abandoned them for good and didn't care. But back then, I decided it was better to focus on the fact that I had a chance to see him, and maybe that would break the concrete wall that had been built between us against my will – our will!

I couldn't sleep the night before. I was too excited, worried, happy and scared – all at the same time. My stomach didn't welcome any food and I felt dizzy all day. I didn't take any appointments, as I couldn't focus. My friend came to pick me up, and I was so nervous. I tried to get into the car through the driver's seat, my hands were shaking and I had to contain a stuttering voice. My smile was unavoidable. Yet, it seemed like a grimace or a contraction because it revealed the mix of joy and terror of a moment that was going to be decisive in one way or the other, good or bad.

We arrived at his school. There were tens of small kids running all around in the playground. We went early to avoid my ex-wife. My friend had talked to the teachers and both had agreed to let me see my boy. We were walking up the corridor to the class and then I saw a young woman with a little boy walking to the door we were heading to. I didn't recognise him. He had grown so much!

My heartbeat went crazy I did not really know how to approach him. But I did not need to know. As soon as he saw me he yelled, "Daddy!" and ran towards me and hugged me. It was one of the most emotional moments I have ever had. I could not contain the tears, neither could my friend or the teacher. We hugged till we couldn't sustain the pressure in our chest anymore. It wasn't enough, but it was more that I had hoped for in many years. I had to leave him, we were both crying. However, I left with the hope that I would see him again. He was so close. That very day my ex-wife complained to the school, then told people that the teachers called the police and they removed me from the school. I haven't seen him since. I'll never understand why some people will go so low by making up stories to hurt others, it will never make any sense to me.

When Lauren fell pregnant we didn't slow down. She worked just as hard, full of energy until she gave birth. Then we would take our baby touring with us. The cruise ships kept me away from my family but it gave me financial stability, and that allowed me to provide for their needs, and although I missed them very much, we would compensate with real quality time.

I still tried to let my boys know that I loved them and missed them, but I never knew whether they received any letters from me. It was like a part of my heart was frozen and numb to the feelings of sadness. I had to care for the rest of my family.

My second wife and I would argue as any other couple does. It wouldn't be about big things. It would be about attention or the girls or simply because we were both very tired. She tried several businesses on her own. She was good at starting businesses, but not that good at maintaining them or following through, which I found very irritating as we wasted a lot of money. She was a good marketer and had the skills, but she lacked the perseverance and I thought that was a pity, because she could do it. There was no tension between us that would predict what happened soon after our second child was born.

One day as any other we had an argument. I don't even remember why we were arguing. Our relationship wasn't in jeopardy at all. It was just an argument. Lauren and I had always been very fiery, we knew that, but the heat of our discussions never lessened our love for each other or our commitment.

We were yelling at each other and could not bring it down. The more words we threw into the argument, the more we found to argue about. It was like chucking dried logs into a crackling bonfire, neither of us was willing to bail. And then she said it.

"I'll leave you and I won't let you see the girls ever again."

The silence was dense and sticky like tar. There was a full stop there. No other sound could be heard for a moment.

I looked her in the eyes. My mouth shut in an expressionless face and my teeth clenching inside. I was frozen, paralysed. My heart stopped dead. Then the bonfire that was burning high between us disappeared and it started to build inside me. I hated her.

That very moment, I hated her so much. She had gone through the pain of losing my two boys with me. She knew how much sorrow and hurt it brought me. She knew that taking my children from me was the worst thing she could ever do to damage my soul in its most abject state. Yet, she was wishing on me the worst of all wrongs and she was willing to use our innocent girls to do it.

I hadn't felt that heat inside for a long time, I went back in time to the moment I attacked Dave with the sword. He was trying to kill my mother's soul and all of our souls. Lauren had just poked my heart with a burning iron and left an open wound. There was no way back from there.

I was now, over twenty years later, standing in front of my

partner as I was then in front of Dave. She was threatening me with the worst pain she knew I could suffer. I wasn't a sixteen-year-old any more and my temper was not a ticking bomb on the edge of an explosion, but I could feel that same rage drowning any good feeling I had for the mother of my children.

She realised what she had said, and there we were standing in front of each other. Saying nothing. I could not empathise with her for a moment. I could not even consider she had made a mistake. All I heard coming from her mouth was that she was willing to hurt my children for the sake of hurting me. At that very moment I stopped loving her. All the magic and love between us had vanished in a few seconds. I did not feel she was my partner anymore.

That night we went to bed. There were apologies and tears. But it was too late. She had betrayed me already, showing me what was inside her. And although I still love her today as the mother of my girls, I would not see her again as the good friend, lover and companion she had been, ever. We drifted apart until the time came to say goodbye. But this time I was leaving sure that the knowledge I needed to build a lasting love relationship had sunk in, and that if I were to meet someone else in the future I'd have a better understanding of how to build stronger foundations for our partnership.

Chapter 34

The Final Beginning

Marinda was blowing the steam away over the coffee cup. I wondered how I hadn't noticed the beauty in her the first time we met. I could sense the effect she had on the crowd of men drinking around us in the piano bar. She was stunning.

I was performing on a cruise ship and she was enjoying a two-week holiday with her friend. There was no instant attraction. She just wasn't my type and neither was I the sort of guy she would go for. But a gentle connection encouraged us to meet the next day.

Time works in a funny way when you are navigating the open sea. There are no other distractions, no appointments or commitments, schedules are generally vague and, aside from performances, days and nights go by just for the sake of the Earth rotating with no further complication. Time on a cruise ship is about relaxing and food.

And so, we talked over a splendid meal, a not-so-good coffee, a few drinks and then another meal. My time was devoted to her for a few days, to her voice with its stories, her hands unfolding a napkin or gently grabbing a glass of wine and her body imperceptibly leaning towards me, closer every time. Her companionship felt so right. The unease I suddenly sensed the day we arrived at the next port was a painful and sweet premonition. I did not want to say goodbye.

She was holding her cup with both hands and raised her eyes to meet mine with a smile. After a sip of her coffee she asked, "But why did they call him Daddy?"

Honesty is so important, honesty and loyalty. I might have failed terribly at honesty, I admit it, but that is in the past. I stake my pride on loyalty, although it hasn't always been sported on the right side of integrity but again, that is something buried in a distant time. We wouldn't hide anything from each other. That was settled. We were tired of unwrapping unpleasant surprises in our past relationships, and in a sense everybody is, even when the past is no more. We vowed for openness and so it was imperative she knew who I was.

"That is the way it was. He was called Daddy because he was sort of a leader and everybody feared him. There were more daddies, they would get into fights between each other to prove who was the boss."

She offers me a cheeky smile. After the initial shock, I know she finds my stories attractive. I like that, I must admit, it brings me an adolescent sense of conquest, and who doesn't like to experience a little teenage passion every now and then. Though, once I get over that vain feeling I don't brag about my stories.

I enjoy narrating them because I am certain that, if I put them out there, many lost souls could see a way ahead. I do not say it will light the way and a whole world will open up before them, because when one comes from so far down the way up tends to be crowded in clutter that hardly lets you see beyond.

That is why it is important that the mind learns to envision that which might seem to be from another world. At the start I was not sure how Marinda would take it, but now I can sense her interest. She looks into my eyes and I can feel the warmth inside. She deserves a good man. I know now that I am.

"And you didn't get into trouble with them, right?"

"Of course I did."

The laughter escapes from her lips.

"Sure you did."

I smile and try to keep a certain seriousness as I remember the daddy jumping on me back in the detention centre. But it is hard not to share her amusement, her presence is hypnotic and joy floats among us.

"Well, it wasn't that funny when it happened, and it definitely wasn't clever..."

She shies up a bit and says sorry, but her eyes are still smiling at me.

"I was in the dining room on cleaning duty. I was wiping a table and then he came with those two thugs of his, one at each side..."

Marinda straightens up and leaves the coffee on the saucer, she looks a bit suspicious, or perplexed, or surprised. Sometimes I don't know. My life has been so different from hers. I am not the type of guy she would normally choose as a partner, she told me that. And yet here I am, the successful professional with a turbulent past – the rogue hypnotist.

Since the beginning she seemed to put some effort into not looking surprised or terrorised by the stories of my past. Maybe she thought I would be offended. Didn't she realise that while I was being honest I was also concerned she might change her mind about me? Or was I?

Confidence is something that sometimes vanishes when you love someone, even before you know you love them. Your heart goes ahead and your mind starts a process of doubts based on the fear of losing what you don't yet have.

Then she developed that look, which I could discern from her other gestures but its meaning was still not clear to me. Oh, how much I liked this woman.

"Why did he have two thugs if he was the leader of the bad guys? Why would he need protection?"

"He didn't need protection, it is about power. It was about having the power to command others. Do you see?"

She nods, grabs the coffee again and invites me to keep going with a soft movement of her chin.

"I was wiping the table and he came to me and said, 'Give me the fucking cloth!' So I said, 'Leave me the fuck alone.' He said again, 'Give me the fucking cloth! You fucking cunt!' And I turned around and said, 'You get fucked, fucking cunt!' And then he jumped on me and grabbed me by the throat and lifted me in the air...'"

Can I see concern in her eyes, even though she tries to

disguise it in her voice?

"And what did you do, Mark?"

I shrugged and offered her a cocky smile.

"I just put on my Cheshire Cat smile."

"When life gives you lemons, don't just make lemonade, take the lemon seeds, keep planting the seeds, watch each one grow and leave a legacy."

Mark Anthony

My tour van aka Black Beauty, she took us for many thousands of kilometres up and down Australia, performing shows in outback towns, cities and many bizarre places. She's still going strong, and can still be seen driving around the Gold Coast by her new owner.

Top: One of the many theatres that I now perform in, to thousands of people who enjoy laughter at it's best by watching volunteers doing the most bizarre but hilarious antics whilst hypnotised.

Bottom: Some of my wonderful volunteers onboard a cruise ship, sleeping like babies.

Top: My infamous 'adults only' show, probably 'the' most recognised hypnosis show in Australia, and full of good, clean, adult fun.

Bottom: Another ship, another show. Performing to many hundreds of passengers on a luxurious cruise ship in the middle of the ocean. Not bad for a mindless delinquent who was told that he'd never get anywhere in life many times by others!

Time out from shows on another luxury cruise ship. Being on cruise ships had been something I had envisioned many years ago, keep visualising your dreams and goals, what we imagine can many times become a reality!

Top: Cruising in the middle of the ocean near the Isle of Pines, New Caledonia... Who knew!

Bottom: From the infamous Ferrier Estate, Southeast London, to the very famous Honolulu Hawaii... How life has changed!

Top: One of the proudest moments of my life... Becoming a Father to Oliver my first-born son, I'm now a proud Father of four children, all of whom I love more than words could ever say.

Bottom: My beautiful wife Marina, who I met on a ship through an acquaintance and will from that moment on live a happy, healthy life together with our children, and our animals in our family home, traveling to many parts of the world and following many dreams and goals which we now talk about and write together.

Top: A stage packed full of willing volunteers, ready to be hypnotised live on stage and entertain many hundreds of onlookers.

Bottom: Me at Surfers Paradise beach on the lovely Gold Coast in Australia, my home for the last 16 years, and I believe to be the most beautiful country in the world. If a mindless delinquent, street Rogue from the Concrete Jungle in South East London can do it… So can you: Follow your dreams, and never give up!

Chapter 35

Miracle is Mind

As I go through life, I look back with wiser eyes. These memories have come back to me in a random fashion. Sometimes I would remember that day I wanted to kill Dave while recalling a ghost in our Victorian house in London. Six months later, I would come back to that memory and the place of its occurrence had changed. Now I could clearly see that we were in Covent Garden Markets.

When I work with my patients I use a timeline to travel back to a moment where their problem wasn't there. However, while writing this book, my own timeline was so erratic that I would see me in the right place with the wrong age or in the wrong place with an impossible age. Names were flying all over the timeline and I would think of people that I met after the memory I had recalled them in. A puzzle. The mind is a puzzle.

And yet, that puzzle is the miracle. If you play well with the pieces, if you do your best to put them together, you've got it. I have worked with my mind since before I even knew I could use it. My ambition of a better life was stronger than the force dragging me to the jaws of a senseless existence.

I have taken all my chances to be a better person. That meant to accept all my mistakes, swallow them with the dressing of pride and ego they come with, and work hard to walk out of the puddle of tar one can get stuck in. That mire of self-pity and guilt. There is no other way to move ahead, and only by moving ahead can you leave things behind.

The miracle is allowing your purpose to come to light and guide you. The puzzle is not difficult in itself; the solution is within your mind. The difficulty lies in overriding the sentinel that doesn't allow you to get in and pick up the right pieces, the pieces that fit together at a given moment. That sentinel is called the conscious mind.

All the times I envisioned having a conversation with my eldest son since his mother and I separated, since she stopped allowing me to see him, years passing by fruitlessly in my relationship with him, every single time the sentinel would jump in and yell cruelly, *You'll never see him again. He hates you. Give up!*

The sentinel is cruel, albeit quite stupid too. I do not know when we decided to make the conscious mind the decision maker. We gave it the power to ruin our lives. Don't get me wrong, your conscious mind is most necessary to function in this world and relate to others. It will be your saviour in so many instances. But the power we bestow on it is far too high for it to manage. We have overrated it.

I learned to surpass my conscious mind instinctively, which after all makes a lot of sense. My desire for another life was so strong that no common sense would divert me from my path, but if I had listened to my conscious mind all the time I can guarantee I wouldn't be here. The sentinel tends to be defeated upon adversity; it's just not strong enough. And it might drag you with it if you are not careful.

I have been very careful. Because I know first hand what being careless can lead you to. I knew I would see my son. I knew in my mind we could be friends again. And every time the sentinel tried to push me down, I distracted it to keep the image of what would be – my son and I together again.

Miracle is mind, but the mind also plays in time and space. I am glad I was patient enough to enjoy lunch with my eldest son. I didn't give up on that vision. And I picture an encounter with his brother in the future as strong and vivid as if it were happening now. Things come to you when you are willing to receive them, and that willingness means having to accept the time it takes.

Of all things, this is what hypnosis has taught me – miracle is mind. So far I have witnessed three remarkable miracles in my life, and I am looking forward to seeing the next one.

The first time, the rush of adrenaline almost made me jump from my chair.

I was broadcast on a show called *Today Tonight* on Channel Seven. After I appeared live on TV, the phone wouldn't stop ringing at my hypnotherapy clinic. I was booked for months and I couldn't handle any more patients. My receptionist was struggling to content people on the other end of the line. Only a week after my appearance on the show I was booked for the next six months.

There was a woman who kept calling. She tried for a whole week to get an appointment with me. She wanted to lose weight fast and insisted on seeing me. My receptionist told her on every occasion an appointment wasn't possible in the next six months, but she didn't get tired of trying. Eventually I decided to call her personally and talk to her. I explained to her an appointment wasn't possible at the moment, but if I had any cancellations, I would assist her.

Sure enough, I got a cancellation. And this is how the universe works beyond our expectations.

She was a woman in her fifties. When I saw her walking into the room I unconsciously became fixated with her arm. It was stuck on her chest in a "mea culpa" fashion. I couldn't help asking about her arm. She had polio when she was a child at the age of two, and while she was having a bath, her arm got fused to her body. It had been paralysed since then and never moved no matter what she tried.

I was fascinated by her arm. Although she wanted me to help her lose weight fast, I was not interested at all in what I thought a banal need at that moment. I wanted to know why that arm hadn't moved for over forty-eight years. I had no reason to believe that it could move at all, but I was feeling impatient about solving a problem like weight loss instead of treating the arm. My intuition was imperative at that moment.

I worked with her and her weight loss request, but before she could go, I asked her humbly if I could try something with her arm. At first, she became very defensive. Her husband was a top traumatologist and had already tried everything in his power to help her but with no success. I didn't insist or ask twice. Instead, as she calmed down from her first reaction, she suddenly thought she had nothing to lose and accepted my proposal.

I took her back along her timeline and asked her to recall the moment her arm became fused to her body. She went into a deep state of trance very fast. I could see the manners of a child in her gestures. The arm seemed to become smaller and the expression on her face more innocent.

Then I asked her to move back in time, just a bit earlier, to when she could move her arm.

By no means did I expect it to happen. I was holding on to the idea that something could be done, my intuition had pressed me strongly enough to request from my patient a trial that wasn't of her own interest. But when her arm started to shake and pull away from her chest, a current of vibrant energy rushed from my toes to the top of my head. The excitement filled my stomach with butterflies, as if I were a teenager in love. I couldn't believe what I was seeing…or could I?

I brought her back from her trance. The amazement had left her speechless. She still couldn't move her arm fully. The distance between the fist and her chest was hardly half an inch, but it was half an inch further that it had ever been.

She came back, and I treated her for further sessions. Her arm was improving in what her doctor reluctantly called a miracle. I had tapped into her unconscious mind and surpassed her conscious mind. Even her mind would remember the time the arm could move, and without inhibitions of any kind, it would try to move it, over and over. She was improving at a rapid pace.

Unfortunately, our appointments had to come to an end. She became obsessed with our sessions, insisting that she got in, no matter how busy my receptionist told her I was. She was not content if my receptionist told her the diary was full and ended up abusing my staff. That was something I could not allow. I called her and explained to her I could not treat her anymore, and I don't know whether she maintained the mobility she had gained in the arm.

It was frustrating for me as a therapist, but as a man of integrity, I could not approve of abusive behaviour towards my staff. Respect is a must, and I wouldn't have been able to work properly with her after she disrespected us.

The second miracle I witnessed was even more notorious and, in the end, again frustrating. But I can only help as much as someone lets me. It is not my job, or anyone else's for that matter, to decide for others. I guide people to find their own potential, to solve their own problems. I do not solve them myself. I am the tool, the one who opens the mind to allow for another perception. I can help to change beliefs and behaviours, I have the key for the change. But that is all. The work, the effort, the desire to change or heal comes from within, from the patient not the therapist.

I had a friend from New Zealand that used to spend holidays on the Gold Coast. One day I received a phone call from her. Her mother had suffered a stroke and her left side was completely paralysed.

I instantly knew I could help. As soon as I heard the bad news, I felt a strong confidence in my skills to improve the life of my friend's mum. So I told her I could assist her if that was their wish.

I was flown to New Zealand immediately and I spent three days with my friend's mum. On those three days, we worked hard with her subconscious. It was exhausting for both of us, but the results were incredible. By just the second session she could move the left leg, slightly lift the right arm and draw an asymmetric smile. By the third session we were getting even better results. We were very satisfied with the outcome.

Unfortunately, it isn't enough to tap into the subconscious

mind to affect a change. Any substantial change requires continual work, a drill. The sentinel always has the last word, and we have been training it for years to do so, indeed our entire lives .

We need to align the subconscious mind with the conscious mind so they can negotiate a way to a better outcome. It is not easy, but it is not impossible. It requires will and drive.

The third miracle came as a Christmas present.

In December 2016, after three years of missing my appointment with the oncologist, I again entered that tube with its metallic humming. The iciness of the room didn't scare me any more. There was no chill wrapping my bones as I lay on the freezing bench. The single-tone vibration drilling my eardrums was no more than a fleeting nuisance. It was over. I felt it.

Christmas passed by and my focus was on work and my wedding with Marinda. My tumour was not even a secondary worry. It ranked so far down I would only remember it if I looked at the doctor's appointment in my diary. The date was there but held no significance and I felt like deleting the event in my calendar. It was just plain slackness, to be honest.

Marinda prompted me to attend my appointment with the oncologist. I wanted her to feel confident she was marrying a responsible man, so I battled my unjustified negligence and went to the clinic.

I had seen my tumour before and was familiar with it. Every time I entered the oncologist's examination room my MRI results would be exposed on the lightened screen showing that obnoxious lump in my head. It was an irregular white spot I had learnt to clearly differentiate over the years among the other shades of white. I was expecting to see it again when I looked on the screen.

I must remark that my conscious mind does not differ from many others in that it is a sentinel that criticises and questions everything. While I was inside the giant magnet getting a picture from inside my head, I was certain everything I had to do there was already over. I knew I had no reason to be there anymore. It was the certainty that only the guts can feel, so the conscious mind didn't get it straight away.

The MRI scan exposed over the oncologist's desk was empty. I thought it was someone else's and didn't pay it any further attention when I greeted my doctor. I sat down in front of him and he gave me a serious look,

"Mark, did you have chemo?"

I stuttered at the unexpected question, "Err...No. I haven't had any chemo, why?"

"Mark, did you have an operation?"

"No, why is that?"

"This is very bizarre. It is very rare that a thing like this happens, but...Mark, the tumour is not there."

I looked at the scan on the light box. It was mine.

At that very moment I got it. Yes, it was over. The tumour had disappeared. I had no need to search for an explanation, because for me the explanation was simple and clear. To change your life, you have to constantly change your mind. Since I have seen paralysed members moving again, I have no doubt tumours can disappear by themselves. I am living proof of it, and according to my doctor it is some bizarre event scientists haven't been able to explain yet.

Almost four years have passed since I decided to write this memoir. There were difficulties along the way. I was let down and betrayed, I rekindled my relationship with my already adult son with huge success and I broke my engagement with the most beautiful person I have in my life. But as I wrote my story, I could see again all the milestones I passed to get to where I am now.

The years go slow when you don't want to live them. They drag, making your feet heavy and your soles sticky. If you get stuck in the tar of your frustration, you won't get any further. If you keep wallowing in the shit from your past, you won't move forwards. Your sight should always be looking ahead, your focus is getting out, doing what it takes and only looking back to remember the lessons.

Success doesn't come from external circumstances. Success is a mental state. If you dare to own it, time will prove to you it was your right all along.

"Slow and steady doesn't always win the race, but perseverance and effort eventually does"

Mark Anthony

Anyone there...?

Reach Out

When you think that times are getting tough, they get even tougher before getting better, just keep going...

Mark Anthony

Too often I would find myself in trouble not knowing how or who to ask for help. Here are some phone numbers and websites where you will find the help and support you need. Do not hesitate in asking for help if you are in need, it's very IMPORTANT that you reach out for help and support. There is an abundance of good will out there to assist you in your way out and up.

Any kind of EMERGENCY 000

The National Sexual Assault, Family & Domestic Violence Counselling Line 1800 RESPECT or 1800 737 732
https://www.1800respect.org.au/

LGBT support line 1800 184 527 https://qlife.org.au/

National Centre Against Bullying
https://www.ncab.org.au/get-help/

Kids Helpline 1800 551 800

Lifeline (Crisis support and suicide prevention) 13 11 14 www.lifeline.org.au

Grief Counselling 1300 554 786

Beyond Blue (Advice and support for anxiety and depression) 1300 22 4636 www.beyondblue.org.au

Headspace (Specialist advice and support for young people aged 12-25) 1800 650 890 www.eheadspace.org.au

Reachout (Helps with tough times, sex, friends and drugs) au.reachout.org

For help with any other issues please use a search engine on the internet i.e.:

www.Google.com.au

www.Yahoo.com.au

Please be advised that the websites listed are for reference only, and I have no ties to any of them, they are just good recommendations as per my research.

Inspirational Books to Read

"Life is all about choices, and it's you who makes those choices!"

Mark Anthony

The Magic Of Thinking Big

Think and Grow Rich

The Richest Man In Babylon

The Art Of The Deal - Donald Trump

Richard Branson´s books

Emile Coue

Psychology Of Winning - Denis Waitly

See You At The Top – Zig Ziglar

Wealth Magic - Peter Spann

Keep Going For It – Victor Kiam

Psycho-Cybernetics – Maxwell Maltz

This website link is full of daily inspirational quotes and videos
www.TheRogueHypnotist.com/DailyQuotes

"No reasons, no excuses."

Mark Anthony

www.ingramcontent.com/pod-product-compliance
Lightning Source LLC
LaVergne TN
LVHW051822080426
835512LV00018B/2682